The California Health Bar Drink Guide

The California Health Bar Drink Guide

SALLY ANN BERK

PHOTOGRAPHS BY GEORGE G. WIESER, JR.

BLACK DOG & LEVENTHAL PUBLISHERS
NEW YORK

Published by

Black Dog & Leventhal Publishers, Inc.
151 W. 19th Street
New York, New York 10011

Distributed by

Workman Publishing Company
708 Broadway
New York, New York 10003
Manufactured in Hong Kong

ISBN: 1-884822-27-4

h g f e d c b a

CONTENTS

INTRODUCTION

Over the past several years, we have seen the popularity of canned and bottled juices, teas, and soft drinks soar. Juice bars have become as ubiquitous as coffee bars. People are choosing to drink less alcohol, or are eliminating it completely, and are clamoring for variety in their choice of alcohol-free beverages.

The *California Health Bar Drink Guide* offers over seven hundred alcohol-free, delicious, and healthy recipes for everyone. Everything from breakfast drinks to cocktail-style drinks is here for every palate. Fresh fruit punches and vegetable drinks, cold-weather hot drinks and hot-weather refreshers are all offered in easy-to-follow instructions.

You no longer have to buy those beverages advertised as being made from the finest ingredients on the planet. You can make your own. They will taste incomparably better because they'll be made with freshly-made juices and won't be loaded with unnecessary preservatives and sweeteners. Nature, in her infinite wisdom, has supplied us with lots of very sweet fruit. We don't need high-fructose corn syrup and neither do our kids.

Many of the recipes in this book are quite adaptable to bartending. If you are entertaining, your guests who do not drink alcohol need no longer be limited to sparkling mineral water or cranberry juice. With the addition of a few basic ingredients, your wet bar can make interesting and appealing alcohol-free cocktails to please any guest.

Of course, we all indulge ourselves every once in a while, so I have included recipes for ice cream drinks and coffee drinks.

Have fun with these drinks. Experiment with ingredients and make up some of your own recipes. After a while, you'll have an idea of what ingredients mix well together. Soon, that craving for a chocolate bar may translate itself into a desire for a nice, tall glass of cucumber and carrot juice.

A NOTE ON THE RECIPE NAMES

Anyone interested in California culture and history may notice that many recipes are named for people, places and things that are unique to California. I have done this for a few reasons. First of all, it's fun. Secondly, I hope you will look up some of these names and read about the fascinating aspects of the history and culture of the Golden State.

INGREDIENTS

All ingredients, unless specified, should be chilled well.

FRUITS, FRUIT JUICES, AND PUREES

APPLES AND APPLE JUICE

The ubiquitous apple is a good source of vitamin C and pectin. If you have a juice extractor, you can make your own juice. However, fresh, unfiltered apple juice is readily available at most supermarkets and natural food stores. Buy the kind found in the produce section or refrigerator case in plastic bottles; it is fresher and much more flavorful than the canned or unrefrigerated bottled juice. Fresh-pressed apple juice made without preservatives will keep in the refrigerator for about one week before starting to ferment. If you have the freezer space, you may want to stock up on the fresh juice being pressed from the fall harvest. The juice can be frozen in the plastic bottle for several months.

APRICOT JUICE OR NECTAR

This rich liquid, loaded with beta-carotene, potassium, and vitamins A, C, E, and K, is readily available in supermarkets and natural food stores. Make sure that the juice you buy is sweetened only with other juices, if at all. You can also make your own with a juicer when apricots are in season in the summer. The best apricot nectar is called Star Valley Splash, made by Star Valley Farm in Vacaville, California. It is certified organic and tastes better than any other apricot juice I've ever tried. It can be found at the local Farmer's Market in San Rafael, Marin County, and at a few natural food stores in San Francisco. If you live in the Bay Area, it's worth the drive to Marin to stock up. If you don't, try to get a friend or relative who lives nearby to ship you some. This stuff is incredible.

BANANAS

Bananas are a critical ingredient in many smoothies. They add good flavor and thickness. A frozen banana helps give a drink an icy, frappe-like consistency. Making frozen bananas is quite simple. Peel a banana, wrap it in plastic wrap and place in the freezer. It will keep for several weeks. You can't juice bananas, but you can use them in your blender. They are full of potassium, as well as vitamins A, B-Complex, C, and E.

BERRIES (EXCEPT FOR STRAWBERRIES AND CRANBERRIES)

Raspberries, blackberries, boysenberries, marion berries, huckleberries, and blueberries are all good sources of vitamin C, magnesium and potassium. You can make berry puree in your blender or food processor, or juice them in a centrifugal juicer. Stock up on berries when they are in season. They freeze well. Most supermarkets and natural food stores sell frozen berries year-round, and they work quite well in these recipes. Blueberry juice, made by After The Fall, is available in most natural food stores.

CHERRIES AND CHERRY JUICE

Most cherries, unless specified as sour, are very sweet little stone fruits. They are good sources of vitamin C and potassium. Unsweetened cherry juice is sweet enough without any additional sweetener, so it is the only kind called for in this book. You can buy bottled unsweetened cherry juice or cider in a natural food store or supermarket. You can make your own cherry juice in a juicer, but it is very tedious to pit cherries and you get very little juice for a lot of effort.

CITRUS AND CITRUS JUICES

The citrus season in California starts around mid-November and continues until late February or early March. In addition to oranges, mandarin oranges, tangerines, tangelos, blood oranges, pomelos (Asian grapefruits), and many other varieties are in abundance at farmers' markets, supermarkets and natural food stores. California citrus is shipped all over the world, so if you want to buy blood oranges or organic satsumas, ask your green grocer or produce manager to order them for you.

There is simply nothing better than fresh citrus juice. It is delicious and loaded with vitamin C, as well as B1. Electric citrus reamers are inexpensive and easy to use. All of these recipes recommend fresh squeezed juice. If you must substitute pre-made orange juice, use the juice packaged in milk cartons labeled "not from concentrate" found in the dairy case at supermarkets. Some supermarkets and natural food stores sell freshly squeezed, unpasteurized orange and grapefruit juices in plastic bottles. It is a little pricey, but worth it since it is usually as good as juice you'd make at home.

The fresh-squeezed rule goes for limes and lemons as well. Do not use reconstituted juices. Some recipes call for Meyer lemons. These are lemons which are slightly sweeter than regular lemons. If you can't find them, add a little sweetener to fresh lemon juice.

COCONUT

Coconut milk and cream of coconut are both available in supermarkets and natural food stores. If you're watching your weight, go easy on the coconut. It has lots of fat.

CRANBERRIES

Cranberries are loaded with vitamin C. When a recipe in this book calls for cranberry juice cocktail, it is referring to the kind which is sweetened with other fruit juices and is readily available in most supermarkets and natural food stores. Do not buy cranberry juice cocktail that is sweetened with sugar or high-fructose corn syrup. Always read the label. When unsweetened cranberry juice is needed, the recipe specifies this. Unsweetened cranberry juice is extremely tart, with a fresh, biting flavor. It can usually be found in natural food stores and some large supermarkets. R.W. Knudsen makes an unsweetened cranberry juice called Just Cranberry. You can also juice your own using fresh cranberries. If a drink is too sweet, a small amount of unsweetened cranberry juice can add a delightful tartness.

DRIED FRUIT

Some of these recipes call for raisins or dates. To prepare them for the recipe, soak in a bowl hot water for about twenty to thirty minutes. Remove from water and proceed with the recipe.

GRAPES AND GRAPE JUICE

Purple grape juice is the most familiar, but red and white grape juices are also available in most supermarkets and natural food stores. When buying juice, purchase bottled juice or frozen concentrate. Use canned grape juice only as a last resort. Each recipe specifies which kind of grape juice to use. White grape juice imparts little flavor of its own and is often used as a sweetener. If you live in a wine-grape growing region, you can often find fresh pressed juice made from wine grapes at the time of the fall harvest, usually at you local farmer's market. Take advantage of your geographical good fortune. These grapes make excellent, subtle tasting juices. You can also buy wine grapes in the fall and make your own juice in a juicer. Grapes are a good source of vitamins B1, C, and E, as well as potassium.

GUAVA

See mango and papaya. Lakewood Products of Miami, Florida, makes a good bottled guava nectar that is 100% juice. I have also found guava juice frozen concentrate, which is quite good. Guava has lots of potassium and vitamin C.

KIWI FRUIT

Kiwi fruit is now grown domestically, so the price has gone down and availability is high. Kiwi fruit juice is not available commercially, but if you don't have a juicer, peel and puree them in a food processor or blender and then strain the mixture. They are a good source of vitamin C.

MANGO

Mango nectar is available in paper cartons in the dairy case in most supermarkets and natural food stores. Canned juice is also available, but use it only as a last resort. I have also found frozen mango chunks in the frozen food section. If you have a juicer, you can make your own. The fruit is usually available year-round. It makes a very thick juice, so you may have to thin it with some white grape juice. It is a good source of vitamins A, B6, C, and E.

MELONS (CANTALOUPE, HONEYDEW, WATERMELON)

Melons make wonderful drinks, alone or in recipes. They are good sources of vitamins A and C. Watermelons also contain vitamin B6. Since melons have a high water content, you get a lot of juice from the fruit. I have been unable to find any kind of melon juice sold commercially. If you have a juicer, make your own. If not, try pureeing the melon and then straining out the juice.

PAPAYA

Like mango, papaya is also available in cartons in the dairy case and in cans. Papaya is a good source of vitamins A and C and beta-carotene.

PASSION FRUIT

You can buy this juice in frozen concentrate and in glass bottles. I prefer the concentrate. If your natural food store doesn't have it, ask them to order it for you.

PEACHES, NECTARINES, AND PLUMS

There is nothing like a fresh, ripe peach or a juicy nectarine. If you have a juicer, I highly recommend making your own juice when stone fruits are in season. You can freeze them (remove the stone) to get you through the long, peach-less winter. Imported peaches, plums and nectarines are available in the winter, but I find them to be rather tasteless and very expensive. My rule of thumb is that the farther a piece of fruit (with the exception of citrus) has to travel, the more flavor it loses. Most supermarkets sell frozen peaches and plums year-round and these are perfectly fine, but not as good as the genuine article. Peach juice and nectar are available in bottles and work well in these recipes. Again, read the label. Make sure that if you buy sweetened peach juice, it has been sweetened with other juices and not sugar or high-fructose corn syrup. Plum and nectarine juices are delicacies, so you'll have to make your own.

PEAR

Pears make great juice that is an asset to many drinks. Make your own if you can. If not, pear juice is becoming increasingly available in natural food stores and supermarkets.

PINEAPPLE

Always buy 100% pineapple juice that has no added sweeteners. Pineapple juice is sweet enough on its own. If you buy juice in the 32-ounce can, pour it into a glass bottle and refrigerate. This will help eliminate some of the flat, metallic flavor canned juices can acquire. Fresh pineapple is available year-round, and if you have a juicer, it is worth it to make your own. Canned pineapple is fine for these recipes as long as you use the kind that is packed in its own juices. Pineapple is a good source of vitamins B1 and C.

POMEGRANATE

Unsweetened pomegranate juice is available in most natural food stores. If your local store doesn't carry it, ask them to order it for you. Juice Creations of Chico, California, makes a juice called

"Old-Fashioned Pomegranate Juice" under its Heinke's label. It is available in most natural food stores. In the fall, some growers sell it at local farmers' markets. It is worth searching for this juice since it is very tedious to make your own. Sweet and tart at the same time, it is a great drink component, full of vitamin C and potassium.

PRUNE

Bottled prune juice is just fine. Read the label to make sure there is no added sugar or high-fructose corn syrup in the juice. Prune juice has lots of vitamin B6, copper and potassium.

RHUBARB

I always chop and cook rhubarb before using it in a recipe. Never use the green tops. They are toxic.

STRAWBERRIES, STRAWBERRY PUREE, AND STRAWBERRY JUICE

Making strawberry puree :
1 pint fresh or frozen strawberries

Wash strawberries in cold water, if using fresh. Remove stems and halve the berries. Place in blender and puree until smooth. Makes about one cup of puree. This will keep in the refrigerator for about one week, and in the freezer for at least two months.

Note: If using frozen berries, let thaw and then place in blender.

I have been unable to find strawberry juice in a store, but it can be made with a centrifugal juicer. Strawberries are loaded with vitamins C and K.

VEGETABLES AND VEGETABLE JUICES

AVOCADO

An avocado is really a fruit, but it's commonly thought of as a vegetable so here we are. You can't juice it, but like bananas, avocados can be used with great success in a variety of smoothies and other blender drinks. I prefer Haas avocados for flavor and consistency. Make sure you have ripe ones, almost squishy. A hard, underripe avocado is a big disappointment in the flavor arena. Avocados are filled with vitamins, minerals and beta-carotene.

BEET

Beet juice is very strong, but if used sparingly it gives excellent color and flavor to many alcohol-free drinks. It is the key ingredient in borscht. If you have a juicer, make your own. You can also use a food processor. Puree the beets and then strain the juice. You may be able to find fresh beet juice in larger natural food stores. Beets are brimming with vitamins C and K, as well as folate and magnesium.

CABBAGE

Cabbage juice, in small quantities, adds a unique flavor to many of these recipes. It is not available commercially, but you can make your own in your juicer. It's a good source of vitamins C, E, and K.

CARROT

Nothing beats fresh carrot juice, so if you have a juicer, by all means, make your own. However, most natural food stores and some supermarkets now sell fresh-pressed carrot juice. You can find it in the refrigerated or produce section. Canned carrot juice is not recommended, but will do in a pinch. The carrot reigns supreme when it comes to beta-carotene. It is also packed with vitamins A, B1, B6, C, and K, as well as folate and potassium.

CELERY

A refreshing, light juice, you will be hard-pressed to find this in any store. If you have a juicer, make your own. Celery juice mixes well with just about everything. Celery is a good way to get vitamins A, B6, C, and K, as well as potassium and calcium.

CUCUMBER

I love cucumber juice. It is cool, refreshing and very low in calories, as well as being a fine source of vitamins C and K. You'll have to make your own. I use English cucumbers, but the garden variety works just as well.

GARLIC

Garlic is delicious and good for you! It is bursting with vitamins B1 and C, as well as many required minerals. It is a natural weapon against bacteria. The Delaney Sisters eat raw garlic every day, and as of this writing they are 103 and 105 years old and have just published their second book. Garlic puree and juice add great flavor to many drinks. You can make your own garlic juice in a centrifugal juicer, or use puree.

GINGER

Ginger root is strong and tangy. A little juice goes a long way. Make this in your juicer. It contains vitamins B6 and C, and makes a good digestive tonic.

HORSERADISH

Horseradish is strong. I only use the white kind. Red horseradish is colored with beet juice and often has added sugar. Buy it in the store. Making your own horseradish is unnecessary. You don't use much, so what's the point in dragging out the food processor just to make a little bit? White horseradish in jars is perfectly fine, and a good source of potassium.

LETTUCES

Make your own lettuce juice. I recommend leaf lettuce or mesclun mix. Lettuce, depending on the variety, can be a good source of vitamins A, B1, C, and K. Don't use iceberg lettuce, as it is not as flavorful as some varieties.

ONIONS AND SCALLIONS

Onions put the zip in many of these recipes. It is not impossible to find onion juice commercially, but it is very difficult. Make your own. Onions and scallions are good sources of vitamin C, and, as with garlic, they fight bacteria.

PARSLEY

Parsley makes a great, green addition to many recipes. You can make parsley juice in your juicer. It has lots of vitamins—A,C,E— and is loaded with minerals. Treat other fresh herbs (mint, cilantro) like parsley in your juicer. In all cases, remember that the juice will be strong and the flavor highly concentrated.

BELL PEPPERS (SWEET)

A bit of bell pepper juice makes many of these recipes unique. Make your own in a juicer. Bell peppers contain vitamins A, B6, C, and E, as well as potassium.

JALAPEÑO AND SERRANO PEPPERS (HOT)

These little guys are full of fire. Use their juice sparingly, and always remove the seeds before juicing. They are available year-round and one can be used in place of the other. I love fiery foods. You may want to adjust the amount of hot pepper juice called for in these recipes if you are not similarly inclined.

PUMPKIN

Pumpkin is a beta-carotene champ and is full of fiber and vitamin C. You cannot juice pumpkin. It is too tough and fibrous. You can buy or make pumpkin puree. If you're buying, make sure it is 100% pumpkin, not pumpkin pie filling. If you make your own puree, good for you! It freezes well.

RADISHES

Like hot peppers, a little goes a long way. Sharp, white or red, radishes add a good zip to many vegetable cocktails and contain vitamin C and potassium. Make your own in a juicer.

SPINACH

Spinach is the green leaf vegetable of champions. It is loaded with iron and other minerals, as well as vitamins A, B2, B6, C, E, and K. You'll have to make your own juice. Try using baby spinach for a more delicate flavor.

SPROUTS AND WHEAT GRASS

Sprouts are great in salads and sandwiches, and they make good, nutritious juice. Most supermarkets sell sprouts. Buy organic and make your own juice. They have lots of vitamin C, B2, and many trace minerals.

Wheat grass juice is a great pick-me-up. Larger natural food store make it fresh, and I recommend you buy this. It is highly perishable, so only buy what you are going to use.

TOMATO

Tomato juice is available everywhere. Buy organic juice that has no preservatives or added salt. You'll notice the difference. Tomatoes are loaded with vitamins A and C. In the summer, when tomatoes are in their wonderful season, make your own juice. It is fabulous.

OTHER INGREDIENTS

ALCOHOL-FREE FLAVOR EXTRACTS

Frontier Natural, of Norway, Iowa, makes twenty-five natural-flavor extracts without alcohol. You can find these in natural food stores. Other companies are beginning to make extracts without alcohol. I have seen alcohol-free vanilla and almond extracts in supermarkets, and I'm sure other flavors will follow.

ALOE-VERA JUICE

This is the juice of the aloe plant. Aloe-vera gel is used in many skin treatments as a healing agent for burns and abrasions, to remedy dry skin, and as a first aid product. The juice is practically flavorless and has virtually no calories. It is an excellent internal cleanser.

BEE POLLEN

Some smoothies call for bee pollen. This is an exceptional nutritional supplement and you can buy it in any natural food store.

BITTER-LEMON SODA

Bitter-lemon soda is a great mixer, terrific on its own or over ice and a personal favorite. Unfortunately, it is difficult to find in some parts of the United States. Cadbury-Schweppes has scaled back its domestic production in recent years. If you find some, stock up. You shouldn't have a problem finding it in larger urban areas, but even in the Bay Area, I have had to drive to Sacramento to buy it. If you can't find it, call a local soft-drink distributor and see if they can order it for you.

When I can't get bitter lemon soda, I use Limonata, a carbonated lemon beverage made by San Pellegrino. It is a little sweeter than bitter lemon, but serves well as a substitute. You can find this in Italian grocery stores, and in better stocked supermarkets and gourmet stores.

BOUILLON

Buy bouillon cubes at your natural food store. You can find beef, chicken and vegetable cubes or concentrate that have no MSG or other nasty additives.

FLAVORED SYRUPS (ITALIAN SYRUPS)

These syrups are basically sugar syrups with natural flavorings added. They are increasingly easy to find since many coffee aficionados like to flavor their coffee drinks with these syrups. The Torani company makes dozens of flavors, from vanilla to kiwi, and just about any other flavor you can imagine.

HONEY

Many of these recipes call for honey. Honey, because of its viscosity, can be difficult to work with when making cold drinks. If you have a microwave, remove the lid of the honey jar and place the jar in the microwave for about 45 seconds. This will thin the honey and make it and easier to work with. You can also dilute honey with a little boiling water to thin it, or place the jar, with the lid off, in a saucepan of boiling water and heat it until the honey turns watery.

MILK, ICE CREAM, YOGURT, AND NON-DAIRY SUBSTITUTES

If you are avoiding dairy products, you can substitute soy milk, rice milk or any other non-dairy substitute whenever milk is called for in a recipe. Toffuti, or other non-dairy frozen desserts may be substituted for ice cream and frozen yogurt. There are soy-based substitutes for yogurt, and these will work in recipes calling for yogurt.

SWEETENERS

Most of these recipes avoid refined sugar and use honey or maple syrup instead. Try brown rice syrup, fruit sugar, or other natural sweeteners found in abundance at natural food stores to see which you prefer. The selection is really dizzying. Never use artificial sweeteners, like saccharin or aspartame.

TABASCO SAUCE

Tabasco sauce now comes in red and green. The green sauce is made with jalapeño peppers. Both are available just about everywhere.

TEAS

Some of these recipes call for different teas as ingredients. Most herbal teas are available packaged in tea bags or boxes at natural food stores. I usually buy my teas from the bulk section. It is less expensive, and I prefer to brew my teas from loose tea. For all of these recipes, you should brew your tea double-strength so its delicate and distinct flavor will not be lost when diluted with ice, soda or juice.

EQUIPMENT AND TOOLS

BLENDER

An electric blender is essential for many of these drinks. A one-speed model is fine for mixing and cracking ice. An immersion blender is also useful in mixing drinks, whipping cream, and blending single servings.

JUICE EXTRACTOR OR CENTRIFUGAL JUICER

Some of these recipes call for juices that are not available commercially, or that are just plain better when you make them yourself. You will need a centrifugal juicer to make them. It extracts the juice from the fruit or vegetable and separates the pulp. A decent non-commercial juicer is about eighty dollars. If you don't have a juicer and don't want to buy one, you can puree the fruit or vegetable in a blender or food processor, and then strain the puree. This will not work with all fruits or vegetables, but you should be able to achieve satisfactory results with fruits and vegetables that have a high water content.

CITRUS JUICER OR REAMER

Electric citrus reamers are very reasonably priced and save a lot of time and energy. Hand-held reamers are also acceptable, but you can get very tired juicing several oranges by hand.

FOOD PROCESSOR

A food processor is not essential for these recipes, however, it is a fine tool for making purees and for blending.

You will also need the following non-electric tools:

Cocktail Shaker   you can substitute a large glass jar with a tight lid.

Mixing glass   generally a pint-sized glass with a wide mouth.

Measuring spoons

Measuring cups

Mortar and pestle   not essential, but good for grinding spices.

SOURCES

Many juices and other ingredients used in these recipes are readily available in supermarkets. You'll have no problem finding juices made from nationally-known companies such as Tropicana, Ocean Spray, or Dole, but you might want to consider going organic, for both health and flavor reasons. The following companies manufacture natural, organic juices that are available nationwide. If you can't find them in your supermarket or natural food store, ask them to order the product for you. I have also listed other products that may be difficult to find, with their manufacturer or distributor. I have found that if I give my grocer the name of a company and the product I want, he will usually be able to get it for me.

JUICES

After the Fall Products, Inc.
Brattleboro, VT 05301

Cascadian Farm, Inc.
719 Metcalf Street
Sedro Wooley, WA 98284
206-855-0100

Epicurean International, Inc.
(coconut milk)
P.O. Box 13242
Berkeley, CA 94701

Heinke's
5365 Clark Road
Paradise, CA 95969-6399
916-877-4847

Kern's
R.W. Knudsen & Sons
Box 369
Chico, CA 95926
916-891-1517

Lakewood Products
Miami, FL 33242-0708

Lily of the Desert (aloe-vera juice)
8726 Royal Lane
Irving, TX 75063
800-229-5459

S. Martinelli and Co. (sparkling juices)
Watsonville, CA 95078

Mountain Sun Organic and
Natural Juices
Dolores, CO 81323

Mrs. Wiggles Rocket Juice Co.
(refrigerated juices)
Santa Rosa, CA 95404

Naked Foods (refrigerated juices)
Glendora, CA 91741

Muir Glen (tomato products)
P.O. Box 1498
Sacramento, CA 95812

Odwalla (refrigerated juices)
Davenport, CA 95017
Seattle, WA 98168

Pyramid Juice Company
Box 1303
Ashland, OR 97520
503-482-2292

Rainbow Valley Orchards
Rainbow, CA

Santa Cruz Naturals
Box 369
Chico, CA 95927

Sowden Brothers (natural prune juice)
8888 Township Road
Live Oak, CA 95953
916-695-3750

Trader Joe's (California and Arizona only)
South Pasadena, CA 91301

Velma Rose's Farm
Yakima, WA

FROZEN-JUICE CONCENTRATES

Knudsen (see juices)

Cascadian Farms (see juices)

Carabik Sun
P. Campofresco, Inc.
Box 755
Santa Isabel, PR 00757
809-834-4760

CARBONATED BEVERAGES

Limonata
Importer: San Pellegrino USA, Inc.
P.O. Box 1367
New York, NY 10101-1367

Bitter Lemon Soda
Schweppes U.S.A.
A Division of Cadbury Beverages, Inc.
Stamford, CT 06905-0800
203-329-0911

SPARKLING MINERAL WATER (PLAIN AND NATURALLY FLAVORED)

Calistoga Mineral Water Co.
Great Spring Waters of America
Calistoga, CA 94515

ALTERNATIVE SWEETENERS

Arrowhead Mills
Box 2059
Hereford, TX 79045-2059
806-364-07390

Bronner's Sweeteners (barley malt syrup)
P.O. Box 28
Escondido, CA 92025
619-745-7069

Fruitsource (Granular sweetener made from fruit and whole grains)
1803 Mission Street, Suite 404
Santa Cruz, CA 95060

Eden Foods, Inc. (brown rice syrup)
Clinton, MI 49236
Nature's Best (fructose, date sugar)
Brea, CA 92621

NutraSource
4005 Sixth Ave. South
Seattle, WA 98108
206-467-7190

Lundberg Family Farms (Brown Rice Syrup)
Richvale, CA 95974-0369

Sucanat (sugar cane juice)
Sucanat N.A. Corp.
58 Meadowbrook Parkway
Milford, NH 03055

Westbrae Natural Foods (brown rice syrup, barley syrup)
Carson, CA 90746

VEGETABLE BOUILLON

Dr. Bronner's Balanced Mineral Bouillon (liquid concentrate)
Box 28
Escondido, CA 92033

Hugli (cubes)
Imported by:
Efco Importers
Jenkintown, PA 19046

Morga (cubes and powdered concentrate)
Imported by:
Liberty Richter, Inc.
Carlstadt, NJ 07072

Hidden Valley Mills (liquid concentrate)
Bernard Jensen Products
Solana Beach, CA 92075

ORGANIC TEAS AND DRIED HERBS

Celestial Seasonings, Inc.
4600 Sleepytime Drive
Boulder, CO 80301-3292
800-525-0347

Garden of the Andes
1993 Traditional Teas /
Traditional Medicinals, Inc.
4515 Ross Road
Sebastopol, CA 95472

Good Earth Teas
Wildcraft Herbs
831 Almar Ave.
Santa Cruz, CA 95060

Lhasa Karnak Herb Company
2513 Telegraph Ave.
Berkeley, CA 94704
510-548-0380

Republic of Tea
San Rafael, CA 94901
San Francisco Herb and Natural
Food Co.
Emeryville, CA 94608

Seeelect Tea Company
P.O. Box 1969
Camarillo, CA 93011

ALCOHOL-FREE FLAVOR EXTRACTS

Cook Flavoring Co.
Cook's Choice Extracts
P.O. Box 890
Tacoma, WA 98401
206-627-5499

Frontier Cooperative Herbs
Box 69
Norway, IA 53218
General Distributors of Natural
Foods

Mountain People's Warehouse
12745 Earhart Ave.
Auburn, CA 95602
800-679-8735

NFS
Natural Food
Systems/Cornucopia
260 Lake Road
Danville, CT 06241
215-624-3559

A

ABSOLUTELY APRICOT

8 parts apricot nectar
   (4 oz.)
4 parts fresh-squeezed orange juice
   (2 oz.)
Lemon slice, for garnish

Combine juices with cracked ice in a cocktail shaker and shake well. Strain into a chilled cocktail glass and garnish with the lemon slice. Serves one.

89 calories; 2 gm fat; 2% calories from fat; 0 mg cholesterol; 4.5 mg sodium; 22.2 gm carbohydrate; 0.8 gm protein; 13.8 mg calcium; 0.5 mg iron; 160.4 RE vitamin A; 28.9 mg vitamin C

ADAM'S RIB

8 parts nonfat milk (4 oz.)
8 parts apple juice (4 oz.)
10 strawberries, hulled and sliced

Combine all ingredients in a blender and blend until smooth. Pour into chilled old-fashioned glasses. Serves two.

69 calories; 0.4 gm fat; 5% calories from fat; 0.9 mg cholesterol; 31.6 mg sodium; 14.6 gm carbohydrate; 2.4 gm protein; 84.3 mg calcium; 0.5 mg iron; 36.8 RE vitamin A; 66.1 mg vitamin C

AFTERNOON DELIGHT

8 parts apple juice (4 oz.)
8 parts strawberry puree (4 oz.)
4 parts carrot juice (2 oz.)
Whole strawberries, for garnish

Combine puree and juices in a blender and blend until frothy. Pour into chilled wineglasses and garnish with strawberries. Serves two.

88 calories; 0.1 gm fat; 1% calories from fat; 0 mg cholesterol; 12.9 mg sodium; 22.3 gm carbohydrate; 1.3 gm protein; 10.9 mg calcium; 1.1 mg iron; 730.1 RE vitamin A; 67.7 mg vitamin C

AFTER-SCHOOL SPECIAL

8 parts red grape juice (4 oz.)
Sparkling white grape juice

Combine red grape juice and ice cubes in a chilled highball glass. Fill glass with sparking white grape juice and stir gently. Serves one.

112.4 calories; 0.1 gm fat; 1% calories from fat; 0 mg cholesterol; 5.1 mg sodium; 25.4 gm carbohydrate; 1 gm protein; 15.3 mg calcium; 0.4 mg iron; 1.3 RE vitamin A; 0.2 mg vitamin C

AFTERSHOCK

10 parts pineapple juice
   (5 oz.)
2 parts red radish juice (1 oz.)
2 parts parsley juice (1 oz.)
Fresh parsley sprig, for garnish

Combine juices with cracked ice in a cocktail shaker and shake well. Strain into a chilled highball glass and garnish with the parsley sprig. Serves one.

131 calories; 0.7 gm fat; 6% calories from fat; 0 mg cholesterol; 40.4 mg sodium; 24.2 gm carbohydrate; 2.3 gm protein; 107.5 mg calcium; 3.9 mg iron; 295.8 RE vitamin A; 97.1 mg vitamin C

ALAN'S SAVORY GARLIC SMOOTHIE

6 parts cucumber juice
 (3 oz.)
2 parts tomato juice (1 oz.)
8 parts plain nonfat yogurt (4 oz.)
2 garlic puree
1 tbsp. fresh basil, minced
½ tsp. ground cumin
Salt, to taste
Freshly ground black pepper, to taste
Fresh parsley sprigs, for garnish

Combine all ingredients except the
salt, pepper, and parsley in a blender
and blend until smooth. Pour into
chilled wineglasses, add salt and pepper to taste, and garnish with the
parsley sprigs. Serves two.

*83 calories; 0.2 gm fat; 3% calories
from fat; 1.2 mg cholesterol; 322.6
mg sodium; 8.7 gm carbohydrate;
4.1 gm protein; 134.7 mg calcium;
0.5 mg iron; 13.6 RE vitamin A;
6.9 mg vitamin C*

ALEXANDER

4 parts half-and-half (2 oz.)
4 parts coffee, cold (2 oz.)
1 tbsp. sweetened cocoa powder
1 tsp. alcohol-free brandy extract

Combine ingredients with cracked ice
in a blender. Blend until slushy and
pour into a chilled wineglass.
Serves one.

*199 calories; 12 gm fat; 54% calo-
ries from fat; 20.1 mg cholesterol;
51.4 mg sodium; 17.1 gm carbohydrate; 5.9 gm protein; 84.8 mg calcium; 2.5 mg iron; 105 RE vitamin
A; 0.5 mg vitamin C*

ALPHABET JUICE

12 parts apple cider (6 oz.)
8 parts celery juice (4 oz.)
4 parts beet juice (2 oz.)
Celery sticks, for garnish

Combine all ingredients except celery
sticks with cracked ice in a cocktail
shaker and shake vigorously. Strain
into chilled old-fashioned glasses and
garnish with celery sticks. Serves two.

*112 calories; 0.3 gm fat; 2% calo-
ries from fat; 0 mg cholesterol;
101.2 mg sodium; 29.6 gm carbohydrate; 1.3 gm protein; 47.7 mg
calcium; 1.4 mg iron; 11.9 RE vitamin A; 8.9 mg vitamin C*

AMADOR APRICOT

10 parts apricot nectar
 (5 oz.)
8 parts fresh-squeezed orange
 juice (4 oz.)
2 parts coconut milk (1 oz.)
1 tbsp. honey
½ tsp. alcohol-free almond extract
Ground nutmeg, for garnish

Combine all ingredients except the
nutmeg in a blender and blend until
smooth. Pour into a chilled collins
glass and sprinkle with nutmeg.
Serves one.

*276 calories; 8.5 gm fat; 27% calo-
ries from fat; 0 mg cholesterol; 10.3
mg sodium; 50.5 gm carbohydrate;
2.2 gm protein; 26.9 mg calcium;
1.3 mg iron; 209.7 RE vitamin A;
104.2 mg vitamin C*

AMAZING GRAPE

10 parts red grape juice
 (5 oz.)
6 parts grapefruit juice (3 oz.)
6 parts unsweetened cherry
 juice (3 oz.)
4 parts fresh-squeezed lime
 juice (2 oz.)
Lime slices, for garnish

Combine all ingredients except lime
slices with cracked ice in a cocktail
shaker. Shake well and strain over ice
cubes into chilled highball glasses.
Garnish with lime slices. Serves two.

*118 calories; 0.8 gm fat; 6% calo-
ries from fat; 0 mg cholesterol; 2.8
mg sodium; 28.8 gm carbohydrate;
1.6 gm protein; 23.2 mg calcium;
0.5 mg iron; 16.5 RE vitamin A;
29.6 mg vitamin C*

AMBROSIA

10 parts coconut milk (5 oz.)
1 banana, sliced
2 tbsp. honey
Pineapple juice (optional)

Combine all ingredients except
pineapple juice in a blender and blend
until smooth. If drink is too thick, add
pineapple juice until desired consistency is achieved. Pour into chilled
wineglasses. Serves two.

*313 calories; 20.4 gm fat; 57%
calories from fat; 0 mg cholesterol;
11.5 mg sodium; 32.6 gm carbohydrate; 2.6 gm protein; 10.9 mg
calcium; 1.2 mg iron; 4.6 RE vitamin A; 5.4 mg vitamin C*

*(Pineapple juice not included in
nutritional analysis.)*

ANGEL'S CAMP
SPARKLER

8 parts peach juice (4 oz.)
4 parts apple juice (2 oz.)
½ tsp. alcohol-free almond extract
6 whole raspberries
5 strawberries, hulled and sliced
Sparkling mineral water

Combine all ingredients except mineral water in a blender and blend until
well-mixed. Divide mixture into two
chilled highball glasses. Fill glasses
with sparkling mineral water and stir
gently. Serves two.

*97 calories; 0.4 gm fat; 3% calories
from fat; 0 mg cholesterol; 6.3 mg
sodium; 24.4 gm carbohydrate; 1.2
gm protein; 17.4 mg calcium; 0.9
mg iron; 22 RE vitamin A; 50.2 mg
vitamin C*

ANNE'S SPECIAL
CUCUMBER
SMOOTHIE

10 parts cucumber juice (5 oz.)
2 parts fresh-squeezed lemon
    juice (1 oz.)
2 parts scallion juice (1 oz.)
2 parts mint juice (1 oz.)
1 banana, sliced

½ tsp. dried dill, crushed
3-5 dashes green Tabasco sauce
Salt, to taste

Combine all ingredients except salt
in a blender and blend until smooth.
If mixture is too thick, add more
cucumber juice until desired consistency is achieved. Pour into chilled
collins glasses. Add salt to taste.
Serves two.

*64 calories; 0.4 gm fat; 4% calories
from fat; 0 mg cholesterol; 7.8 mg
sodium; 16.4 gm carbohydrate; 1
gm protein; 16.9 mg calcium; 0.5
mg iron; 8.5 RE vitamin A; 15.2
mg vitamin C*

ANYTHING GOES

8 parts tomato juice (4 oz.)
8 parts pineapple juice (4 oz.)
6 parts mango nectar (3 oz.)

Combine all ingredients with cracked
ice in a blender and blend well. Strain
into chilled collins glass over ice
cubes. Serves two.

*175 calories; 0.5 gm fat; 3% calo-
ries from fat; 0 mg cholesterol;
412.5 mg sodium; 44.5 gm carbohydrate; 2 gm protein; 43.9 mg calcium; 1.2 mg iron; 615.6 RE vitamin A; 60.4 mg vitamin C*

ANZA BORREGO
FRAPPE

8 parts fresh-squeezed orange
    juice (4 oz.)
8 parts papaya juice (4 oz.)
8 parts coconut milk (4 oz.)
1 banana, sliced
Shredded coconut

Combine all ingredients except shredded coconut in a blender and blend
until smooth. Pour into a chilled
collins glass and sprinkle with shredded coconut. Serves two.

*546 calories; 33.8 gm fat; 54%
calories from fat; 0 mg cholesterol;
28.6 mg sodium; 59.2 gm carbohydrate; 5.4 gm protein; 41.2 mg calcium; 2.5 mg iron; 44.5 RE vitamin A; 70.4 mg vitamin C*

APPLE-ALOE SMOOTHIE

APPLE-BERRY TREAT

12 parts apple juice (6 oz.)
8 fresh strawberries, or 6 parts
    strawberry puree (3 oz.)

Combine all ingredients except for one whole strawberry (for garnish) with cracked ice in a blender and blend until slushy. Pour into a chilled highball glass and garnish with the remaining strawberry. Serves two.

125 calories; 0.2 gm fat; 1% calories from fat; 0 mg cholesterol; 7.8 mg sodium; 31.6 gm carbohydrate; 1 gm protein; 11.9 mg calcium; 1.3 mg iron; 0 RE vitamin A; 107.6 mg vitamin C

APPLE-ALOE SMOOTHIE

2 tart apples, peeled,
    cored, and chopped
Juice of one lemon
2 parts aloe-vera juice (1 oz.)
1 banana, sliced
1 tbsp. bee pollen
1 tbsp. honey
White grape juice

Combine all ingredients except grape juice in a blender and blend until smooth. Slowly add grape juice through top of blender jar until milkshake-like consistency is achieved. Pour into chilled glasses and serve with drinking straws. Serves two.

215 calories; 0.7 gm fat; 3% calories from fat; 0 mg cholesterol; 1.3 mg sodium; 55.4 gm carbohydrate; 3.4 gm protein; 10.6 mg calcium; 0.5 mg iron; 10.7 RE vitamin A; 20.9 mg vitamin C

(Aloe-vera juice and bee pollen not included in nutritional analysis.)

APPLE BLAST

8 parts strong-brewed ginseng tea,
    chilled (4 oz.)
4 parts unsweetened cranberry
    juice (2 oz.)
Sparkling apple juice

Combine ginseng tea, cranberry juice, and ice cubes in a chilled highball glass. Fill the glass with sparkling juice and stir gently. Serves one.

84 calories; 0.3 gm fat; 3% calories from fat; 0 mg cholesterol; 3.9 mg sodium; 22.3 gm carbohydrate; 0.5 gm protein; 14.5 mg calcium; 0.5 mg iron; 5.2 RE vitamin A; 38.5 mg vitamin C

APPLE BLUSH

10 parts apple juice (5 oz.)
6 parts carrot juice (3 oz.)
3 parts beet juice (1½ oz.)

Combine juices with cracked ice in a cocktail shaker and shake well. Strain over ice cubes into a chilled highball glass. Serves two.

113 calories; 0.3 gm fat; 3% calories from fat; 0 mg cholesterol; 50.6 mg sodium; 27.3 gm carbohydrate; 1.4 gm protein; 35 mg calcium; 1.1 mg iron; 2,191 RE vitamin A; 66.4 mg vitamin C

APPLE-CHUTNEY SMOOTHIE

12 parts nonfat yogurt
(6 oz.)
10 parts apple juice (5 oz.)
2 tbsp. mango chutney
1 tbsp. honey
1 tsp. fresh-squeezed lemon juice

Combine all ingredients in a blender and blend until smooth. If mixture is too thick, add more apple juice until desired consistency is achieved. Pour into a chilled collins glass. Serves two.

331 calories; 0.2 gm fat; 0% calories from fat; 3.7 mg cholesterol; 129.2 mg sodium; 75.7 gm carbohydrate; 9.9 gm protein; 356.5 mg calcium; 1 mg iron; 0.1 RE vitamin A; 60.7 mg vitamin C

APPLE COBBLER

14 parts apple cider (7 oz.)
2 tbsp. damson plum jam
5 fresh mint leaves, bruised
2 whole cloves
Cinnamon stick
Ground nutmeg, for garnish

Combine all ingredients except nutmeg in a saucepan over medium heat until mixture is very hot but not boiling, stirring to dissolve jam. Strain into a warmed mug and sprinkle with nutmeg on top. Serves two.

213 calories; 0.6 gm fat; 2% calories from fat; 0 mg cholesterol; 12.1 mg sodium; 56 gm carbohydrate; 0.5 gm protein; 24.4 mg calcium; 1.5 mg iron; 1.5 RE vitamin A; 3.2 mg vitamin C

APPLE EGGNOG

32 parts whole milk (16 oz.)
32 parts apple cider (16 oz.)
16 parts egg substitute (8 oz.)
4 parts sugar (2 oz.)
1 tsp. alcohol-free almond extract
1 tsp. alcohol-free vanilla extract
Whipped cream, for garnish
Ground nutmeg, for garnish

Combine all ingredients except
whipped cream and nutmeg in a large
punch bowl and stir well. Serve in
chilled punch cups with a dollop of
whipped cream and sprinkled with
nutmeg. Serves eight.

*169 calories; 8.5 gm fat; 44% calo-
ries from fat; 28.33 mg cholesterol;
85.4 mg sodium; 18.4 gm carbohydrate; 5.6 gm protein; 96.1 mg calcium; 0.9 mg iron; 148.3 RE vitamin A; 1.2 mg vitamin C*

APPLE FIZZ

8 parts apple juice (4 oz.)
1 tsp. sugar syrup
½ tsp. fresh-squeezed lemon juice
Sparkling mineral water

Combine all ingredients except
sparkling water with cracked ice in a
cocktail shaker and shake well. Strain
over ice cubes into a chilled highball
glass and fill with sparkling mineral
water. Serves one.

APPLE FIZZ

*80 calories; 0 gm fat; 0% calories
from fat; 0 mg cholesterol; 4 mg
sodium; 20.4 gm carbohydrate; 0
gm protein; 9.8 mg calcium; 0.5
mg iron; 0 RE vitamin A; 3 mg vitamin C*

APPLE-MINT SPARKLER

6 parts apple juice (3 oz.)
1 tsp. alcohol-free mint extract
Sparkling mineral water
Fresh mint sprig, for garnish

Stir apple juice and mint extract
together in a mixing glass. Pour over
ice cubes into a chilled highball glass
and fill with sparkling mineral water.
Stir gently and garnish with the mint
sprig. Serves one.

*55 calories; 0.1 gm fat; 2% calories
from fat; 0 mg cholesterol; 38 mg
sodium; 11.4 gm carbohydrate;
0.1 gm protein; 6 mg calcium; 0.3
mg iron; 0 RE vitamin A; 34.9 mg
vitamin C*

APPLE PIE

10 parts apple cider
    (5 oz.)
1 tsp. brown sugar
1 tsp. fresh-squeezed lemon juice
½ tsp. ground cinnamon
¼ tsp. ground nutmeg
Ginger ale
Cinnamon stick, for garnish

Combine apple cider, brown sugar,
lemon juice, and ground spices in a
blender and blend well. Pour over ice
cubes into a chilled collins glass. Fill
glass with ginger ale and stir gently.
Garnish with cinnamon stick.
Serves one.

*156 calories; 1 gm fat; 6% calories
from fat; 0 mg cholesterol; 16 mg
sodium; 39.7 gm carbohydrate;
0.3 gm protein; 49.2 mg calcium;
2 mg iron; 0.9 RE vitamin A; 4.5
mg vitamin C*

APPLE-RAISIN SMOOTHIE

16 parts apple juice (8 oz.)
4 parts rehydrated raisins (2 oz.)
1 banana, sliced
1 tbsp. honey
½ tsp. cinnamon

Combine all the ingredients in a blender and blend until smooth. If mixture is too thick add more apple juice. Pour into chilled highball glasses. Serves two.

224 calories; 0.5 gm fat; 2% calories from fat; 0 mg cholesterol; 43 mg sodium; 57.3 gm carbohydrate; 1.6 gm protein; 32.5 mg calcium; 1.6 mg iron; 5.2 RE vitamin A; 52.7 mg vitamin C

APPLE SALAD

12 parts apple juice (6 oz.)
6 parts carrot juice (3 oz.)
6 parts celery juice (3 oz.)
Carrot stick, for garnish
Celery stick, for garnish

Combine juices with cracked ice in a cocktail shaker and shake well. Strain over ice cubes into a chilled collins glass. Garnish with the carrot and celery sticks. Serves one.

132 calories; 0.5 gm fat; 3% calories from fat; 0 mg cholesterol; 128 mg sodium; 31.9 gm carbohydrate; 1.8 gm protein; 77.7 mg calcium; 1.5 mg iron; 2,104 RE vitamin A; 85 mg vitamin C

APPLE SPRITZER

10 parts apple juice
  (5 oz.)
4 parts fresh-squeezed lime
  juice (2 oz.)
Sparkling mineral water
Lime slice, for garnish

Combine juices in a mixing glass and stir well. Pour over ice cubes into a chilled collins glass and fill the glass with sparkling mineral water. Stir gently and garnish with the lime slice. Serves one.

82 calories; 0.2 gm fat; 2% calories from fat; 0 mg cholesterol; 4.8 mg sodium; 21.7 gm carbohydrate; 0.3 gm protein; 15 mg calcium; 0.5 mg iron; 0.6 RE vitamin A; 74.8 mg vitamin C

APPLE ZINGER

10 parts apple juice
  (5 oz.)
4 parts fresh-squeezed lemon
  juice (2 oz.)
½ tsp. ginger juice
Cinnamon stick, for garnish

Combine all ingredients except cinnamon stick in a saucepan. Heat well over medium temperature but do not boil. Pour into a warmed mug and garnish with the cinnamon stick. Serves one.

91 calories; 0.3 gm fat; 2% calories from fat; 0 mg cholesterol; 6.6 mg sodium; 23.6 gm carbohydrate; 0.5 gm protein; 16.3 mg calcium; 0.6 mg iron; 1.1 RE vitamin C; 84.9 mg vitamin C

APPLES AND ORANGES

6 parts apple cider (3 oz.)
6 parts fresh-squeezed orange
  juice (3 oz.)
2 parts unsweetened cranberry
  juice (1 oz.)
Apple slice, for garnish

Combine apple cider and orange juice with cracked ice in a cocktail shaker and shake well. Strain into chilled collins glass. Slowly pour cranberry juice into the mixture to create a red, swirling effect. Do not stir. Garnish with the apple slice. Serves one.

106 calories; 0.4 gm fat; 3% calories from fat; 0 mg cholesterol; 4.1 mg sodium; 27 gm carbohydrate; 0.7 gm protein; 16.6 mg calcium; 0.7 mg iron; 18.6 RE vitamin A; 54.5 mg vitamin C

APRICOT BLUSH

10 parts apricot nectar (5 oz.)
4 parts strawberry puree (2 oz.)
4 parts aloe-vera juice (2 oz.)

Combine ingredients with cracked ice in a cocktail shaker and shake well. Strain into a chilled highball glass. Serves two.

114 calories; 0.5 gm fat; 4% calories from fat; 0 mg cholesterol; 5.4 mg sodium; 28.4 gm carbohydrate; 1.2 gm protein; 25.9 mg calcium; 1 mg iron; 190 RE vitamin A; 111.6 mg vitamin C

(Aloe vera juice not included in nutritional analysis.)

APRICOT CHILL

10 parts apricot nectar (5 oz.)
10 parts milk (5 oz.)
1 tbsp. coconut syrup
2 scoops vanilla ice cream

Combine the ingredients in a blender and blend until smooth. Pour into a chilled collins glass. Serves two.

455 calories; 12 gm fat; 23% calories from fat; 42.5 mg cholesterol; 219 mg sodium; 78.8 gm carbohydrate; 11.6 gm protein; 427.7 calcium; 1.5 mg iron; 310.7 RE vitamin A; 49.9 mg vitamin C

APRICOT FRAPPE

6 parts apricot nectar
  (3 oz.)
4 parts pineapple juice (2 oz.)
2 parts fresh-squeezed lime
  juice (1 oz.)
2 parts cherry syrup (1 oz.)

Combine all ingredients with cracked
ice in a blender. Blend until slushy
and pour into a chilled collins glass.
Serves one.

224 calories; 0.2 gm fat; 1% calories from fat; 0 mg cholesterol; 32.6 sodium; 39.2 gm carbohydrate; 0.7 gm protein; 26.7 calcium; 0.8 mg iron; 126.9 RE vitamin A; 49.6 mg vitamin C

APRICOT SPARKLER

APRICOT-PRUNE NECTAR

8 parts apricot nectar
  (4 oz.)
8 parts prune juice (4 oz.)
1 tbsp. fresh-squeezed lemon juice

Combine the ingredients with cracked
ice in a cocktail shaker and shake
well. Strain into chilled old-fashioned
glasses. Serves two.

74 calories; 0.1 gm fat; 1% calories from fat; 0 mg cholesterol; 4 mg sodium; 18.7 gm carbohydrate; 2 gm protein; 11.3 mg calcium; 0.9 mg iron; 75.1 RE vitamin A; 24.8 mg vitamin C

APRICOT-RASPBERRY FIZZ

8 parts apricot nectar (4 oz.)
4 parts raspberry juice or puree (2 oz.)
Lime-flavored sparkling mineral water

Combine apricot nectar and raspberry
juice with cracked ice in a cocktail
shaker and shake well. Strain into a
chilled highball glass. Fill the glass
with mineral water and stir gently.
Serves one.

86 calories; 0.2 gm fat; 2% calories from fat; 0 mg cholesterol; 3.7 mg sodium; 21.6 gm carbohydrate; 0.7 gm protein; 15.5 mg calcium; 0.6 mg iron; 169.5 RE vitamin A; 49.6 mg vitamin C

APRICOT SHAKE

8 parts apricot nectar (4 oz.)
4 parts unsweetened apricot
  preserves (2 oz.)
10 parts plain nonfat yogurt (5 oz.)
1 tsp. bee pollen
Nonfat milk (optional)*

Combine all ingredients except milk
in a blender and blend until smooth.
If shake is too thick, add nonfat milk
until desired consistency is achieved.
Pour into a chilled collins glass.
Serves two.

226 calories; 0.2 gm fat; 1% calories from fat; 3.6 mg cholesterol; 121.3 mg sodium; 48.8 gm carbohydrate; 14 gm protein; 329.6 mg calcium; 0.7 mg iron; 167.8 RE vitamin A; 38.7 mg vitamin C

(Bee pollen and nonfat milk not included in nutritional analysis.)

APRICOT SPARKLER

4 parts apricot nectar (2 oz.)
2 parts fresh-squeezed lemon
  juice (1 oz.)
Sparkling mineral water
Lemon peel, for garnish

Combine all ingredients except
sparkling mineral water with cracked
ice in a mixing glass. Stir well. Strain
over ice cubes into a chilled highball
glass. Top off with sparkling mineral
water and stir. Twist lemon peel over
glass and drop in. Serves one.

31

ARCATA SUNSET

43 calories; 0 gm fat; 0% calories from fat; 0 mg cholesterol; 2.1 mg sodium; 11.6 gm carbohydrate; 0.3 gm protein; 6.5 mg calcium; 0.2 mg iron; 83.3 RE vitamin A; 35 mg vitamin C

ARCATA SUNSET

6 parts cranberry juice
  cocktail (3 oz.)
2 parts fresh-squeezed lime
  juice (1 oz.)
Lime slice, for garnish
Fresh mint sprig, for garnish

Combine cranberry juice and lime juice with crushed ice in a cocktail shaker and shake well. Pour into a chilled wineglass. Garnish with lime slice and mint sprig. Serves one.

62 calories; 0.1 gm fat; 1% calories from fat; 0 mg cholesterol; 4 mg sodium; 16.4 gm carbohydrate; 0.1 gm protein; 24.3 mg calcium; 0.1 mg iron; 0.3 RE vitamin A; 42.6 mg vitamin C

ATOMIC FREEZE

16 parts pineapple juice (8 oz.)
10 parts apple juice (5 oz.)
8 parts strawberry puree (4 oz.)
1 tsp. alcohol-free almond extract
Whole strawberries, for garnish

Combine all ingredients except whole
strawberries with cracked ice in a
blender and blend until slushy. Pour
into chilled highball glasses and garnish with the whole strawberries.
Serves two.

*134 calories; 0.2 gm fat; 1% calo-
ries from fat; 0 mg cholesterol; 5.1
mg sodium; 32.5 gm carbohydrate;
1 gm protein; 24.3 mg calcium; 1
mg iron; 0.5 RE vitamin A; 66.4
mg vitamin C*

AUGUST MOON

16 parts apple juice
   (8 oz.)
16 parts raspberry juice (8 oz.)
1 tbsp. fresh-squeezed lime juice
1 tbsp. honey

Combine all ingredients in a blender
and blend until smooth. Pour over ice
cubes into chilled highball glasses.
Serves two.

*132 calories; 0.6 gm fat; 4% calo-
ries from fat; 0 mg cholesterol; 4 mg
sodium; 33.2 gm carbohydrate;
1 gm protein; 29.5 mg calcium;
0 mg iron; 12 RE vitamin A;
71.9 mg vitamin C*

AUTUMN HARVEST

8 parts prune juice (4 oz.)
6 parts white grape juice (3 oz.)
6 parts pomegranate juice (3 oz.)

Combine juices with cracked ice in a
cocktail shaker and shake well. Strain
over ice cubes into a chilled highball
glass. Serves one.

*162 calories; 0.1 gm fat; 1% calo-
ries from fat; 0 mg cholesterol; 5.9
mg sodium; 39.7 gm carbohydrate;
1.5 gm protein; 16 mg calcium; 1.7
mg iron; 0.4 RE vitamin A; 6.9 mg
vitamin C*

AVOCADO SMOOTHIE

10 parts nonfat yogurt
   (5 oz.)
8 parts cucumber juice (4 oz.)
1 part fresh-squeezed lime
   juice (½ oz.)
1 Haas avocado, peeled, pitted, and
   sliced

Combine ingredients in a blender and
blend until smooth. Pour into a
chilled collins glass. Serves two.

*414 calories; 30.3 gm fat; 61%
calories from fat; 3.1 mg cholesterol; 125.6 mg sodium; 31.1 gm
carbohydrate; 13 gm protein;
332.8 mg calcium; 2.7 mg iron;
114.4 RE vitamin A; 28.5 mg
vitamin C*

BABY BELLINI

4 parts peach nectar (2 oz.)
2 parts fresh-squeezed lemon
   juice (1 oz.)
Sparkling apple cider, chilled
Fresh mint sprig, for garnish

Pour the peach nectar and lemon
juice into a chilled champagne flute
and stir well. Fill the glass with the
sparkling cider and stir gently.
Garnish with mint sprig. Serves one.

103 calories; 0.1 gm fat; 1% calories from fat; 0 mg cholesterol; 5.9 mg sodium; 28.4 gm carbohydrate; 0.4 gm protein; 12.8 gm calcium; 0.7 mg iron; 16.6 RE vitamin A; 18.5 mg vitamin C

BABY BELLINI

BABYLON BY THE BAY

Lemonade (see Traditional Lemonade,
   page 207)
Ginger beer
Lemon wedge, for garnish

Slowly pour equal amounts of lemonade and ginger beer into a chilled pilsner glass. Do not stir. Squeeze lemon
wedge over drink and drop in. Serves
one.

80 calories; 0 gm fat; 0% calories from fat; 0 mg cholesterol; 15.4 mg sodium; 21.3 gm carbohydrate; 0.6 gm prottein; 19.2 mg calcium; 0.1 mg iron; 1.8 RE vitamin A; 42 mg vitamin C

BAJA TOMATO

12 parts tomato juice
   (6 oz.)
6 parts fresh-squeezed orange
   juice (3 oz.)
4 parts pineapple juice (2 oz.)
Pineapple spear, for garnish

Combine juices with cracked ice in a
cocktail shaker and shake well. Strain
over ice cubes into chilled highball
glasses and garnish with a pineapple
spear. Serves two.

68 calories; 0.3 gm fat; 2% calories from fat; 0 mg cholesterol; 307.5 mg sodium; 16.6 gm carbohydrate; 0.1 gm protein; 19.8 mg calcium; 0.8 mg iron; 56.9 RE vitamin A; 37.1 mg vitamin C

BAKERSFIELD SPECIAL

4 parts sparkling apple
   cider
   (2 oz.)
2 parts apricot nectar (1 oz.)
2 part fresh-squeezed lemon
   juice (1 oz.)
Lemon twist, for garnish

Combine all ingredients with cracked
ice in a mixing glass, and shake well.
Pour into chilled old-fashioned glass
and garnish with a lemon twist. Serves
one.

74 calories; 0.1 gm fat; 1% calories from fat; 0 mg cholesterol; 4.4 mg sodium; 20.2 gm carbohydrate; 0.4 gm protein; 10.1 mg calcium; 0.5 mg iron; 83.1 RE vitamin A; 14.9 mg vitamin C

BAKERSFIELD SPECIAL

BALBOA SMOOTHIE

1 banana, sliced
8 parts vanilla nonfat
   yogurt (4 oz.)
Fresh-squeezed orange juice

Combine the banana and vanilla yogurt in a blender and blend until smooth. While running the blender at its lowest speed, slowly add the orange juice through the top of blender until desired consistency is achieved. Pour into a chilled collins glass. Serves one.

220 calories; 0.7 gm fat; 3% calories from fat; 2.5 mg cholesterol; 71.4 mg sodium; 50.1 gm carbohydrate; 7.1 mg protein; 213 mg calcium; 0.5 mg iron; 20.5 RE vitamin A; 38.7 mg vitamin C

BANANA-BERRY SMOOTHIE

4 parts fresh raspberries
   (2 oz.)
4 parts fresh blackberries (2 oz.)
4 parts fresh strawberries, sliced (2 oz.)
1 banana, sliced
½ tsp. ginger juice
White grape juice

Combine fresh fruits and ginger juice in a blender and blend until smooth. While running the blender at its lowest speed, slowly add the grape juice through the top of the blender until desired consistency is achieved. Pour into a chilled collins glass. Serves two.

214 calories; 1.3 gm fat; 5% calories from fat; 0 mg cholesterol; 3.3 mg sodium; 53 gm carbohydrate; 2.8 gm protein; 50.7 mg calcium; 1.3 mg iron; 27.9 RE vitamin A; 68.6 mg vitamin C

BANANA-MOCHA FRAPPE

8 parts nonfat milk (4 oz.)
8 parts strong-brewed coffee, cold (4 oz.)
1 banana, sliced
1 scoop chocolate ice cream
Cocoa powder, for garnish

Combine all the ingredients except cocoa in a blender and blend until smooth. Pour into a chilled collins glass and sprinkle with cocoa. Serves two.

393 calories; 13.3 gm fat; 29% calories from fat; 39.7 mg cholesterol; 147.5 mg sodium; 64.6 gm carbohydrate; 9.5 gm protein; 272.8 mg calcium; 1.5 mg iron; 212.6 RE vitamin A; 12.3 mg vitamin C

BANANARAMA

12 parts apricot juice (6 oz.)
5 parts coconut milk (2½ oz.)
1 banana, sliced

Combine the ingredients in a blender and blend until smooth. Pour into a chilled highball glass. Serves two.

393 calories; 17.6 gm fat; 40% calories from fat; 0 mg cholesterol; 18 mg sodium; 55.1 gm carbohydrate; 3.4 gm protein; 30 mg calcium; 2.2 mg iron; 232.8 RE vitamin A; 13.2 mg vitamin C

BANANA SHAKE

12 parts nonfat milk (6 oz.)
1 banana, sliced
1 scoop vanilla ice cream (or frozen yogurt)
Ground cinnamon, for garnish

Combine all ingredients except cinnamon in a blender and blend until smooth. Pour into chilled collins glass and sprinkle with cinnamon. Serves two.

324 calories; 5.7 gm fat; 15% calories from fat; 18.2 mg cholesterol; 184.8 mg sodium; 61 gm carbohydrate; 11.3 gm protein; 378 mg calcium; 0.6 mg iron; 166.7 RE vitamin A; 12.9 mg vitamin C

(Nutritional analysis represents totals when using vanilla ice cream.)

BANANA SMOOTHIE

12 parts fresh-squeezed orange juice (6 oz.)
12 parts plain nonfat yogurt (6 oz.)
1 banana, sliced
½ tsp. alcohol-free vanilla extract
1 tbsp. honey

Combine all ingredients in a blender and blend until smooth. If mixture is too thick, add more orange juice until desired consistency is achieved. Pour into chilled highball glasses. Serves two.

192 calories; 0.4 gm fat; 2% calories from fat; 1.9 mg cholesterol; 54.1 mg sodium; 44 gm carbohydrate; 5.3 gm protein; 163.1 mg calcium; 0.4 mg iron; 21.6 RE vitamin A; 47.7 mg vitamin C

BANANA SPLIT

10 parts nonfat milk (5 oz.)
4 parts chocolate syrup (2 oz.)
2 parts unsweetened cherry juice (1 oz.)
2 scoops vanilla frozen yogurt
1 banana, sliced

Combine all ingredients in a blender and blend until smooth. (For a thinner drink, add more nonfat milk.) Pour into chilled highball glasses. Serves two.

264 calories; 4.8 gm fat; 15% calories from fat; 3.15 cholesterol; 114.9 mg sodium; 53.3 gm carbohydrate; 6.5 gm protein; 200.4 mg calcium; 0.9 mg iron; 92 RE vitamin A; 20 mg vitamin C

BANANARAMA

BANANA-STRAWBERRY FREEZE

1 banana, frozen and sliced
8 parts strawberries, frozen (4 oz.)
White grape juice

Combine the banana and strawberries in a blender. While running the blender at its lowest speed, slowly add the grape juice through the top of blender until desired consistency is achieved. Pour into a chilled collins glass. Serves two.

197 calories; 0.7 gm fat; 3% calories from fat; 0 mg cholesterol; 5.8 mg sodium; 49.8 gm carbohydrate; 2.1 gm protein; 32.8 mg calcium; 1.4 mg iron; 14.9 RE vitamin A; 57.1 mg vitamin C

BANDWAGON

12 parts apple juice (6 oz.)
8 parts carrot juice (4 oz.)
8 parts pineapple juice (4 oz.)
1 Haas avocado, peeled, pitted, and chopped

Combine all ingredients in a blender and blend until smooth. Pour into chilled highball glasses.
Serves two.

247 calories; 15.2 gm fat; 52% calories from fat; 0 mg cholesterol; 30 mg sodium; 29 gm carbohydrate; 2.6 gm protein; 38.7 mg calcium; 1.7mg iron; 1513 RE vitamin A; 52.7 mg vitamin C

BEACHCOMBER

BARBARA'S SPARKLING BERRY PUNCH

8 parts blackberry juice (4 oz.)
8 parts raspberry juice (4 oz.)
8 parts strawberry juice (4 oz.)
2 750-ml bottles of de-alcoholized
  sparkling wine, well-chilled
Whole berries, for garnish

Combine juices in a punch bowl. Just before serving, pour in the bottles of wine, stirring gently. Float fresh berries on top for garnish. Serves ten.

82 calories; 0.1 gm fat; 2% calories from fat; 0 mg cholesterol; 23.7 mg sodium; 21.2 gm carbohydrate; 0.3 gm protein; 12.4 mg calcium; 0.3 mg iron; 3.7 RE vitamin A; 11.7 mg vitamin C

BARBIE'S BEACH TREAT

8 parts fresh-squeezed
  orange juice (4 oz.)
8 parts fresh raspberries (4 oz.)
4 parts unsweetened cranberry
  juice (2 oz.)
Fresh raspberries, for garnish

Combine all ingredients except raspberries with cracked ice in a blender and blend until slushy. Pour into chilled highball glasses and garnish with fresh raspberries. Serves two.

67 calories; 0.5 gm fat; 6% calories from fat; 0 mg cholesterol; 0.7 mg sodium; 16.1 gm carbohydrate; 1 gm protein; 20.7 mg calcium; 0.5 mg iron; 20 RE vitamin A; 46.4 mg vitamin C

BARTON PINK

8 parts guava nectar (4 oz.)
4 parts fresh-squeezed
   lemon juice (2 oz.)
Ginger ale

Combine juices with cracked ice in a cocktail shaker and shake well. Strain over ice cubes into a chilled collins glass and fill the glass with ginger ale. Stir gently. Serves one.

86 calories; 0.2 gm fat; 2% calories from fat; 0 mg cholesterol; 30.7 mg sodium; 21.2 gm carbohydrate; 1.5 gm protein; 43.2 mg calcium; 1.5 mg iron; 12.5 RE vitamin A; 198.7 mg vitamin C

BEACHCOMBER

10 parts guava nectar
   (5 oz.)
2 parts raspberry syrup (1 oz.)
4 parts fresh-squeezed lime
   juice (2 oz.)

Combine all ingredients with cracked ice in a cocktail shaker and shake well. Pour into a chilled collins glass. Serves two.

215 calories; 0.9 gm fat; 3% calories from fat; 0 mg cholesterol; 32.8 mg sodium; 55.5 gm carbohydrate; 1.4 gm protein; 4.3 mg calcium; 0.7 mg iron; 112.9 RE vitamin A; 277.9 mg vitamin C

BEAR'S CHOICE

6 parts Granny Smith apple juice
   (3 oz.)*
12 parts lemonade (6 oz.) (see
   Traditional Lemonade, page 207)

Combine all ingredients together in a mixing glass. Strain over ice cubes into a chilled collins glass. Serves two.

51 calories; 0 gm fat; 0% calories from fat; 0 mg cholesterol; 6.7 mg sodium; 14.4 gm carbohydrate; 0.2 gm protein; 6.4 mg calcium; 0.2 mg iron; 1.2 RE vitamin A; 28 mg vitamin C

*If you are juicing your own apple juice, use Granny Smith apples. Otherwise any store-bought apple juice may be used.

BEDAZZLED

6 parts fresh-squeezed
   orange juice (3 oz.)
4 parts pineapple juice (2 oz.)
1 tbsp. fresh-squeezed lime juice
Ginger ale
Orange twist, for garnish

Combine juices with cracked ice in a cocktail shaker and shake well. Strain over ice cubes into a chilled collins glass and slowly fill glass with ginger ale. Stir gently and garnish with the orange twist. Serves one.

93 calories; 0.2 gm fat; 2% calories from fat; 0 mg cholesterol; 5.4 mg sodium; 23 gm carbohydrate; 0.8 gm protein; 22 mg calcium; 0.4 mg iron; 17.4 RE vitamin A; 53.1 mg vitamin C

BEETLEJUICE

8 parts beet juice (4 oz.)
8 parts kiwi juice (4 oz.)
4 parts cucumber juice (2 oz.)
Sparkling mineral water
Cucumber slices, for garnish

Combine juices with cracked ice in a cocktail shaker and shake well. Strain into chilled collins glasses and fill the glasses with sparkling mineral water. Stir gently and garnish with cucumber slices. Serves two.

58 calories; 0.3 gm fat; 5% calories from fat; 0 mg cholesterol; 31.5 mg sodium; 13.5 gm carbohydrate; 1.4 gm protein; 27 mg calcium; 0.7 mg iron; 12.6 RE vitamin A; 60.7 mg vitamin C

BEFORE AND AFTER

8 parts prune juice (4 oz.)
6 parts white grape juice (3 oz.)
1 tbsp. fresh-squeezed lemon juice

Combine juices with cracked ice in a cocktail shaker and shake well. Strain over ice cubes into a chilled highball glass. Serves two.

136 calories; 0.1 gm fat; 1% calories from fat; 0 mg cholesterol; 7.2 mg sodium; 33.8 gm carbohydrate; 1.2 gm protein; 22.3 mg calcium; 1.5 mg iron; 1.4 RE vitamin A; 11.7 mg vitamin C

BERRY-BERRY MANGO

8 parts mango juice
 (4 oz.)
4 parts blueberry juice (2 oz.)
4 parts raspberry juice (2 oz.)
Sparkling mineral water

Combine juices in a blender and blend until smooth. Pour over ice cubes into chilled collins glass and fill the glass with sparkling mineral water. Stir gently. Serves two.

134 calories; 0.8 gm fat; 5% calories from fat; 0 mg cholesterol; 33.9 gm carbohydrate; 1.5 gm protein; 27.4 mg calcium; 0.6 mg iron; 454.6 RE vitamin A; 52.9 mg vitamin C

BETA BOOSTER

12 parts carrot juice (6 oz.)
6 parts unsweetened cherry
 juice (3 oz.)
4 parts celery juice (2 oz.)
2 parts red-cabbage juice (1 oz.)

Combine juices with cracked ice in a cocktail shaker and shake well. Strain over ice cubes into chilled old-fashioned glasses. Serves two.

77 calories; 0.6 gm fat; 7% calories from fat; 0 mg cholesterol; 52.4 mg sodium; 17.8 gm carbohydrate; 1.9 gm protein; 52.5 mg calcium; 0.8 mg iron; 2,204 RE vitamin A; 28.4 mg vitamin C

BEVERLY HILLS SPARKLER

4 parts black-currant syrup (2 oz.)
1 tsp. alcohol-free anise extract
Sparkling mineral water
Fresh mint sprig, for garnish

Combine the black-currant syrup and the anise extract in a chilled collins glass. Fill the glass about two-thirds full with the sparkling mineral water and stir gently. Add ice cubes and garnish with the mint sprig. Serves one.

163 calories; 0 gm fat; 0% calories from fat; 0 mg cholesterol; 2.8 mg sodium; 39.9 gm carbohydrate; 0 gm protein; 34 mg calcium; 2 mg iron; 0 RE vitamin A; 0 mg vitamin C

BIG BEAR COCOA

2 heaping tsp. unsweetened
 cocoa powder
½ tsp. ground cinnamon
2 tbsp. honey
16 parts hot milk (8 oz.)
Whipped cream, for garnish
Ground nutmeg, for garnish
Cinnamon stick, for garnish

Combine the cocoa, cinnamon, and honey in a warmed mug. Add the hot milk and stir until blended. Top with a dollop of whipped cream, sprinkle with nutmeg, and garnish with the cinnamon stick. Serves one.

410 calories; 14.9 gm fat; 32% calories from fat; 35.8 mg cholesterol; 126 mg sodium; 60 gm carbohydrate; 11.9 gm protein; 300 mg calcium; 2.8 mg iron; 148.5 RE vitamin A; 2.5 mg vitamin C

BITE OF THE APPLE

BIG ONE

12 parts pear juice (6 oz.)
12 parts plum juice (6 oz.)
1 banana, sliced
1 tbsp. honey
Cinnamon sticks, for garnish

Combine all ingredients except cinnamon sticks in a blender and blend until smooth. Pour into chilled highball glasses and garnish with cinnamon sticks. Serves two.

182 calories; 0.8 gm fat; 0% calories from fat; 0 mg cholesterol; 4 mg sodium; 46 gm carbohydrate; 1 gm protein; 11 mg calcium; 0.5 mg iron; 31.8 RE vitamin A; 14.2 mg vitamin C

BITE OF THE APPLE

10 parts apple juice (5 oz.)
2 parts fresh-squeezed
   lime juice (1 oz.)
1 part orgeat (almond) syrup (½ oz.)
1 tbsp. unsweetened apple sauce
Ground cinnamon, for garnish

Combine all ingredients except cinnamon with cracked ice in a blender and blend at medium speed until smooth. Pour into a chilled pilsner glass and sprinkle with cinnamon. Serves one.

150 calories; 0.2 gm fat; 1% calories from fat; 0 mg cholesterol; 19.4 mg sodium; 45.5 mg carbohydrate; 39.2 gm calcium; 0.3 gm protein; 1.5 mg iron; 1.3 RE vitamin A; 67.3 mg vitamin C

41

BITTER-ORANGE FIZZ

8 parts fresh-squeezed
   orange juice (4 oz.)
1 part unsweetened cranberry
   juice (½ oz.)
Bitter-orange or bitter-lemon soda

Combine juices with cracked ice in a
cocktail shaker and shake well. Strain
over ice cubes into a a chilled collins
glass and fill with bitter-orange or
bitter-lemon soda. Stir gently.
Serves one.

*99 calories; 0.3 gm fat; 2% calories
from fat; 0 mg cholesterol; 10.5 gm
sodium; 24.2 carbohydrate; 0.9 gm
protein; 16.1 mg calcium; 0.3 mg
iron; 24 RE vitamin A; 60.5 mg
vitamin C*

BITTERSWEET UNION

4 parts passion-fruit juice (2 oz.)
4 parts mango nectar (2 oz.)
Bitter-lemon soda
Lime wedge, for garnish

Combine juices with cracked ice in a
cocktail shaker and shake well. Strain
over ice cubes into a a chilled collins
glass. Fill the glass with the bitter-
lemon and stir gently. Garnish with
the lime wedge. Serves one.

*112 calories; 0.3 gm fat; 3% calo-
ries from fat; 0 mg cholesterol; 11.3
mg sodium; 28.6 gm carbohydrate;
0.8 gm protein; 12 mg calcium;
0.4 mg iron; 467.7 RE vitamin A;
60. 5 mg vitamin C*

BLACK AND TAN

Ginger ale, chilled
Ginger beer, chilled
Lime wedge, for garnish

Pour equal parts of the ginger ale and
ginger beer into a chilled pilsner glass.
Do not stir. Garnish with the lime
wedge. Serves one.

*106 calories; 0 gm fat; 0% calories
from fat; 0 mg cholesterol; 26.3 mg
sodium; 27.3 gm carbohydrate;
0 gm protein; 11.3 mg calcium;
0.3 mg iron; 0 RE vitamin A; 0 mg
vitamin C*

BLACK-AND-WHITE MILKSHAKE

16 parts milk (8 oz.)
1 scoop chocolate ice cream
1 scoop vanilla ice cream
2 tbsp. chocolate syrup
1 tsp. alcohol-free vanilla extract

Combine all ingredients in a blender
and blend until smooth. Pour into
chilled highball glasses. Serves two.

*473 calories; 22.8 gm fat; 42%
calories from fat; 81.1 mg cholesterol; 120.3 mg sodium; 61.2 gm
carbohydrate; 10.3 gm protein;
340.6 mg calcium; 1.2 mg iron;
242.6 RE vitamin A; 2.2 mg vitamin C*

BLACKBERRY BLOSSOM

8 parts blackberry puree
   (4 oz.)
10 parts rose-hip tea, chilled (5 oz.)
2 parts fresh-squeezed lemon
   juice (1 oz.)
1 tsp. sugar or to taste
2 fresh mint sprigs, for garnish

Combine all ingredients except mint
sprigs with cracked ice in a cocktail
shaker and shake well. Strain over ice
cubes into two old-fashioned glasses.
Add more sugar if desired. Garnish
with mint sprigs. Serves two.

*42 calories; 0.2 gm fat; 4% calories
from fat; 81.1 mg cholesterol; 120.3
mg sodium; 10.7 gm carbohydrate;
0.5 gm protein; 20.6 mg calcium;
0.4 mg iron; 9.6 RE vitamin A;
18.4 mg vitamin C*

BLACK AND TAN

BLACKBERRY BRAMBLE

8 parts apple juice (4 oz.)
4 parts blackberry puree (2 oz.)
2 parts maple syrup (1 oz.)
1 tbsp. fresh-squeezed lemon juice
Fresh blackberries, for garnish

Combine all ingredients except fresh blackberries with cracked ice in a blender and blend until slushy. Pour into chilled old-fashioned glasses and garnish with fresh blackberries. Serves two.

79 calories; 0.2 gm fat; 2% calories from fat; 0 mg cholesterol; 12.3 mg sodium; 20.1 gm carbohydrate; 0.3 gm protein; 28.3 mg calcium; 0.4 mg iron; 4.8 RE vitamin A; 18.4 mg vitamin C

BLACK-CURRANT BLISS

8 parts nonfat milk (4 oz.)
8 parts nonfat plain yogurt (4 oz.)
4 parts black-currant syrup (2 oz.)
4 parts blackberry juice (2 oz.)
½ tsp. alcohol-free anise extract

Combine all ingredients in a blender and blend until smooth. Pour into a chilled collins glass. Serves two.

285 calories; 0.4 gm fat; 1% calories from fat; 4.3 mg cholesterol; 126.3 mg sodium; 61 gm carbohydrate; 10.8 gm protein; 416.7 mg calcium; 2.4 mg iron; 78.8 RE vitamin A; 32.7 mg vitamin C

BLADE RUNNER

8 parts lemonade (4 oz.)
  (see Traditional Lemonade, page 207)
4 parts cucumber juice (2 oz.)
Sparkling white grape juice
Fresh mint sprig, for garnish

Combine lemonade and cucumber juice with cracked ice in a cocktail shaker and shake well. Strain over ice cubes into a chilled collins glass and fill the glass with sparkling grape juice. Stir gently and garnish with the fresh mint sprig. Serves one.

104 calories; 0.1 gm fat; 1% calories from fat; 0 mg cholesterol; 12 mg sodium; 28.8 gm carbohydrate; 1.1 gm protein; 20.6 mg calcium; 0.4 mg iron; 5.3 RE vitamin A; 58.7 mg vitamin C

BLENDER BENDER

12 parts plain nonfat yogurt (6 oz.)
10 parts carrot juice (5 oz.)
4 parts broccoli juice (2 oz.)
4 parts cucumber juice (2 oz.)

Combine all ingredients in a blender and blend until smooth. Pour into chilled highball glasses. Serves two.

85 calories; 0.2 gm fat; 2% calories from fat; 1.9 mg cholesterol; 12.9 mg sodium; 15.7 gm carbohydrate; 12.9 mg sodium; 0.7 mg iron; 1,870 RE vitamin A; 33.8 mg vitamin C

BLOODY ORANGE

8 parts fresh-squeezed
  orange juice (4 oz.)
6 parts unsweetened cherry
  cider (3 oz.)
1 tbsp. fresh-squeezed lemon juice
Orange slice, for garnish

Combine the juices with cracked ice in a cocktail shaker and shake well. Strain over ice cubes into a chilled highball glass and garnish with the orange slice. Serves one.

95 calories; 0.8 gm fat; 7% calories from fat; 0 mg cholesterol; 4.3 mg sodium; 22.5 gm carbohydrate; 1.5 gm protein; 21.8 gm calcium; 0.5 mg iron; 35.2 RE vitamin A; 67.7 mg vitamin C

BLUE-ANGEL COCKTAIL

8 parts blueberry juice (4 oz.)
12 parts watermelon juice (6 oz.)
Lemon twists, for garnish

Combine the juices with cracked ice in a cocktail shaker and shake well. Strain into chilled cocktail glasses and garnish with lemon twists. Serves two.

66 calories; 0.6 gm fat; 8% calories from fat; 0 mg cholesterol; 4.3 mg sodium; 16 gm carbohydrate; 1 gm protein; 10.8 gm calcium; 0.3 mg iron; 36.5 RE vitamin A; 17.2 mg vitamin C

BLUEBERRY SHAKE

8 parts frozen blueberries (4 oz.)
16 parts milk
2 scoops vanilla ice cream
Fresh blueberries, for garnish

Combine all ingredients except fresh blueberries in a blender and blend until slushy. Pour into a chilled collins glasses and garnish with fresh blueberries. Serves two.

BLUEBERRY SHAKE

472 calories; 23.4 gm fat; 45% calories from fat; 91.2 mg cholesterol; 227.1 mg sodium; 56.2 gm carbohydrate; 13.1 gm protein; 470.1 mg calcium; 0.4 mg iron; 238.7 RE vitamin A; 5.9 mg vitamin C

BLUEBERRY SMOOTHIE

8 parts blueberries, fresh or
    frozen-thawed (4 oz.)
8 parts vanilla nonfat yogurt (4 oz.)
4 parts nonfat milk (2 oz.)
1 tsp. bee pollen
1 banana, sliced

Combine all ingredients in a blender and blend until smooth. If drink is too thick, add more nonfat milk until desired consistency is achieved. Pour into chilled highball glasses. Serves two.

139 calories; 0.5 gm fat; 3% calories from fat; 1.7 mg cholesterol; 123.6 mg sodium; 31.5 gm carbohydrate; 4.7 gm protein; 141.8 gm calcium; 0.3 mg iron; 27.6 RE vitamin A; 12.8 mg vitamin C

(Bee pollen not included in nutritional analysis.)

BLUEBERRY TART

12 parts blueberry puree (6 oz.)
6 parts unsweetened cranberry
    juice (3 oz.)
Ginger ale

Combine blueberry puree and cranberry juice in a cocktail shaker and
shake well. Pour into a chilled collins
glass and fill the glass with ginger ale.
Serves two.

*168 calories; 0.6 gm fat; 3% calo-
ries from fat; 0 mg cholesterol; 20
mg sodium; 42.5 gm carbohydrate;
0.9 gm protein; 14.6 mg calcium;
0.5 mg iron; 14.5 RE vitamin A; 49
mg vitamin C*

BLUSHING PEACH
SMOOTHIE

12 parts peach juice (6 oz.)
8 parts raspberry puree
    (4 oz.)
8 parts coconut milk (4 oz.)
1 banana, sliced
1 tbsp. ginger juice
Mint sprigs, for garnish

Combine all ingredients except mint
sprigs in a blender and blend until
smooth. Pour into chilled highball
glasses and garnish with mint sprigs.
Serves two.

*284 calories; 16.7 gm fat; 51%
calories from fat; 0 mg cholesterol;
19.1 mg sodium; 33.4 gm carbohydrate; 3.7 gm protein; 25.5 mg
calcium; 1.4 mg iron; 33.5 RE
vitamin A; 23.8 mg vitamin C*

BODEGA BAY

10 parts grapefruit juice (5 oz.)
8 parts cranberry juice cocktail
    (4 oz.)
1 part white grape juice (½ oz.)

Combine all ingredients with cracked
ice in a cocktail shaker and shake
well. Strain over ice cubes into a
chilled collins glass. Serves one.

*144 calories; 0.1 gm fat; 1% calo-
ries from fat; 0 mg cholesterol; 10.9
mg sodium; 35.1 gm carbohydrate;
2.1 gm protein; 30.2 mg calcium;
0.3 mg iron; 1.4 RE vitamin A;
113.8 mg vitamin C*

BORDER
PATROL

8 parts mango juice
    (4 oz.)
4 parts fresh-squeezed orange
    juice (2 oz.)
1 scoop lemon sorbet
Sparkling mineral water
Lemon twist, for garnish

Combine all ingredients except mineral water and lemon twist in a
blender and blend until smooth. Pour
into a chilled collins glass and fill the
glass with sparkling water. Stir gently
and garnish with the lemon twist.
Serves one.

*194 calories; 0.2 gm fat; 2% calo-
ries from fat; 0 mg cholesterol; 2.1
mg sodium; 44.7 gm carbohydrate;
5.6 gm protein; 66.9 mg calcium;
0.3 mg iron; 245.1 RE vitamin A;
48.2 mg vitamin C*

BOTTLED SUNSHINE

10 parts pineapple juice
    (5 oz.)
4 parts strawberry puree (2 oz.)
4 parts fresh-squeezed lemon juice
    (2 oz.)
Pineapple spear

Combine all ingredients with cracked
ice in a cocktail shaker and shake
well. Strain over cracked ice into a a
chilled collins glass and garnish with
the pineapple spear. Serves one.

111 calories; 0.3 gm fat; 2% calories from fat; 0 mg cholesterol; 2.6 mg sodium; 28.5 gm carbohydrate; 1 gm protein; 36 mg calcium; 0.6 mg iron; 3.5 RE vitamin A; 73.4 mg vitamin C

BREAKFAST NOG

10 parts nonfat milk
    (5 oz.)
8 parts fresh-squeezed orange
    juice (4 oz.)
6 parts egg substitute (3 oz.)
Ground cinnamon, for garnish

Combine all ingredients except cinnamon in a blender and blend until
smooth. Pour into a chilled collins
glass and sprinkle with cinnamon.
Serves one.

178 calories; 3.4 gm fat; 17% calories from fat; 3.2 mg cholesterol; 224.9 mg sodium; 21.1 gm carbohydrate; 15.9 gm protein; 260.1 mg calcium; 2.9 mg iron; 293.7 RE vitamin A; 58.7 mg vitamin C

BRIGHT EYES

10 parts carrot juice (5 oz.)
4 parts plain aloe-vera
    juice (2 oz.)
1 tbsp. parsley juice
1 tbsp. bee pollen
Fresh parsley sprig, for garnish
Carrot stick, for garnish

Combine all ingredients except parsley
sprig and carrot stick in a blender and
blend until well mixed. Pour into a
chilled highball glass and garnish
with parsley and carrot stick.
Serves one.

59 calories; 0.3 gm fat; 4% calories from fat; 0 mg cholesterol; 45.3 mg sodium; 13.7 gm carbohydrate; 1.6 gm protein; 44.3 calcium; 1.1 mg iron; 3,689 RE vitamin A; 22.1 mg vitamin C

(Bee pollen not included in nutritional analysis.)

BROWN PELICAN

10 parts sparkling apple cider
    (5 oz.)
5 parts ginger beer (2½ oz.)

Combine all ingredients in a mixing
glass and stir gently. Pour over ice
cubes into a chilled highball glass.
Serves one.

87 calories; 0.2 gm fat; 2% calories from fat; 0 mg cholesterol; 8 mg sodium; 20.5 gm carbohydrate; 0.2 gm protein; 10.4 mg calcium; 0.7 mg iron; 0 RE vitamin A; 1.4 mg vitamin C

C

CABO COOLER

8 parts pineapple juice
   (4 oz.)
4 parts kiwi juice (2 oz.)
4 parts papaya juice (2 oz.)
Fresh mint sprigs, for garnish

Combine juices in a blender with
cracked ice and blend until smooth.
Pour into chilled wineglasses and
garnish with mint sprigs. Serves two.

*60 calories; 0.2 gm fat; 3% calories
from fat; 0 mg cholesterol; 2.8 mg
sodium; 14.8 gm carbohydrate;
0.6 gm protein; 23.8 mg calcium;
0.3 mg iron; 62.3 RE vitamin A;
51.4 mg vitamin C*

CAFÉ ANISE

12 parts coffee, hot (6 oz.)
4 parts hot licorice-root tea (2 oz.)
½ tsp. alcohol-free anise extract
½ tsp. alcohol-free orange extract
Honey, to taste
Steamed milk (optional)

Combine all ingredients together in a
warmed mug. Add steamed milk and
honey if desired. Serves one.

*82 calories; 0 gm fat; 0% calories
from fat; 0 mg cholesterol; 5 mg
sodium; 19.6 gm carbohydrate; 0.2
gm protein; 5.6 mg calcium; 0.2
mg iron; 0 RE vitamin A; 0.2 mg
vitamin C*

*(Steamed milk not included in
nutritional analysis.)*

CAFÉ AU LAIT

Hot coffee
Hot milk
Sugar (optional)

Combine equal parts of each liquid in
a warmed mug. Sweeten with sugar to
taste. Serves one.

*168 calories; 8.1 gm fat; 43% calo-
ries from fat; 33 mg cholesterol;
122.3 mg sodium; 15.9 gm carbo-*

*hydrate; 8.1 gm protein; 293.3 mg
calcium; 0.1 mg iron; 92.2 RE vitamin A; 2.2 mg vitamin C*

*(Sugar not included in nutritional
analysis.)*

CAFÉ MOCHA

4 parts espresso (2 oz.), or 8 parts
   strong-brewed coffee (4 oz.)
1 tbsp. sweetened cocoa powder
Steamed or hot milk
Whipped cream, for garnish
Ground cinnamon, for garnish

In a warmed mug, combine the
espresso or coffee with the cocoa until
completely blended. Fill the mug with
steamed milk and top with a dollop of
whipped cream. Sprinkle with
cinnamon. Serves one.

*116 calories; 6.1 gm fat; 47%
calories from fat; 12.3 mg cholesterol; 50.7 mg sodium; 11.3 gm
carbohydrate; 4.4 gm protein; 96.1
mg calcium; 1.5 mg iron; 59.7 RE
vitamin A; 0.7 mg vitamin C*

CALAVERAS COUNTY
CIDER

16 parts apple cider (8 oz.)
16 parts black tea, hot (8 oz.)
2 parts fresh-squeezed orange
   juice (1 oz.)
2 parts fresh-squeezed lemon
   juice 1 oz.)
2 tbsp. honey
½ tsp. ground cinnamon
Ground nutmeg
Cinnamon sticks

Combine all ingredients except nutmeg and cinnamon sticks in a
saucepan over medium heat and
bring to a boil. Reduce heat quickly
and simmer for ten minutes. Pour
into warmed mugs and garnish with
ground nutmeg and cinnamon sticks.
Serves two.

*102 calories; 0.3 gm fat; 2% calo-
ries from fat; 0 mg cholesterol; 7.7*

mg sodium; 27.8 gm carbohydrate;
0.3 gm protein; 15.9 mg calcium;.
9 mg iron; 3.3 RE vitamin A; 15
mg vitamin C

CALICO COOLER

4 parts carrot juice
  (2 oz.)
4 parts fresh-squeezed orange
  juice (2 oz.)
4 parts unsweetened cherry
  juice (2 oz.)
Sparkling mineral water
Orange slice, for garnish

Combine juices with cracked ice in a
cocktail shaker and shake well. Strain
over ice cubes into a chilled collins
glass and fill the glass with sparkling
water. Garnish with the orange slice.
Serves one.

89 calories; 0.7 gm fat; 7% calories
from fat; 0 mg cholesterol; 16.9 mg
sodium; 20.6 gm carbohydrate;
1.6 gm protein; 28.1 mg calcium;
0.6 mg iron; 1,483 RE vitamin A;
37.2 mg vitamin C

CALIFORNIA CHAI

32 parts water (16 oz.)
5 whole cloves
3 cardamom seeds
3 cinnamon sticks
1 tsp. dried orange peel
1 tsp. fennel seeds
1 tsp. chopped fresh ginger
4 tbsp. loose black tea
Honey (optional)
Steamed milk (optional)

Place water and spices in a saucepan
and bring to a boil. Lower the heat
and simmer for about twenty minutes.
Turn off the heat and add the tea
leaves let steep for ten minutes. Strain
into warmed mugs and serve with
honey and milk. Serves two.

106 calories; 1.9 gm fat; 15% calo-
ries from fat; 3.3 mg cholesterol;
23.9 mg sodium; 18.4 gm carbo-
hydrate; 4.9 gm protein; 61.4 mg
calcium; 2.5 mg iron; 12.1 RE
vitamin A; 2.8 mg vitamin C

(Honey and steamed milk are
included in nutritional analysis.)

CALIFORNIA
ORANGE SUPREME

4 parts fresh-squeezed
  navel-orange juice (2 oz.)
4 parts fresh satsuma
  mandarin-orange juice (2 oz.)
4 parts fresh-squeezed
  Valencia-orange juice (2 oz.)
4 parts fresh-squeezed
  Meyer-lemon juice (2 oz.)
4 parts fresh-squeezed
  blood-orange juice (2 oz.)

Combine all except blood-orange
juice in a mixing glass. Stir well and
pour into a chilled highball glass.
Slowly pour blood orange-juice into
glass. Do not stir. Serves one.

125 calories; 0.5 gm fat; 4% calo-
ries from fat; 0 mg cholesterol; 2.5
mg sodium; 30.7 gm carbohydrate;
1.9 gm protein; 31 mg calcium;
0.5 mg iron; 50.7 RE vitamin A;
150 mg vitamin C

CALIFORNIA
SPLIT

12 parts tomato
  juice (6 oz.)
2 parts spinach juice (1 oz.)
2 parts fresh-squeezed lemon
  juice (1 oz.)
Freshly ground pepper, to taste
Fresh parsley sprig, for garnish

Combine all ingredients except parsley
sprig with cracked ice in a blender and
blend until slushy. Pour into a chilled
highball glass and garnish with the
parsley sprig. Serves one.

64 calories; 0.6 gm fat; 7% calories
from fat; 0 mg cholesterol; 675.9
mg sodium; 14.9 gm carbohydrate;
4.1 gm protein; 123.4 mg calcium;
5 mg iron; 632.4 RE vitamin A;
85.1 mg vitamin C

CAMEL BARN COOLER

8 parts peach juice (4 oz.)
4 parts strawberry juice
(2 oz.)
Sparkling white grape juice
Fresh mint sprig, for garnish

Combine peach and strawberry juices with cracked ice in a cocktail shaker and shake well. Strain into a chilled collins glass and fill the with the sparkling grape juice. Stir gently and garnish with the fresh mint sprig. Serves one.

130 calories; 0.6 gm fat; 4% calories from fat; 0 mg cholesterol; 6.4 mg sodium; 32.6 gm carbohydrate; 0.12 gm protein; 28 mg calcium; 0.9 mg iron; 4.3 RE vitamin A; 85.8 mg vitamin C

CANDLELIGHT COMFORTER

8 parts strong-brewed chamomile tea, hot (4 oz.)
8 parts hot milk (4 oz.)
2 parts honey (1 oz.)
10 fresh mint leaves
Fresh mint sprig, for garnish

Muddle the mint leaves and the honey in the bottom of a warmed mug. Add the hot chamomile tea and stir until the honey is dissolved. Add the milk and stir again. Garnish with the mint sprig. Serves one.

157 calories; 3.7 gm fat; 21% calories from fat; 15.3 mg cholesterol; 58.3 mg sodium; 28.8 gm carbohydrate; 3.8 gm protein; 138.9 mg calcium; 0.2 mg iron; 42.8 RE vitamin A; 1.3 mg vitamin C

CANTALOUPE COOLER

8 parts cantaloupe, diced
(4 oz.)
8 parts fresh-squeezed orange
juice (4 oz.)
2 parts fresh-squeezed lime
juice (1 oz.)
Lime slice, for garnish

Combine all ingredients except lime slice in a blender and blend until smooth. Pour into old-fashioned glasses and garnish with the lime slice. Serves one.

94 calories; 0.4 gm fat; 3% calories from fat; 0 mg cholesterol; 24 mg sodium; 23.2 gm carbohydrate; 1.9 gm protein; 29.5 mg calcium; 0.5 mg iron; 453.8 RE vitamin A; 107.3 mg vitamin C

CAPE SPLIT CLAM COCKTAIL

6 parts clam juice (3 oz.)
2 parts celery juice (1 oz.)
1 part fresh-squeezed lemon juice (½ oz.)
½ tsp. white horseradish
Cocktail onion, for garnish

Combine all ingredients except cocktail onion with cracked ice in a cocktail shaker. Shake well and strain into chilled cocktail glass. Garnish with the cocktail onion. Serves one.

48 calories; 0.1 gm fat; 2% calories from fat; 0 mg cholesterol; 391.4 mg sodium; 11.7 gm carbohydrate; 1 gm protein; 24 mg calcium; 0.6 mg iron; 22.6 RE vitamin A; 12.5 mg vitamin C

CAPTAIN COOK'S COOLER

4 parts fresh-squeezed lime
juice (2 oz.)
2 parts fresh-squeezed orange
juice (1 oz.)
1 tsp. sugar syrup
Sparkling mineral water
Lime slice, for garnish

Combine juices and sugar syrup in a cocktail shaker and shake well. Strain over ice cubes into chilled highball glass and fill the glass with sparkling water. Stir gently and garnish with the lime slice. Serves one.

45 calories; 0.1 gm fat; 2% calories from fat; 0 mg cholesterol; 1.1 mg sodium; 12.4 gm carbohydrate; 0.4 gm protein; 12 mg calcium; 0.3 mg iron; 6.2 RE vitamin A; 30.8 mg vitamin C

CARROT-APPLE NECTAR

8 parts apple juice (4 oz.)
8 parts carrot juice (4 oz.)
Carrot stick, for garnish

Combine juices with cracked ice in a cocktail shaker. Shake well and strain into chilled highball glass. Garnish with the carrot stick. Serves one.

98 calories; 0.2 gm fat; 2% calories from fat; 0 mg cholesterol; 34.5 mg. calcium; 23.8 gm carbohydrate; 0.9 mg iron; 1.1 gm protein; 36 mg sodium; 29.2 RE vitamin A; 10.7 mg vitamin C

CARROT BLUSH

8 parts carrot juice (4 oz.)
8 parts celery juice (4 oz.)
1 tbsp. beet juice
Celery stick, for garnish
Carrot stick, for garnish

Combine juices with cracked ice in a cocktail shaker. Shake well and strain into chilled highball glass. Garnish with celery stick and carrot sticks. Serves one.

106 calories; 0.4 gm fat; 3% calories from fat; 0 mg cholesterol; 191 mg sodium; 24.3 gm carbohydrate; 3.5 gm protein; 77.5 mg calcium; 1.7 mg iron; 2,935 RE vitamin A; 20.7 mg vitamin C

CARROT COCKTAIL

6 parts pineapple juice
  (3 oz.)
4 parts crushed pineapple
  (2 oz.)
6 parts carrot juice (3 oz.)
Pineapple spear, for garnish
Carrot stick, for garnish

Combine the juices and pineapple with cracked ice in a blender and blend until slushy. Pour into a chilled highball glass. Garnish with the pineapple spear and carrot stick. Serves one.

CARROT COCKTAIL

113 calories; 0.4 gm fat; 3% calories from fat; 0 mg cholesterol; 26.5 mg sodium; 28.2 gm carbohydrate; 1.3 gm protein; 35.9 mg calcium; 0.8 mg iron; 2,194 RE vitamin A; 24.1 mg vitamin C

CARROT-PEACH NECTAR

16 parts carrot juice
  (8 oz.)
8 parts peach juice (4 oz.)
2 parts fresh-squeezed lemon
  juice (1 oz.)
2 parts aloe-vera juice (1 oz.)
Lemon slices, for garnish

Combine juices with cracked ice in a cocktail shaker and shake well. Strain over ice cubes into chilled old-fashioned glasses. Garnish with the lemon slices. Serves two.

83 calories; 0.2 gm fat; 2% calories from fat; 0 mg cholesterol; 35.1 mg sodium; 20.7 gm carbohydrate; 1.2 gm protein; 30.7 mg calcium; 0.7 mg iron; 2,920 RE vitamin A; 16.8 mg vitamin C

(Aloe vera juice not included in nutritional analysis.)

CARROT SNAP

10 parts carrot juice
   (5 oz.)
1 tbsp. fresh-squeezed lemon juice
Ginger ale
Lemon slice, for garnish

Combine juices with cracked ice in a
mixing glass and stir well. Strain over
ice cubes into a chilled collins glass.
Fill with ginger ale and stir gently.
Garnish with the lemon slice.
Serves one.

*99 calories; 0.2 gm fat; 2% calories
from fat; 0 mg cholesterol; 49.1 mg
sodium; 24.3 gm carbohydrate;
1.4 gm protein; 38.4 mg calcium;
0.8 mg iron; 3,650 RE vitamin A;
19.1 mg vitamin C*

CARROT SOUR

6 parts carrot juice
   (3 oz.)
4 parts sauerkraut juice (2 oz.)
1 tsp. fresh-squeezed lime juice
Carrot curl, for garnish
Lime peel, for garnish

Combine juices with cracked ice in a
cocktail shaker and shake well. Strain
into chilled sour glass and garnish
with the carrot curl and the lime peel.
Serves one.

*46 calories; 0.2 gm fat; 4% calories
from fat; 0 mg cholesterol; 399.5
mg sodium; 10.8 gm carbohydrate;
1.3 gm protein; 37.9 mg calcium;
1.2 mg iron; 2,191 RE vitamin A;
17.1 mg vitamin C*

CARROT TOP

12 parts carrot
   juice (6 oz.)
4 parts celery juice (2 oz.)
Juice of one lime

Combine juices with cracked ice in a
cocktail shaker and shake well. Strain
over ice cubes into a chilled collins
glass. Serves one.

*90 calories; 0.4 gm fat; 3% calories
from fat; 0 mg cholesterol; 99 mg
sodium; 22.1 gm carbohydrate; 2.2
gm protein; 67.7 mg calcium; 1 mg
iron; 4,388 RE vitamin A; 32 mg
vitamin C*

CARROT ZEST

8 parts carrot juice
   (4 oz.)
2 parts fresh-squeezed lemon
   juice (1 oz.)
3–5 dashes Tabasco sauce
Dash soy sauce
Freshly ground black pepper, for
   garnish
Lemon peel, for garnish

Combine juices, Tabasco, and soy
sauce with cracked ice in a cocktail
shaker and shake well. Strain into
chilled cocktail glass and sprinkle
with pepper. Twist lemon peel over
drink and drop it in. Serves one.

*55 calories; 0.2 gm fat; 3% calories
from fat; 0 mg cholesterol; 37.9 mg
sodium; 13.6 gm carbohydrate;
33.5 mg calcium; 0.8 mg iron; 1.3
gm protein; 2,921 RE vitamin A;
24.6 mg vitamin C*

CASCADE COOLER

2 scoops lemon sorbet
Ginger ale
Lemon twist, for garnish

Place sorbet in a chilled highball glass
and slowly fill the glass with ginger
ale. Do not stir. Garnish with the
lemon twist. Serves one.

*189 calories; 0.2 gm fat; 4% calo-
ries from fat; 0 mg cholesterol; 72
mg sodium; 38.7 gm carbohydrate;
0 gm protein; 1.7 mg calcium; 6.9
mg iron; 0 RE vitamin A; 25.4 mg
vitamin C*

CASTRO STREET LEMONADE

CASTRO STREET LEMONADE

4 parts fresh-squeezed lemon
 juice (2 oz.)
4 parts fresh-squeezed lime
 juice (2 oz.)
1 tsp. bar sugar
2 tsp. passion-fruit syrup
Sparkling mineral water
Orange peel, for garnish
Lime slice, for garnish

Combine juices, bar sugar, and passion-fruit syrup with cracked ice in a cocktail shaker. Shake well. Strain into a chilled highball glass nearly filled with ice cubes and fill the glass with sparkling water. Stir gently and garnish with thr orange peel and lime slice. Serves one.

80 calories; 0 gm fat; 0% calories from fat; 0 mg cholesterol; 10.4 mg sodium; 23.2 gm carbohydrate; 0.4 gm protein; 12.1 mg calcium; 0.1 mg iron; 1.7 RE vitamin A; 42.6 mg vitamin C

CATALINA SMOOTHIE

CATALINA SMOOTHIE

1 banana, sliced thin
8 parts fresh strawberries (4 oz.)
3 parts honey (1½ oz.)
16 parts fresh-squeezed orange
   juice (8 oz.)
1 whole strawberry, for garnish

Combine fruits and honey in a
blender and blend until smooth. Add
orange juice and cracked ice and
blend until smooth. Pour into a
chilled collins glass and garnish with
the strawberry. Serves one.

341 calories; 1.4 gm fat; 4% calories from fat; 0 mg cholesterol; 5.6 mg sodium; 85.1 gm carbohydrate; 3.7 gm protein; 51.4 mg calcium; 1.4 mg iron; 61.9 RE vitamin A; 198.9 mg vitamin C

CAT'S PAW

8 parts apricot nectar
  (4 oz.)
2 parts fresh-squeezed lemon juice
  (1 oz.)
1 tsp. honey
Lemon twist, for garnish

Combine ingredients in a blender and blend until frothy. Pour into a chilled cocktail glass. Garnish with the lemon twist. Serves one.

92 calories; 0.1 gm fat; 1% calories from fat; 0 mg cholesterol; 4 mg sodium; 24.5 gm carbohydrate; 0.5 gm protein; 10.3 mg calcium; 0.5 mg iron; 150.1 RE vitamin A; 50.9 mg vitamin C

CAZADERO CONNECTION

10 parts carrot juice (5 oz.)
4 parts beet juice (2 oz.)
4 parts cucumber juice (2 oz.)
Carrot sticks, for garnish

Combine juices in a blender and blend until smooth. Pour into chilled old-fashioned glasses and garnish with carrot sticks. Serves two.

98 calories; 0.4 gm fat; 3% calories from fat; 0 mg cholesterol; 85 mg sodium; 22.2 gm carbohydrate; 2.9 gm protein; 59.1 mg calcium; 1.5 mg iron; 3,656 RE vitamin A; 27.1 mg vitamin C

CELEBRATED JUMPING FROG

8 parts carrot juice
  (4 oz.)
4 parts cabbage juice (2 oz.)
2 parts parsley juice (1 oz.)
1 tbsp. apple cider vinegar or
  fresh-squeezed lemon juice
Fresh parsley sprig, for garnish

Combine juices and vinegar with cracked ice in a cocktail shaker. and shake well. Strain over ice cubes into a chilled highball glass. Garnish with the parsley sprig. Serves one.

84 calories; 0.6 gm fat; 6% calories from fat; 0 mg cholesterol; 67.3 mg sodium; 19.1 carbohydrate; 3.2 gm protein; 114.5 mg calcium; 2.8 mg iron; 3,081 RE vitamin A; 102.2 mg vitamin C

CELEBRATION PUNCH

32 parts grapefruit juice (16 oz.)
16 parts sugar syrup (8 oz.)
8 parts fresh-squeezed lemon
  juice (4 oz.)
4 parts raspberry syrup (2 oz.)
2 liters ginger ale
Fresh raspberries, for garnish

Combine all ingredients except ginger ale and raspberries in a large punch bowl and stir well. Chill mixture for at least two hours. Just before serving, add ice and the ginger ale. Stir gently and float raspberries on top. Serves twenty.

84 calories; 0 gm fat; 0% calories from fat; 0 mg cholesterol; 8.2 mg sodium; 21.5 gm carbohydrate; 0.2 gm protein; 14.7 mg calcium; 0.7 mg iron; 0.7 RE vitamin A; 12 mg vitamin C

CELERY COCKTAIL

8 parts celery juice (4
  oz.)
1 tbsp. fresh-squeezed lime juice
1 tbsp. onion juice
Cocktail onion, for garnish

Combine juices with cracked ice in a cocktail shaker and shake well. Strain into chilled cocktail glass and garnish with the cocktail onion. Serves one.

39 calories; 0.2 gm fat; 3% calories from fat; 0 mg cholesterol; 96.1 mg sodium; 9.3 gm carbohydrate; 1.2 gm protein; 65.1 mg calcium; 0.7 mg iron; 14 RE vitamin A; 15.5 mg vitamin C

CELERY TONIC

8 parts celery juice (4 oz.)
Sparkling mineral water
Lemon wedge, for garnish

Pour celery juice over ice cubes into a chilled highball glass. Fill glass with sparkling mineral water and stir gently. Squeeze lemon over drink and drop it in. Serves one.

34 calories; 0.3 gm fat; 7% calories from fat; 0 mg cholesterol; 185 mg sodium; 7.8 gm carbohydrate; 1.6 gm protein; 85.3 mg calcium; 0.9 mg iron; 27 RE vitamin A; 14.9 mg vitamin C

CHARLIE'S ANGEL

10 parts pineapple juice (5 oz.)
4 parts grapefruit juice (2 oz.)
4 fresh strawberries, hulled and sliced
1 banana, sliced
1 whole strawberry, for garnish

Combine all ingredients except whole strawberry in a blender and blend until smooth. If mixture is too thick, add more pineapple or grapefruit juice until desired consistency is achieved. Pour into a chilled collins glass and garnish with the strawberry. Serves one.

229 calories; 1 gm fat; 4% calories from fat; 0 mg cholesterol; 3.7 mg sodium; 56.7 gm carbohydrate; 2.4 gm protein; 46.6 mg calcium; 1.1 mg iron; 12.5 RE vitamin A; 89.3 mg vitamin C

CHERRY FROTH

2 scoops vanilla frozen yogurt
Natural cherry soda

Place frozen yogurt in a chilled highball glass and slowly fill the glass with the cherry soda. Do not stir. Serves one.

275 calories; 27% calories from fat; 4 mg cholesterol; 135 mg sodium; 45.8 gm carbohydrate; 5.9 gm protein; 206 mg calcium; 0.4 mg iron; 82 RE vitamin A; 1.2 mg vitamin C

CHERRY MOON

8 parts apple juice (4 oz.)
6 parts unsweetened cherry
   juice (3 oz.)
Sparkling mineral water
Lime slice, for garnish

Combine juices with cracked ice in a cocktail shaker and shake well. Strain over ice cubes into a chilled collins glass and fill glass with sparkling mineral water. Stir gently and garnish with the lime slice. Serves one.

176 calories; 1.8 gm fat; 8% calories from fat; 0 mg cholesterol; 3.4 mg sodium; 41.5 gm carbohydrate; 2.1 gm protein; 33 mg calcium; 1.1 mg iron; 37 RE vitamin A; 58.5 mg vitamin C

CHERRY-RASPBERRY SHAKE

CHERRY ZEST

CHERRY-
RASPBERRY
SHAKE

8 parts unsweetened cherry cider
(4 oz.)
8 parts raspberry sorbet (4 oz.)
1 tsp. fresh-squeezed lemon juice

Combine all ingredients in a blender
and blend until slushy. Pour into a
chilled collins glass. Serves one.

*205 calories; 2.3 gm fat; 10%
calories from fat; 5.9 mg cholesterol; 38.8 mg sodium; 46.8 gm
carbohydrate; 1.4 gm protein; 60
mg calcium; 0.5 mg iron; 16.1 RE
vitamin A; 69 mg vitamin C*

CHERRY ZEST

8 parts unsweetened cherry
cider (4 oz.)
2 parts fresh-squeezed lime
juice (1 oz.)
Sparkling mineral water
Lemon slice, for garnish

Combine cherry cider, lime juice, and
sparkling mineral water over ice into
a chilled highball glass. Stir and garnish with the lemon slice. Serves one.

*56 calories; 0 gm fat; 0% calories
from fat; 0 mg cholesterol; 3.6 mg
sodium; 14.4 gm carbohydrate; 0.2
gm protein; 8.7 mg calcium; 0.4
mg iron; 0.9 RE vitamin A; 70.2
mg vitamin C*

CHICKEN SHOT

and stir well. Chill overnight. Serve in old-fashioned glasses and garnish with cinnamon sticks. Serves four.

119 calories; 0.7 gm fat; 5% calories from fat; 2.5 mg cholesterol; 39.7 mg sodium; 27.5 gm carbohydrate; 2.3 gm protein; 96.5 mg calcium; 0.3 mg iron; 40.8 RE vitamin A; 9.8 mg vitamin C

CHILL OUT

12 parts pineapple juice
  (6 oz.)
2 parts fresh-squeezed lemon
  juice (1 oz.)
1/2 banana, sliced
Pineapple spear, for garnish

Combine juices and banana with cracked ice in a blender and blend until slushy. Pour into a chilled highball glass and garnish with the pineapple spear. Serves one.

245 calories; 1 gm fat; 3% calories from fat; 0 mg cholesterol; 3.8 mg sodium; 62.2 gm carbohydrate; 2.1 gm protein; 43.4 mg calcium; 1.1 mg iron; 12.3 RE vitamin A; 53.5 mg vitamin C

CHINA LAKE MOONSHINE

12 parts apple juice (6 oz.)
8 parts rehydrated dates,
  chopped (4 oz.)
1/2 tsp. ground cinnamon
2 whole cloves

Combine apple juice and dates in a blender and blend until well-mixed. Pour mixture into a saucepan and add remaining ingredients. Simmer over low heat for about thirty minutes. Pour into warmed mugs. Serves two.

211 calories; 0.2 gm fat; 1% calories from fat; 0 mg cholesterol; 5.7 mg sodium; 51.4 gm carbohydrate; 1.5 gm protein; 47.7 mg calcium; 1 mg iron; 13.5 RE vitamin A; 35.5 mg vitamin C

CHICKEN SHOT

4 parts chicken bouillon,
  chilled (2 oz.)
4 parts vegetable bouillon, chilled
  (2 oz.)
1 part fresh-squeezed lemon
  juice (1/2 oz.)
Tabasco sauce, to taste
Worcestershire sauce, to taste
Freshly ground black pepper, to taste
Celery salt, to taste
Lime wedge, for garnish

Combine all ingredients except lime wedge with cracked ice in a mixing glass. Stir well. Pour into chilled old-fashioned glass and garnish with the lime wedge. Serves one.

19 calories; 0.3 gm fat; 14% calories from fat; 2.8 mg cholesterol; 711 mg sodium; 2.8 gm carbohydrate; 2 gm protein; 11.2 mg calcium; 0.4 mg iron; 1.4 RE vitamin A; 10.9 mg vitamin C

CHILLED CHAI

32 parts California Chai (16 oz.)
  (see recipe California Chai, page 49)
16 parts warm milk (8 oz.)
8 parts honey (4 oz.)
Cinnamon sticks, for garnish

Prepare the recipe for California Chai, but strain the mixture into a heat-proof pitcher. Add the milk and honey

CHOCOLATE-RASPBERRY SHAKE

12 parts nonfat milk (6 oz.)
8 parts raspberry juice (4 oz.)
2 tbsp. chocolate syrup
2 scoops vanilla frozen yogurt
1 banana, sliced
½ tsp. alcohol-free almond extract

Combine all ingredients in a blender and blend until smooth. If mixture is too thick, add more nonfat milk. Pour into chilled highball glasses. Serves two.

257 calories; 4.8 gm fat; 16% calories from fat; 3.4 mg cholesterol; 117.2 mg sodium; 50 gm carbohydrate; 6.9 gm protein; 221.1 mg calcium; 0.9 mg iron; 101.7 RE vitamin A; 14.3 mg vitamin C

CHUCK'S GINGER COOLER

6 parts pineapple juice (3 oz.)
4 parts strawberry puree (2 oz.)
2 parts fresh-squeezed lemon juice (1 oz.)
1 tsp. ginger juice
Ginger ale

Combine all ingredients except the ginger ale with cracked ice in a cocktail shaker and shake well. Strain mixture equally over ice cubes into two chilled collins glasses. Fill the glasses with ginger ale and stir gently. Serves two.

55 calories; 0.2 gm fat; 3% calories from fat; 0 mg cholesterol; 4.7 mg sodium; 13.9 gm carbohydrate; 0.5 mg protein; 14.7 mg calcium; 0.3 mg iron; 1.3 RE vitamin A; 27.5 mg vitamin C

CIDER FREEZE

12 parts apple cider
   (6 oz.)
2 parts ginger juice (1 oz.)
2 tbsp. unsweetened applesauce
1 tbsp. maple syrup
1 tsp. fresh-squeezed lemon juice
½ tsp. alcohol-free vanilla extract

Combine ingredients with cracked ice
in a blender and blend until slushy.
Pour into a chilled highball glass.
Serves one.

154 calories; 0.2 gm fat; 1% calories from fat; 0 mg cholesterol; 8.1 mg sodium; 40.2 gm carbohydrate; 0.3 gm protein; 31.5 mg calcium; 1.1 mg iron; 0.1 RE vitamin A; 14.9 mg vitamin C

CINCO DE MAYO AGUA FRESCA

8 parts fresh-squeezed
   orange juice (4 oz.)
8 parts pineapple juice (4 oz.)
8 parts strawberry puree (4 oz.)
Pineapple spears, for garnish
Whole strawberries, for garnish

Combine juices and puree with
cracked ice in a blender and blend
until slushy. Pour into chilled wineglasses. Garnish with pineapple spears
and whole strawberries. Serves two.

89 calories; 0.5 gm fat; 5% calories from fat; 0 mg cholesterol; 2 mg sodium; 21.4 gm carbohydrate; 1.1 gm protein; 27.6 mg calcium; 0.6 mg iron; 14.1 RE vitamin A; 79.7 mg vitamin C

CITRUS COCKTAIL

8 parts fresh-squeezed
   orange juice (4 oz.)
2 parts grapefruit juice (1 oz.)
1 tbsp. fresh-squeezed lemon juice
Lime twist, for garnish

Combine juices with cracked ice in a
cocktail shaker and shake well. Strain
into chilled cocktail glass and garnish
with the lime twist. Serves one.

66 calories; 0.3 gm fat; 3% calories from fat; 0 mg cholesterol; 1.4 mg sodium; 21.4 gm carbohydrate; 1 gm protein; 45 mg calcium; 1.4 mg sodium; 0.3 mg iron; 23.3 RE vitamin A; 74.5 mg vitamin C

CITRUS COOLER

4 parts fresh-squeezed
   orange juice (2 oz.)
1 tbsp. fresh-squeezed lemon juice
1 tbsp. fresh-squeezed lime juice
Sparkling mineral water
Orange slice, for garnish
Lemon slice, for garnish
Lime slice, for garnish

Combine juices in a cocktail shaker
and shake well. Strain over ice cubes
into a chilled collins glass and fill
with sparkling mineral water. Stir
gently and garnish with the fruit
slices. Serves one.

33 calories; 0.1 gm fat; 3% calories from fat; 0 mg cholesterol; 0.8 mg sodium; 8.6 gm carbohydrate; 0.5 gm protein; 30 mg calcium; 0.1 mg iron; 11.8 RE vitamin A; 39.9 mg vitamin C

CITRUS *VINCIT OMNIA*

12 parts fresh-squeezed
   orange juice (6 oz.)
2 parts fresh-squeezed lime
   juice (1 oz.)
2 parts fresh-squeezed
   Meyer lemon juice (1 oz.)

Combine all ingredients in a blender
and blend until frothy. Pour into a
chilled highball glass. Serves one.

91 calories; 0.4 gm fat; 3% calories from fat; 0 mg cholesterol; 1.9 mg sodium; 22.7 gm carbohydrate; 1.4 gm protein; 23.1 mg calcium; 0.4 mg iron; 34.9 RE vitamin A; 106.4 mg vitamin C

CLAM DIGGER

CLAM DIGGER

16 parts Clamato juice
  (8 oz.)
2 parts fresh-squeezed lime
  juice (1 oz.)
3–5 dashes Tabasco sauce
3–5 dashes Worcestershire sauce
Freshly ground pepper, to taste
Celery salt, to taste
¼ tsp. white horseradish
Celery stalk, for garnish
Lime wedge, for garnish

Combine all ingredients except celery
stalk and lime wedge with cracked ice
in a cocktail shaker and shake well.

Strain over ice cubes into a chilled
collins glass and garnish with the
lime wedge and celery stalk.
Serves one.

123 calories; 0.3 gm fat; 2% calories from fat; 0 mg cholesterol; 1,400 mg sodium; 29.9 gm carbohydrate; 1.7 gm protein; 41.1 mg calcium; 1.8 mg iron; 54.5 RE vitamin A; 22.5 mg vitamin C

CLASSIC ICED TEA

CLASSIC ICED COFFEE

32 parts strong-brewed coffee,
 chilled (16 oz.)
1½ tsp. alcohol-free almond extract
Sugar (optional)
Milk (optional)

Combine coffee and almond extract
with cracked ice in a mixing glass and
stir well. Strain equal amounts of the
mixture over ice cubes into two chilled
highball glasses. Add sugar and milk
to taste. Serves two

*12 calories; 0 gm fat; 2% calories
from fat; 0 mg cholesterol; 4.5 mg
sodium; 1.6 gm carbohydrate;
0.2 gm protein; 4.5 mg calcium;
0.1 mg iron; 0 RE vitamin A; 0 mg
vitamin C*

*(Sugar and milk not included in
nutritional analysis.)*

CLASSIC ICED TEA

4 tsp. loose tea, any variety
32 parts water, heated to boiling
  (16 oz.)
Sugar, to taste
Fresh mint sprig, for garnish
Lemon wedge, for garnish

Place loose tea in a heated ceramic teapot and add boiling water. Steep for five minutes. Stir and strain over ice cubes into a chilled collins glass filled. Add sugar to taste and garnish with mint sprig and lemon. Add more ice if necessary. Serves two.

50 calories; 0 gm fat; 0% calories from fat; 0 mg cholesterol; 5.2 mg sodium; 12.8 gm carbohydrate; 0 gm protein; 0 mg calcium; 0 mg iron; 0 RE vitamin A; 0 mg vitamin C

CLASS-M SMOOTHIE

10 parts fresh-squeezed
  orange juice (5 oz.)
8 parts pineapple juice (4 oz.)
4 parts fresh-squeezed lime
  juice (2 oz.)
1 tbsp. honey
1 Haas avocado, peeled, pitted,
  and chopped

Combine all ingredients with cracked ice in a blender and blend until smooth. Pour into chilled wineglasses. Serves two.

256 calories; 15.2 gm fat; 49% calories from fat; 0 mg cholesterol; 12.4 mg sodium; 32.4 gm carbohydrate; 7 gm protein; 29.9 mg calcium; 1.4 mg iron; 67.7 RE vitamin A; 56.8 mg vitamin C

CLOUD HOPPER

8 parts apple cider (4 oz.)
4 parts strawberry puree
  (2 oz.)
2 parts fresh-squeezed lemon
  juice (1 oz.)
1 banana, sliced
8 parts vanilla nonfat yogurt (4 oz.)

Combine all ingredients in a blender and blend until smooth. Pour into a chilled collins glass. Serves one.

276 calories; 0.9 gm fat; 3% calories from fat; 2.5 mg cholesterol; 74.2 mg sodium; 66.3 gm carbohydrate; 7.2 gm protein; 223.6 mg calcium; 1.1 mg iron; 11.3 RE vitamin A; 56.6 mg vitamin C

CLOVERDALE CITRUS FAIR PUNCH

1 recipe Traditional Lemonade
  (see page 207)
64 parts fresh-squeezed orange
  juice (32 oz.)
16 parts grapefruit juice (8 oz.)
Fresh strawberries, hulled and halved,
  for garnish

Prepare Traditional Lemonade recipe and combine with other juices in a large punch bowl. Stir well and add several ice cubes. Float fresh strawberries on top. Serves forty.

205 calories; 0 gm fat; 0% calories from fat; 0 mg cholesterol; 6.4 mg sodium; 10.8 gm carbohydrate 0.2 gm protein; 3.2 mg calcium; 0.1 mg iron; 0,2 RE vitamin A; 15.6 mg vitamin C

COASTAL COOLER

10 parts apple juice (5 oz.)
8 parts cucumber juice (4 oz.)
4 parts celery juice (2 oz.)

Combine juices with cracked ice in a cocktail shaker and shake well. Strain over ice cubes into a chilled collins glass. Serves one.

90 calories; 0.4 gm fat; 4% calories from fat; 0 mg cholesterol; 55.8 mg sodium; 21.9 gm carbohydrate; 1.1 gm protein; 48.5 mg calcium; 1.1 mg iron; 13.1 RE vitamin A; 67.5 mg vitamin C

COCO COLA

4 parts coconut milk (2 oz.)
2 parts fresh-squeezed lime
   juice (1 oz.)
Natural cola
Lime wedge, for garnish

Combine coconut milk and lime juice in a cocktail shaker and shake well. Pour over ice into a chilled highball glass. Fill the glass with cola and garnish with the lime wedge. Serves one.

196 calories; 13.5 gm fat; 62% calories from fat; 0 mg cholesterol; 14.6 mg sodium; 20.4 gm carbohydrate; 1.4 gm protein; 16 mg calcium; 1.9 mg iron; 0.2 RE vitamin A; 9.8 mg vitamin C

COCONUT ORANGEADE

12 parts fresh-squeezed
   orange juice (6 oz.)
4 parts coconut milk (2 oz.)
2 parts fresh-squeezed lime
   juice (1 oz.)
Lime wedge

Combine all ingredients except lime wedge with cracked ice in a blender and blend until slushy. Pour into a chilled collins glass and garnish with the lime wedge. Serves one.

242 calories; 16.4 gm fat; 60% calories from fat; 0 mg cholesterol; 9.6 mg sodium; 21.9 gm carbohydrate; 2.9 gm protein; 26.2 mg calcium; 1.1 mg iron; 34.3 RE vitamin A; 93.4 mg vitamin C

COCONUT PATTY

4 parts coconut milk (2 oz.)
4 parts pineapple juice (2 oz.)
3 parts chocolate syrup (1½ oz.)
1 part coconut syrup (½ oz.)
2 scoops vanilla ice cream
Milk (optional)
Shredded coconut
Pineapple spear, for garnish

Combine all ingredients except milk, shredded coconut, and pineapple spear in a blender and blend until smooth. If shake is too thick, add milk until desired consistency is achieved. Pour into a chilled collins glass and sprinkle with shredded coconut. Serves one.

814 calories; 45.9 gm fat; 49% calories from fat; 205.7 mg cholesterol; 162 mg sodium; 95.8 gm carbohydrate; 11.5 gm protein; 334.2 mg calcium; 2.8 mg iron; 351 RE vitamin A; 7.7 mg vitamin C

(Milk not included in nutritional analysis.)

COCONUT-GINGER FREEZE

8 parts cream of
  coconut (4 oz.)
2 parts ginger juice (1 oz.)
2 parts fresh-squeezed lime
  juice (1 oz.)
1 tsp. bar sugar
Shredded coconut

Combine all ingredients except grated coconut with cracked ice in a blender and blend until slushy. Pour into a chilled wineglass and sprinkle with shredded coconut. Serves one.

483 calories; 39.9 gm fat; 69% calories from fat; 0 mg cholesterol; 10.4 mg sodium; 35.9 gm carbohydrate; 4.4 gm protein; 15.1 mg calcium; 3.4 mg iron; 0.3 RE vitamin A; 13.2 mg vitamin C

COCONUT-MANGO COCKTAIL

6 parts coconut milk (3 oz.)
6 parts mango nectar (3 oz.)

Combine all ingredients in a blender and blend until smooth. Pour into a chilled cocktail glass. Serves one.

292 calories; 24.3 gm fat; 73% calories from fat; 0 mg cholesterol; 13.6 mg sodium; 16.9 gm carbohydrate; 2.8 gm protein; 16.3 mg calcium; 1.2 mg iron; 331.2 RE vitamin A; 23.5 mg vitamin C

COCONUT-MANGO COCKTAIL

COFFEE MILK SHAKE

8 parts nonfat milk (4 oz.)
8 parts strong-brewed coffee,
    chilled (4 oz.)
2 scoops vanilla frozen yogurt
Honey, to taste (optional)

Combine all ingredients in a blender
and blend until smooth but not
watery. Add honey to taste. Pour into a
chilled collins glass. Serves one.

*250 calories; 0.2 gm fat; 1% calories from fat; 1.9 mg cholesterol;
164.5 mg sodium; 51.3 gm carbohydrate; 9.7 gm protein; 142.1 mg
calcium; 0.1 mg iron; 69.4 RE
vitamin A; 1.1 mg vitamin C*

*(Honey not included in nutritional
analysis.)*

COLD-BUSTER

8 parts fresh-squeezed
    orange juice (4 oz.)
4 parts fresh-squeezed lemon
    juice (2 oz.)
4 parts fresh-squeezed lime
    juice (2 oz.)
1 tsp. ginger juice
Honey, to taste

Combine all ingredients except honey
in a saucepan over medium heat.
Heat until very hot, stirring occasionally, but do not boil. Pour into
warmed coffee mug and add honey to
taste. Serves one.

*183 calories; 0.3 gm fat; 1% calories from fat; 0 mg cholesterol; 5.6
mg sodium; 49.7 gm carbohydrate;
1.4 gm protein; 0.7 mg iron; 24.4
RE vitamin A; 100.4 mg vitamin C*

COMMISSARY SPECIAL

10 parts carrot juice (5 oz.)
8 parts apple juice (4 oz.)
6 parts pineapple juice (3 oz.)
1 tsp. ginger juice
½ tsp. ground cinnamon
½ tsp. ground cardamom
Ground nutmeg, for garnish

Combine all ingredients except nutmeg in a blender and blend until
frothy. Pour into chilled wineglasses
and sprinkle with nutmeg. Serves two.

*103 calories; 0.4 gm fat; 4% calories from fat; 0 mg cholesterol; 24.2
mg sodium; 25.2 gm carbohydrate;
0.9 gm protein; 36.2 mg calcium;
1.1 gm iron; 182.5 RE vitamin A;
34.5 mg vitamin C*

COMSTOCK CONCOCTION

8 parts grapefruit juice (4 oz.)
8 parts tomato juice (4 oz.)
3–5 dashes Worcestershire sauce
Lime wedge, for garnish

Combine all ingredients except lime
wedge with cracked ice in a cocktail
shaker and shake well. Strain over
ice cubes into a chilled highball glass
and garnish with the lime wedge.
Serves one.

*75 calories; 0.2 gm fat; 2% calories
from fat; 0 mg cholesterol; 556.8
mg sodium; 17.9 gm carbohydrate;
1.7 gm protein; 35.4 mg calcium;
1.8 mg iron; 69.4 RE vitamin A;
79.2 mg vitamin C*

CONFETTI

8 parts unsweetened cherry
    cider (4 oz.)
2 parts orgeat (almond) syrup (1 oz.)
4 parts fresh apples, peeled and
    chopped (2 oz.)
4 parts fresh pears, peeled and
    chopped (2 oz.)
4 parts fresh peaches, peeled and
    chopped (2 oz.)

Combine all ingredients with cracked
ice in a blender and blend until
smooth. Pour into a chilled highball
glass. (Note: If canned fruit is used, be
sure it is packed in its own juice with
no added sugar.) Serves one.

*228 calories; 0.5 gm fat; 2% calories from fat; 0 mg cholesterol; 23.5
mg sodium; 58.9 gm carbohydrate;
0.8 gm protein; 24 mg calcium;
0.9 mg iron; 34.5 RE vitamin A;
70.1 mg vitamin C*

CONFETTI

COOL AS A CUKE

8 parts carrot juice (4 oz.)
8 parts cucumber juice (4 oz.)
4 parts celery juice (2 oz.)
Celery stick, for garnish
Freshly ground black pepper, for
   garnish

Combine juices with cracked ice in a
cocktail shaker and shake well. Strain
over ice cubes into a chilled collins
glass. Garnish with a celery stick and
sprinkle with pepper. Serves one.

*72 calories; 0.4 gm fat; 5% calories
from fat; 0 mg cholesterol; 84.8 mg
sodium; 1,661 gm carbohydrate;
2.2 gm protein; 70.3 mg calcium;
1.4 mg iron; 2,933 RE vitamin A;
20.3 mg vitamin C*

COOL BREEZE

8 parts grapefruit juice
   (4 oz.)
3 parts fresh-squeezed lime
   juice (1½ oz.)
1 tbsp. peppermint syrup
Sparkling mineral water
Fresh mint sprig, for garnish

Combine juices and peppermint syrup
with cracked ice in a cocktail shaker
and shake well. Strain over ice cubes
into a chilled highball glass and fill
with sparkling water. Stir gently
and garnish with the mint sprig.
Serves one.

*102.6 calories; 0.1 gm fat; 1% calo-
ries from fat; 0 mg cholesterol; 84.8*

67

mg sodium; 26.1 gm carbohydrate; 0.7 mg protein; 24.3 mg calcium; 0.9 mg iron; 1.4 RE vitamin A; 51.4 mg vitamin C

COOL COLLINS

4 parts fresh-squeezed lemon
   juice (2 oz.)
1 tsp. bar sugar
7 fresh mint leaves
Sparkling mineral water
Lemon slice, for garnish
Fresh mint sprigs, for garnish

Pour lemon juice and sugar into a a chilled collins glass. Add the mint leaves and crush them with a spoon. Add ice cubes and fill the glass with sparkling water. Stir gently and garnish with the lemon slice and mint sprigs. Serves one.

23 calories; 0 gm fat; 0% calories from fat; 0 mg cholesterol; 0.5 mg sodium; 7 gm carbohydrate; 0.2 gm protein; 3.9 mg calcium; 0 mg iron; 1.1 RE vitamin A; 26 mg vitamin C

COOL-ECTIVE UNCONSCIOUS

4 parts peach nectar (2 oz.)
6 parts cranberry juice cocktail (3 oz.)
6 parts pineapple juice (3 oz.)
Pineapple spear, for garnish

Add all ingredients except pineapple spear into a a chilled collins glass filled with ice cubes and stir well. Garnish with pineapple spear. Serves one.

126 calories; 0.1 gm fat; 1% calories from fat; 0 mg cholesterol; 8 mg sodium; 31.8 gm carbohydrate; 0.4 gm protein; 19.9 mg calcium; 0.4 mg iron; 15 RE vitamin A; 42.2 mg vitamin C

COOL GREEN FIRE

8 parts celery juice (4 oz.)
8 parts cucumber juice (4 oz.)
1 part serrano chile juice (½ oz.)
Freshly ground black pepper, for garnish

Combine juices over ice cubes in a cocktail shaker and shake well. Strain over ice cubes into chilled highball glass and sprinkle with the ground pepper. Serves one.

40 calories; 0.4 gm fat; 8% calories from fat; 0 mg cholesterol; 105.7 mg sodium; 8.3 gm carbohydrate; 2 gm protein; 66.9 mg calcium; 0.9 mg iron; 52.8 RE vitamin A; 21 mg vitamin C

COOL TOMATO

10 parts tomato juice (5 oz.)
4 parts cucumber juice (2 oz.)
Cucumber slice, for garnish

Combine juices with cracked ice in a cocktail shaker and shake well. Strain into chilled old-fashioned glass and garnish with the cucumber slice. Serves one.

31 calories; 0.2 gm fat; 4% calories from fat; 0 mg cholesterol; 511.9 sodium; 7.6 gm carbohydrate; 1.4 gm protein; 20.7 mg calcium; 1 mg iron; 81.8 RE vitamin A; 14 mg vitamin C

CORONADO SPARKLER

2 parts fresh-squeezed lemon juice (1 oz.)
4 parts fresh-squeezed orange juice (2 oz.)
2 parts papaya juice (1 oz.)
2 parts pineapple juice (1 oz.)
½ tsp. grenadine
Sparkling mineral water
Pineapple spear, for garnish
Orange slice, for garnish

Combine juices and grenadine with cracked ice in a cocktail shaker. Shake well. Pour over ice cubes into a chilled collins glass. Fill the glass with sparkling water and stir gently. Garnish with the pineapple spear and orange slice. Serves one.

71 calories; 0.1 gm fat; 1% calories from fat; 0 mg cholesterol; 3.8 mg sodium; 18 gm carbohydrate; 0.6 gm protein; 16.2 mg calcium; 0.3 mg iron; 15.1 RE vitamin A; 45.2 mg vitamin C

CORONADO SPARKLER

COTTON-CANDY SHAKE

16 parts guava nectar (8 oz.)
8 fresh strawberries, hulled and sliced
2 scoops vanilla frozen yogurt

Combine all ingredients in a blender and blend until smooth. If shake is too thick, add more guava nectar until desired consistency is achieved. Pour into chilled highball glasses. Serves two.

194 calories; 5 gm fat; 22% calories from fat; 2 mg cholesterol; 67.2 mg sodium; 36.2 gm carbohydrate; 4.2 gm protein; 136.1 mg calcium; 0.9 mg iron; 132.9 RE vitamin A; 250.8 mg vitamin C

COUNTERFEIT TRAITOR

8 parts cucumber juice (4 oz.)
2 parts scallion juice (1 oz.)
3–5 dashes Tabasco sauce
Cocktail onion, for garnish

Combine juices and green Tabasco sauce with cracked ice in a cocktail shaker. Shake well. Strain into a chilled cocktail glass and garnish with cocktail onion. Serves one.

32 calories; 0.1 gm fat; 4% calories from fat; 0 mg cholesterol; 10.1 mg sodium; 7.4 gm carbohydrate;

CRANBERRY COOLER

1 gm protein; 37 mg calcium; 0.6 mg iron; 6.3 RE vitamin A; 9.5 mg vitamin C

0.4 gm protein; 18.1 mg calcium; 0.8 mg iron; 3.9 RE vitamin A; 81.3 mg vitamin C

(Sugar not included in nutritional analysis.)

CRANBERRY-APPLE TART

12 parts apple juice (6 oz.)
6 parts unsweetened cranberry
   juice (3 oz.)
1 tbsp. sugar (optional)

Combine apple and cranberry juice in a mixing glass and stir well. Pour over ice cubes into a chilled highball glass. Add sugar if desired. Serves one.

122 calories; 0.4 gm fat; 3% calories from fat; 0 mg cholesterol; 5.9 mg sodium; 30.7 gm carbohydrate;

CRANBERRY COOLER

12 parts cranberry juice
   cocktail (6 oz.)
6 parts apple juice (3 oz.)
1 tbsp. fresh-squeezed lemon juice
Sparkling mineral water
Lime slice, for garnish

Combine juices in a collins glass and stir well. Add ice cubes and fill the glass with sparkling water. Stir gently and garnish with the lime slice. Serves one.

CRANBERRY CREAM COCKTAIL

141 calories; 0.2 gm fat; 1% calories from fat; 0 mg cholesterol; 9.4 mg sodium; 35.7 gm carbohydrate; 0.1 gm protein; 12.1 mg calcium; 0.5 mg iron; 0.3 RE vitamin A; 102.1 mg vitamin C

CRANBERRY CREAM COCKTAIL

5 parts cranberry juice
   cocktail (2½ oz.)
4 parts apple juice (2 oz.)
2 parts fresh-squeezed lime juice (1 oz.)
1 part cream of coconut (½ oz.)
2 dashes grenadine

Combine all ingredients with cracked ice in a blender and blend until smooth. Pour into a chilled wineglass. Serves one.

135 calories; 5.3 gm fat; 35% calories from fat; 0 mg cholesterol; 6.6 mg sodium; 23.2 gm carbohydrate; 0.7 gm protein;10.9 mg calcium; 0.6 mg iron; 0.2 RE vitamin A; 62.1 mg vitamin C

CRANBERRY FREEZE

12 parts cranberry juice
   cocktail (6 oz.)
4 parts cranberry sauce (2 oz.)
2 scoops vanilla frozen yogurt

Combine all ingredients in a blender and blend until smooth. Pour into a chilled collins glass. For a thinner shake, add more cranberry juice cocktail. Serves one.

542 calories; 12.9 mg fat; 21% calories from fat; 6.3 mg cholesterol; 221.6 mg sodium; 101.4 gm carbohydrate; 8.9 gm protein; 331.8 mg calcium; 1.1 mg iron; 130.3 RE vitamin A; 64.4 mg vitamin C.

CRANBERRY SUMMER COOLER

8 parts cranberry juice cocktail (4 oz.)
Tonic water
Lime wedge, for garnish

Pour cranberry juice over ice cubes into a chilled collins glass. Fill the glass with tonic water and stir gently. Squeeze the lime wedge over the drink and drop it in. Serves one.

84 calories; 0.1 gm fat; 1% calories from fat; 0 mg cholesterol; 6.8 mg sodium; 21.3 gm carbohydrate; 0 gm protein; 4 mg calcium; 0.2 mg iron; 0 RE vitamin A; 40.2 mg vitamin C

CRANBERRY TART

8 parts fresh-squeezed orange juice (4 oz.)
4 parts unsweetened cranberry juice (2 oz.)
Lime wedge, for garnish

Pour juices into a collins glass and stir. Add ice cubes and garnish with the lime wedge. Serves one.

83 calories; 0.2 gm fat; 2% calories from fat; 0 mg cholesterol; 3.1 mg sodium; 19.9 gm carbohydrate; 0.7 gm protein; 14 mg calcium; 0.3 mg iron; 22 RE vitamin A; 76.7 mg vitamin C

CRANBERRY TEA

16 parts unsweetened cranberry juice (8 oz.)
1 tbsp. fresh-squeezed lemon juice
1 tbsp. honey
½ tsp. ground cinnamon
16 parts black tea, hot (8 oz.)
Cinnamon sticks, for garnish

Combine all ingredients except black tea and cinnamon sticks in a saucepan over medium heat. Bring to a boil and then simmer for about five minutes. Strain mixture into warmed mugs and fill each mug with hot tea. Stir gently and garnish with the cinnamon sticks. Serves two.

181 calories; 0.5 gm fat; 2% calories from fat; 0 mg cholesterol; 10.1 mg sodium; 48.1 gm carbohydrate; 1 gm protein; 18.6 mg calcium; 0.6 mg iron; 10 RE vitamin A; 37.7 mg vitamin C

CRANBERRY-VERBENA COCKTAIL

8 parts lemon-verbena tea, chilled (4 oz.)
4 parts cranberry-juice cocktail (2 oz.)
Fresh mint sprig, for garnish
Lemon slice, for garnish

Combine tea and cranberry juice with cracked ice in a cocktail shaker and shake well. Strain into a chilled cocktail glass and garnish with the mint sprig and lemon slice. Serves one.

33 calories; 0.1 gm fat; 1% calories from fat; 0 mg cholesterol; 3.4 mg sodium; 8.4 gm carbohydrate; 0 gm protein; 4 mg calcium; 0.2 mg iron; 0 RE vitamin A; 20.1 mg vitamin C

CRAZY MAMA

12 parts pear juice (6 oz.)
12 parts nonfat yogurt (6 oz.)
4 parts rehydrated dates, chopped fine (2 oz.)
1 tbsp. honey
½ tsp. alcohol-free vanilla extract
½ tsp. ground cinnamon

Combine all ingredients in a blender and blend until smooth. Pour into chilled highball glasses. Serves two.

213 calories; 0 gm fat; 0% calories from fat; 1.9 mg cholesterol; 64.4 mg sodium; 49.2 gm carbohydrate; 5.7 gm protein; 188.5 mg calcium; 0.5 mg iron; 6.5 RE vitamin A; 1 mg vitamin C

CREAMSICLE

8 parts fresh-squeezed orange
   juice (4 oz.)
8 parts cream of coconut (4 oz.)
Sparkling mineral water
Orange slices, for garnish

Blend well the orange juice and cream
of coconut in a blender until smooth.
Divide the mixture into two a chilled
collins glasses. Add ice cubes to each
glass and fill the glasses with
sparkling mineral water. Garnish with
orange slices. Serves two.

*442 calories; 39.4 gm fat; 80%
calories from fat; 0 mg cholesterol;
19.2 mg sodium; 21.8 gm carbohydrate; 0.5 gm protein; 10.1 mg
calcium; 0.7 mg iron; 17.6 RE
vitamin A; 28.4 mg vitamin C*

CRIMSON TIDE

6 parts pineapple
   juice (3 oz.)
6 parts apple cider (3 oz.)
4 parts strawberry puree (2 oz.)
1 tbsp. unsweetened cherry cider

Combine juices and puree in a cocktail shaker and shake well. Strain over
ice cubes into a a chilled collins glass.
Serves one.

*148 calories; 0.9 gm fat; 5% calo-
ries from fat; 0 mg cholesterol; 4 mg
sodium; 36.9 gm carbohydrate;
1.4 gm protein; 35.8 mg calcium;
1.1 mg iron; 14.1 RE vitamin A;
46.1 mg vitamin C*

CRUCIFEROUS
COCKTAIL

8 parts broccoli
   juice (4 oz.)
4 parts carrot juice (2 oz.)
1 part fresh-squeezed lemon
   juice (½ oz.)
Salt, to taste
Freshly ground black pepper, to taste
Broccoli floret, for garnish

Combine juices with cracked ice in a
cocktail shaker and shake well. Strain
into a chilled cocktail glass and add
salt and pepper to taste. Garnish with
the broccoli floret. Serves one.

*59 calories; 0.5 gm fat; 6% calories
from fat; 0 mg cholesterol; 505.8
mg sodium; 12.7 gm carbohydrate;
4 gm protein; 73.8 mg calcium;
1.4 mg iron; 1,635 RE vitamin A;
117.6 mg vitamin C*

CUCUMBER
COCKTAIL

8 parts cucumber juice
   (4 oz.)
1 tsp. fresh-squeezed lemon juice
Salt, to taste
Freshly ground black pepper,
   for garnish

Combine all ingredients except black
pepper with cracked ice in a cocktail
shaker and shake well. Strain into a
chilled cocktail glass. Add salt to taste.
Sprinkle with black pepper. Serves one.

*17 calories; 0.2 gm fat; 7% calories
from fat; 0 mg cholesterol; 231.6
mg sodium; 3.9 gm carbohydrate;
0.7 gm protein; 18.6 mg calcium;
0.4 mg iron; 5.8 RE vitamin A; 7.9
mg vitamin C*

CUCUMBER
COOLER

10 parts cucumber juice (5 oz.)
10 parts plain nonfat yogurt (5 oz.)
2 parts wheatgrass juice (1 oz.)
1 tbsp. scallions, chopped fine
   (white part only)
1 tbsp. parsley juice
1 tbsp. fresh-squeezed lime juice
1 tbsp. fresh dill
Salt, to taste

Combine all ingredients except salt in
blender and blend until smooth. Pour
into a chilled collins glass. Add salt to
taste. Serves one.

*117 calories; 0.2 gm fat; 2% calo-
ries from fat; 3.1 mg cholesterol;
337.9 mg sodium; 21.1 gm carbohydrate; 9.4 gm protein; 331 mg
calcium; 0.9 mg iron; 26.8 RE vitamin A; 19.7 mg vitamin C*

CUCUMBER SALAD

10 parts cucumber
   juice (5 oz.)
10 parts plain nonfat yogurt (5 oz.)
2 garlic cloves, chopped fine
1 tsp. chopped parsley
½ tsp. paprika (sweet or hot)
Salt, to taste

Combine all ingredients except salt in
a blender and blend until smooth.
Pour into a chilled collins glass. Add
salt to taste. Serves one.

*103 calories; 0.3 mg fat; 2% calo-
ries from fat; 3.1 mg cholesterol;
333.7 mg sodium; 17.6 gm carbohydrate; 9.3 gm protein; 315.3 mg
calcium; 0.6 mg iron; 26.3 RE vitamin A; 10.4 mg vitamin C*

CURRANT
EVENTS

8 parts fresh-squeezed
   orange juice (4 oz.)
8 parts watermelon juice (4 oz.)
3 parts black-currant syrup (1½ oz.)
Sparkling white grape juice
Orange slices, for garnish

Combine juices and black-currant
syrup with cracked ice in a cocktail
shaker and shake well. Strain mixture
over ice cubes into two chilled highball glasses and fill the glasses with
sparkling grape juice. Stir gently
and garnish with the orange slices.
Serves two.

*84 calories; 0.4 gm fat; 3% calories
from fat; 0 mg cholesterol; 2.3 mg
sodium; 22.9 gm carbohydrate; 0.9
gm protein; 24.8 mg calcium; 0.7
mg iron; 34.8 RE vitamin A; 42.9
mg vitamin C*

CURRANT SPLASH

4 parts grapefruit juice (2 oz.)
4 parts pineapple juice (2 oz.)
1 part black- or red-currant
   syrup (½ oz.)

Combine juices with cracked ice in a
cocktail shaker and shake well. Strain
into a chilled cocktail glass and slowly
pour the currant syrup into the drink.
Do not stir. Serves one.

*91 calories; 0.1 gm fat; 1% calories
from fat; 0 mg cholesterol; 1.8 mg
sodium; 22.7 gm carbohydrate;
0.5 gm protein; 23.2 mg calcium;
0.8 mg iron; 0.8 RE vitamin A;
27.6 mg vitamin C*

CURRIED
CUCUMBER
COCKTAIL

10 parts cucumber juice (5 oz.)
2 parts fresh-squeezed lime
   juice (1 oz.)
½ tsp. curry powder
Fresh mint sprig, for garnish

Combine all ingredients except mint
sprig with cracked ice in a cocktail
shaker and shake well. Strain over ice
cubes into chilled old-fashioned glass
and garnish with the mint sprig.
Serves one.

*27 calories; 0.3 gm fat; 7% calories
from fat; 0 mg cholesterol; 3.3 mg
sodium; 6.9 gm carbohydrate; 0.9
gm protein; 24.4 mg calcium; 0.5
mg iron; 7.8 RE vitamin A; 15 mg
vitamin C*

CURRIED TOMATO
COCKTAIL

8 parts tomato juice (4 oz.)
1 tsp. fresh-squeezed lemon juice
1 tsp. white grape juice
½ tsp. curry powder
Lemon slice, for garnish

Combine all ingredients except lemon
slice with cracked ice in a cocktail
shaker and shake well. Strain into a
chilled cocktail glass and garnish with
the lemon slice. Serves one.

*18 calories; 0.1 gm fat; 7% calories
from fat; 0 mg cholesterol; 180 mg
sodium; 3.8 gm carbohydrate;
0.5 gm protein; 5.3 mg calcium;
0.5 mg iron; 26 RE vitamin A;
9.7 mg vitamin C*

D

DANGEROUS LIAISONS

8 parts pineapple juice (4 oz.)
4 parts red grape juice (2 oz.)
1 tbsp. fresh-squeezed lemon juice
Sparkling mineral water
Pineapple spear, for garnish

Combine juices with cracked ice in a cocktail shaker and shake well. Strain over ice cubes into a chilled collins glass and fill the glass with sparkling mineral water. Stir gently and garnish with the pineapple spear. Serves one.

102 calories; 0.1 mg fat; 1% calories from fat; 0 mg cholesterol; 3 mg sodium; 25.4 gm carbohydrate; 0.7 gm protein; 14.1 mg calcium; 0.5 mg iron; 0.9 RE vitamin A; 57.9 mg vitamin C

DANIEL'S COCKTAIL

4 parts fresh-squeezed
   orange juice (2 oz.)
3 parts fresh-squeezed lime
   juice (1½ oz.)
2 tsp. grenadine

Combine all ingredients with cracked ice in a cocktail shaker and shake well. Strain into a chilled cocktail glass. Serves one.

285 calories; 1 gm fat; 3% calories from fat; 0 mg cholesterol; 14.1 mg sodium; 69.5 gm carbohydrate; 3.8 gm protein; 63.9 mg calcium; 99.9 RE vitamin A; 270.5 mg vitamin C

DAVID'S VALLEJO SPECIAL

8 parts apple juice (4 oz.)
8 parts pear juice (4 oz.)
4 parts fresh-squeezed lemon
   juice (2 oz.)
Apple slice, for garnish

Combine juices with cracked ice in a cocktail shaker and shake well. Strain into a chilled collins glass, garnish with the apple slice and serve with a drinking straw. Serves one.

102 calories; 0.2 gm fat; 2% calories from fat; 0 mg cholesterol; 4.6 mg sodium; 24.4 gm carbohydrate; 0.7 gm protein; 14.1 mg calcium; 0.5 mg iron; 0.9 RE vitamin A; 57.9 mg vitamin C

DAY FOR NIGHT

4 parts passion-fruit juice (2 oz.)
2 parts peppermint syrup (1 oz.)
1 tbsp. fresh-squeezed lime juice
Ginger ale

Combine all ingredients except ginger ale with cracked ice in a cocktail shaker and shake well. Strain into a chilled highball glass and fill the glass with ginger ale. Stir gently. Serves one.

206 calories; 0.1 gm fat; 0 % calories from fat; 0 mg cholesterol; 10.4 mg sodium; 53 gm carbohydrate; 0.4 gm protein; 39.3 mg calcium; 2.3 mg iron; 136.7 RE vitamin A; 14.8 mg vitamin C

DANIEL'S COCKTAIL

DAYDREAM

DAYDREAM

3 parts passion-fruit
  syrup (1½ oz.)
Fresh-squeezed orange juice
Ground nutmeg, for garnish

Pour passion-fruit syrup into a chilled
collins glass filled with ice cubes. Fill
the glass with orange juice and stir.
Sprinkle with nutmeg. Serves one.

*140 calories; 0.8 gm fat; 5% calo-
ries from fat; 0 mg cholesterol; 4.9
mg sodium; 32.5 gm carbohydrate;
1.9 gm protein; 30.5 mg calcium;
6 mg iron; 82.8 RE vitamin A;
137.8 mg vitamin C*

DEATH VALLEY COOLER

10 parts de-alcoholized sparkling
  white wine (5 oz.)
4 parts peppermint syrup (2 oz.)
1 tsp. fresh-squeezed lemon juice
Fresh mint sprig, for garnish

Pour sparkling wine into a chilled
wineglass. Add syrup and lemon juice
and stir gently. Garnish with the mint
sprig. Serves one.

*236 calories; 0.1 gm fat; 0% calo-
ries from fat; 0 mg cholesterol; 7.1
mg sodium; 60.2 gm carbohydrate;
0.8 gm protein; 47.1 mg calcium;
2.4 mg iron; 1.2 RE vitamin A; 2.5
mg vitamin C*

DECOMPRESSION COLA

8 parts ginger ale (4 oz.)
8 parts prune juice (4 oz.)
2 parts black tea, chilled (1 oz.)

Combine all ingredients in a chilled collins glass and stir gently. Add ice if desired. Serves one.

120 calories; 0 gm fat; 0% calories from fat; 0 mg cholesterol; 13.3 mg sodium; 29.7 gm carbohydrate; 0.7 gm protein; 17 mg calcium; 1.5 mg iron; 0.4 RE vitamin A; 4.7 mg vitamin C

DEEP ORANGE

10 parts carrot juice (5 oz.)
6 parts fresh-squeezed orange juice (3 oz.)
6 parts pumpkin puree (3 oz.)
Carrot curls, for garnish

Combine ingredients except carrot curls in a blender and blend until frothy. Pour into chilled highball glasses and garnish with carrot curls. Serves two.

124 calories; 0.6 gm fat; 4% calories from fat; 0 mg cholesterol; 46 mg sodium; 28.9 gm carbohydrate; 2.9 gm protein; 65.3 mg calcium; 2 mg iron; 5,543 RE vitamin A; 58.2 mg vitamin C

DEL NORTE

8 parts cranberry juice cocktail (4 oz.)
8 parts grapefruit juice (4 oz.)
2 parts fresh-squeezed lime juice (1 oz.)
Lime slice, for garnish

Combine juices with cracked ice in a mixing glass. Pour over ice cubes into a chilled collins glass. Garnish with the lime slice. Serves one.

116 calories; 0.2 gm fat; 2 % calories from fat; 0 mg cholesterol; 5.9 mg sodium; 29.3 gm carbohydrate; 0.6 gm protein; 16.1 mg calcium; 0.4 mg iron; 1.4 RE vitamin A; 91.5 mg vitamin C

DELTA CITY COCKTAIL

8 parts tomato juice (4 oz.)
3–5 dashes green Tabasco sauce
3–5 dashes soy sauce
1/8 tsp. hot paprika
Celery salt, to taste
Freshly ground black pepper, to taste
Cocktail onion, for garnish

Combine all ingredients except celery salt, pepper, and the cocktail onion with cracked ice in a cocktail shaker and shake well. Strain into a chilled cocktail glass. Add celery salt and black pepper to taste. Garnish with the cocktail onion. Serves one.

182 calories; 8.8 gm fat; 40% calories from fat; 0 mg cholesterol; 469.1 mg sodium; 16.5 gm carbohydrate; 13 gm protein; 58 mg calcium; 2.1 mg iron; 84.3 RE vitamin A; 10.6 mg vitamin C

DESERT DATE SHAKE

12 parts papaya juice (6 oz.)
8 parts nonfat milk (4 oz.)
4 parts rehydrated dates, chopped (2 oz.)
4 parts coconut milk (2 oz.)
4 parts fresh-squeezed orange juice (2 oz.)
1 tsp. coconut syrup

Combine all ingredients in a blender and blend until smooth. Pour into chilled highball glasses. Serves two.

251 calories; 9.3 gm fat; 29% calories from fat; 0.9 mg cholesterol; 38.2 mg sodium; 41.4 gm carbohydrate; 3.6 gm protein; 101.5 mg calcium; 1.1 mg iron; 60.3 RE vitamin A; 17.3 mg vitamin C

DESERT RUSH

8 parts apricot juice (4 oz.)
4 parts aloe vera-juice (2 oz.)
4 parts unsweetened cherry juice (2 oz.)
1 tsp. bee pollen

DEL NORTE

Combine juices and bee pollen in a blender and blend until smooth. Pour into a chilled highball glass. Serves one.

105 calories; 0.6 gm fat; 5% calories from fat; 0 mg cholesterol; 3.4 mg sodium; 25.7 gm carbohydrate; 1.1 gm protein; 16.3 mg calcium; 0.6 mg iron; 161.7 RE vitamin A; 41.9 mg vitamin C

(Aloe-vera juice and bee pollen not included in nutritional analysis.)

DESERT SOLITAIRE

10 parts pineapple juice (5 oz.)
8 parts mango nectar (4 oz.)
Pineapple spear, for garnish

Combine juices in a blender and blend until smooth. Pour into a chilled highball glass and garnish with the pineapple spear. Serves one.

153 calories; 0.4 gm fat; 2% calories from fat; 0 mg cholesterol; 3.6 mg sodium; 38.9 gm carbohydrate; 1 gm protein; 35.6 mg calcium; 0.5 mg iron; 442.2 RE vitamin A; 46 0.6 mg vitamin C

DESPERADO

8 parts red grape
   juice (4 oz.)
4 parts carrot juice (2 oz.)
4 parts pineapple juice (2 oz.)
4 parts pomegranate juice (2 oz.)
1 tbsp. fresh-squeezed lemon juice
Lemon twists, for garnish

Combine juices with cracked ice in a
blender and blend until slushy. Pour
into chilled wineglasses and garnish
with the lemon twists. Serves two.

*83 calories;0.2 gm fat; 2% calories
from fat; 0 mg cholesterol; 11.1 mg
sodium; 20.5 gm carbohydrate;
1 gm protein; 18.1 mg calcium;
0.4 mg iron; 730.8 RE vitamin A;
10.8 mg vitamin C*

DINUBA DYNAMITE

8 parts peach juice (4 oz.)
4 parts apricot juice (2 oz.)
2 parts unsweetened
   cherry juice (1 oz.)
Sparkling mineral water

Combine juices with cracked ice in a
mixing glass and stir well. Strain over
ice cubes into a chilled collins glass
and slowly fill glass with sparkling
mineral water. Stir gently. Serves one.

*113 calories; 0.3 gm fat; 3% calo-
ries from fat; 0 mg cholesterol; 9.4
mg sodium; 28.7 gm carbohydrate;
0.9 gm protein; 14.1 mg calcium;
0.5 mg iron; 110 RE vitamin A;
26.9 mg vitamin C*

DISCREET
CHARM

8 parts plum
   juice (4 oz.)
1 tbsp. fresh-squeezed lime juice
1 tbsp. honey
Ginger ale

Combine all ingredients except ginger
ale with cracked ice in a cocktail
shaker. Shake vigorously and strain
over ice cubes into a chilled highball
glass. Fill the glass with ginger ale
and stir gently. Serves one.

*149 calories; 0.7 gm fat; 4% calo-
ries from fat; 0 mg cholesterol; 5.2
mg sodium; 38.3 gm carbohydrate;
1 gm protein; 8.7 mg calcium;
0.3 mg iron; 36.4 RE vitamin A;
15.5 mg vitamin C*

DONNER PARTY
PUNCH

64 parts red grape
   juice (32 oz.)
16 parts fresh-squeezed orange
   juice (8 oz.)
8 parts fresh-squeezed lemon
   juice (4 oz.)
8 parts honey (4 oz.)
4 parts ginger juice (2 oz.)
1 tbsp. orange peel, chopped
1 tbsp. lemon peel, chopped
1 tsp. alcohol-free almond extract
½ tsp. allspice
½ tsp. nutmeg
5 cinnamon sticks
10 whole cloves
Orange slices, for garnish

In a large stock pot, combine all
ingredients except orange slices and
simmer over low heat for at least one
hour. Serve hot in warmed mugs garnished with orange slices. Serves six.

*202 calories; 0.2 gm fat; 1% calo-
ries from fat; 0 mg cholesterol; 7.7
mg sodium; 51.5 gm carbohydrate;
1.3 gm protein; 23.3 mg calcium;
0.8 mg iron; 9.7 RE vitamin A;
31.1 mg vitamin C*

DOUBLE HELIX

8 parts pear
   juice (4 oz.)
6 parts passion-fruit juice (3 oz.)
1 tbsp. fresh-squeezed lime juice
Lime slice, for garnish

Combine juices with cracked ice in a
cocktail shaker and shake well. Strain
over ice cubes into a chilled highball
glass. Garnish with the lime slice.
Serves one.

*123 calories; 0.2 gm fat; 1% gm fat;
0 mg cholesterol; 9.3 mg sodium;
31.6 gm carbohydrate; 0.8 gm
protein; 9.7 mg calcium; 0.6 mg
iron; 205 RE vitamin A; 21.2 mg
vitamin C*

DOUBLE-TAKE

4 parts celery juice (2 oz.)
Sparkling apple cider
Lemon twist, for garnish

Pour celery juice into a chilled wine-glass and fill the glass with sparkling cider. Stir gently and garnish with the lemon twist. Serves one.

52 calories; 0.2 gm fat; 3% calories from fat; 0 mg cholesterol; 51.8 mg sodium; 13.8 gm carbohydrate; 0.5 gm protein; 27.8 mg calcium; 0.7 mg iron; 7.4 RE vitamin A; 4.8 mg vitamin C

DRAGONFLY

10 parts apple
   juice (5 oz.)
8 parts cantaloupe juice (4 oz.)
8 parts kiwi juice (4 oz.)
1 tbsp. fresh-squeezed lemon juice
Lemon twists, for garnish

Combine juices in a blender and blend until smooth. Pour into chilled wineglasses and garnish with the lemon twists. Serves two.

176 calories; 0.8 gm fat; 4% calories from fat; 0 mg cholesterol; 32.9 mg sodium; 13.7 gm carbohydrate; 2.3 gm protein; 55.2 mg calcium; 1.2 mg iron; 451 RE vitamin A; 218.6 mg vitamin C

DREAM TIME

8 parts fresh-squeezed
   orange juice (4 oz.)
8 parts strawberry puree (4 oz.)
8 parts plain nonfat yogurt (4 oz.)
4 parts papaya juice (2 oz.)
1 banana, sliced

Combine all ingredients in a blender and blend until smooth. If mixture is too thick, add more orange juice until desired consistency is achieved. Pour into a chilled collins glasses. Serves two.

141 calories; 0.6 gm fat; 4% calories from fat; 1.2 mg cholesterol; 42.9 mg sodium; 31.9 gm carbohydrate; 4.6 gm protein; 132.9 mg calcium; 0.6 mg iron; 20.8 RE vitamin A; 66.5 mg vitamin C

E

EARLY DAWN

8 parts pineapple juice (4 oz.)
6 parts strawberry puree (3 oz.)
2 parts red grape juice (1 oz.)
½ tsp. alcohol-free almond extract

Combine all ingredients in a blender
and blend until smooth. Pour over ice
cubes into a chilled old-fashioned
glass. Serves one.

*57 calories; 0.2 gm fat; 3% calories
from fat; 0 mg cholesterol; 8.3 mg
sodium; 44.7 gm carbohydrate;
0.3 gm protein; 15.3 mg calcium;
0.3 mg iron; 1.6 RE vitamin A;
30.2 mg vitamin C*

EARTHQUAKE WEATHER

EARLY FROST

10 parts apple cider (5 oz.)
8 parts pear nectar (4 oz.)
4 parts red grape juice (2 oz.)

Combine all ingredients with cracked
ice in a blender and blend until
slushy. Pour into a chilled collins
glass. Serves one.

*167 calories; 0.2 gm fat; 1% calo-
ries from fat; 0 mg cholesterol; 8.3
mg sodium; 44.7 gm carbohydrate;
0.5 gm protein; 15.3 mg calcium;
1.1 mg iron; 0 RE vitamin A; 11.7
mg vitamin C*

*105 calories; 0 gm fat; 0 % calories
from fat; 0 mg cholesterol; 7.9 mg
sodium; 27.7 gm carbohydrate;
0.1 gm protein; 20.7 mg calcium;
1.1 mg iron; 0.3 RE vitamin A; 8.3
mg vitamin C*

EAT TO THE BEET

8 parts carrot juice (4 oz.)
4 parts beet juice (2 oz.)
4 parts cucumber juice (2 oz.)
2 parts celery juice (1 oz.)

Combine juices with cracked ice in a
cocktail shaker and shake well. Strain
over ice cubes into a chilled collins
glass. Serves one.

*41 calories; 0.2 gm fat; 4% calories
from fat; 0 mg cholesterol; 61.8 mg
sodium; 9.1 gm carbohydrate;
1.4 gm protein; 32.3 mg calcium;
0.8 mg iron; 737 RE vitamin A;
10.2 mg vitamin C*

EARTHQUAKE
WEATHER

4 parts passion-fruit syrup (2 oz.)
2 parts fresh-squeezed lime
   juice (1 oz.)
Bitter-lemon soda
Lime slice, for garnish

Combine syrup and juice with cracked
ice in a mixing glass. Strain over ice
cubes into a chilled highball glass
and fill with bitter-lemon soda. Stir
gently and garnish with the lime slice.
Serves one.

EGG NOG

EGGNOG

16 parts milk (8 oz.)
4 parts egg substitute (2 oz.)
2 parts banana syrup (1 oz.)
1 tbsp. sugar
¼ tsp. alcohol-free almond extract
¼ tsp. alcohol-free vanilla extract
Whipped cream, for garnish
Freshly ground nutmeg

Combine milk, egg substitute, syrup, sugar, and extracts in a cocktail shaker and shake well. Pour into a chilled mug. Top with a dollop of whipped cream and sprinkle with nutmeg. Serves one.

390 calories; 15.1 gm fat; 35% calories from fat; 50.8 gm cholesterol; 246.1 mg sodium; 49.1 gm carbohydrate; 15.2 gm protein; 339.6 mg calcium; 1.5 mg iron; 262.2 RE vitamin A; 2.3 mg vitamin C

ELECTRIC LADY

6 parts plum juice (3 oz.)
4 parts apple juice (2 oz.)
4 parts white grape juice (2 oz.)
1 tsp. ginger juice
Lemon twist, for garnish

Combine ingredients with cracked ice in a cocktail shaker and shake well. Strain into a chilled wineglass and garnish with the lemon twist. Serves one.

116 calories; 0.6 gm fat; 5% calories from fat; 0 mg cholesterol; 3.9 mg sodium; 28.3 gm carbohydrate; 1 gm protein; 12.5 mg calcium; 0.5 mg iron; 27.7 RE vitamin A; 31.6 mg vitamin C

ELIZABETH'S SPARKLING RASPBERRY PUNCH

16 parts raspberry juice (8 oz.)
8 parts white grape juice (4 oz.)
8 parts peach juice (4 oz.)
4 parts fresh-squeezed lime
  juice (2 oz.)
4 parts raspberry syrup (2 oz.)
1 tbsp. alcohol-free almond extract
2 750-ml. bottles of de-alcoholized
  sparkling wine, well-chilled
Fresh raspberries, for garnish
Lime slices, for garnish

Combine all ingredients except the sparkling wine and fresh fruit in a punch bowl. Just before serving, add the bottles of sparkling wine and stir gently. Add ice and float raspberries and lime slices on top. Serves twelve.

94 calories; 0.1 gm fat; 1% calories from fat; 0 mg cholesterol; 20.9 mg sodium; 23.6 gm carbohydrate; 0.3 gm protein; 12.7 mg calcium; 0.4 mg iron; 5 RE vitamin A; 6.6 mg vitamin C

ELLIE'S GRAPE MILKSHAKE

16 parts milk (8 oz.)
8 parts grape juice (4 oz.)
2 tbsp. grape preserves
2 scoops vanilla ice cream

Combine all ingredients in a blender and blend until smooth but not watery. For a thinner shake, add more milk. Pour into chilled highball glasses. Serves two.

251 calories; 9.5 gm fat; 33% calories from fat; 54.3 mg cholesterol; 85.9 mg sodium; 37.3 gm carbohydrate; 5.9 gm protein; 200.8 mg calcium; 0.5 mg iron; 110.4 RE vitamin A; 1.8 mg vitamin C

EL NIÑO

4 parts pineapple
  juice (2 oz.)
4 parts fresh-squeezed lime
  juice (2 oz.)
2 parts passion-fruit syrup (1 oz.)
½ tsp. orgeat (almond) syrup
Pineapple spear, for garnish

Combine all ingredients except pineapple spear with cracked ice in a cocktail shaker and shake well. Pour into a chilled old-fashioned glass. Garnish with the pineapple spear. Serves one.

151 calories; 0.2 gm fat; 1% calories from fat; 0 mg cholesterol; 5.5 mg sodium; 39.4 gm carbohydrate; 0.8 gm protein; 33.7 mg calcium; 1.4 mg iron; 119.8 RE vitamin A; 31.7 mg vitamin C

ELVIS MILKSHAKE

16 parts buttermilk (8 oz.)
1 banana, sliced
2 tbsp. peanut butter

Combine all ingredients in a blender and blend until smooth. Pour into a chilled collins glass. Serves one.

385 calories; 18.6 gm fat; 41% calories from fat; 8.3 mg cholesterol; 391.9 sodium; 44.2 gm carbohydrate; 17 gm protein; 281.7 mg calcium; 1 mg iron; 31.7 RE vitamin A; 12.5 mg vitamin C

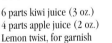
EL NIÑO

EMBRACEABLE YOU

12 parts pear juice (6 oz.)
10 parts nonfat yogurt (5 oz.)
1 tbsp. ginger juice
1 tbsp. honey
½ tsp. alcohol-free mint extract

Combine all ingredients in a blender
and blend until smooth. Pour into a
chilled collins glass. Serves one.

*251 calories; 0 gm fat; 0% calories
from fat; 3.1 mg cholesterol; 107.6
mg sodium; 57.7 gm carbohydrate;
8.4 gm protein; 290 mg calcium;
0.6 mg iron; 0 RE vitamin A; 2.2
mg vitamin C*

EMERALD CITY
COCKTAIL

6 parts kiwi juice (3 oz.)
4 parts apple juice (2 oz.)
Lemon twist, for garnish

Combine juices with cracked ice in a
cocktail shaker and shake well. Strain
into a chilled cocktail glass and garnish with the lemon twist. Serves one.

*83 calories; 0.5 gm fat; 5% calories
from fat; 0 mg cholesterol; 5.6 mg
sodium; 20.2 gm carbohydrate;
1 gm protein; 34.1 mg calcium;
0.6 mg iron; 15.2 RE vitamin A;
114.3 mg vitamin C*

85

EMPEROR'S PASSION

10 parts strong-brewed green
   tea, chilled (5 oz.)
8 parts white grape juice (4 oz.)
1 tsp. fresh-squeezed lime juice
Sugar, to taste
Lime slice, for garnish

Combine green tea and juices with
cracked ice in a cocktail shaker and
shake well. Strain over ice cubes into a
chilled collins glass and garnish with
the lime slice. Add sugar to taste.
Serves one.

*72 calories; 0.1 gm fat; 1% calories
from fat; 0 mg cholesterol; 4.9 mg
sodium; 17.7 gm carbohydrate;
0.7 gm protein; 13.5 mg calcium;
0.4 mg iron; 0.9 RE vitamin A;
1.6 mg vitamin C*

*(Sugar not included in nutritional
analysis.)*

ENCINO JUICE

8 parts loganberry
   juice (4 oz.)
8 parts pineapple juice (4 oz.)
1 part fresh-squeezed lime
   juice (½ oz.)

Combine all ingredients in a mixing
glass with cracked ice and stir well.
Strain over ice cubes into a chilled
collins glass. Serves one.

*130 calories; 0.5 gm fat; 3% calo-
ries from fat; 0 mg cholesterol; 2.4
mg sodium; 31.7 gm carbohydrate;
2.1 gm protein; 50 mg calcium;
1 mg iron; 4.7 RE vitamin A; 33.7
mg vitamin C*

ERIC'S VEGGIE COCKTAIL

6 parts carrot juice (3
   oz.)
4 parts cabbage juice (2 oz.)
4 parts red bell-pepper juice (2 oz.)
1 part scallion juice (½ oz.)
Salt, to taste
Freshly ground black pepper, to taste
Lemon peel, for garnish

Combine juices with cracked ice in a
cocktail shaker and shake well.
Strain over ice cubes into chilled old-
fashioned glasses. Add salt and pepper
to taste and garnish with the lemon
peels. Serves two.

*36 calories; 0.1 gm fat; 3% calories
from fat; 0 mg cholesterol; 657.1
mg sodium; 8.5 gm carbohydrate;
0.8 gm protein; 27 mg calcium;
0.8 mg iron; 1,107 RE vitamin A;
17.7 mg vitamin C*

F

FAIRFAX AVENUE BORSCHT

8 parts beet juice (4 oz.)
8 parts carrot juice (4 oz.)
4 parts celery juice (2 oz.)
4 parts onion juice (2 oz.)
3 parts cabbage juice (1½ oz.)
1 tbsp. fresh-squeezed lemon juice
Salt, to taste
Sour cream or plain nonfat yogurt,
    for garnish

Combine all ingredients except salt
and sour cream in a saucepan over
medium heat. Heat until just boiling,
then reduce heat and simmer for
about twenty minutes, stirring occasionally. Add salt to taste. Serve in
warmed mugs with a dollop of sour
cream or nonfat yogurt on top for
garnish. Serves one.

*84 calories; 1.9 gm fat; 18% calo-
ries from fat; 3.2 mg cholesterol;
206.5 mg sodium; 16 gm carbohydrate; 2.4 gm protein; 54.3 mg
calcium; 0.9 mg iron; 1,484 RE
vitamin A; 17.6 mg vitamin C*

FARM-STAND SPECIAL

6 parts peach
    nectar (3 oz.)
6 parts nectarine juice (3 oz.)
6 parts plum juice (3 oz.)
4 parts raspberry juice or puree (2 oz.)
3 parts apricot nectar (1½ oz.)

Combine all ingredients with cracked
ice in a cocktail shaker and shake
well. Strain over ice cubes into a
chilled collins glass. Serves one.

*194 calories; 1.3 gm fat; 6% calo-
ries from fat; 0 mg cholesterol; 7.5
mg sodium; 47.6 gm carbohydrate;
2.4 gm protein; 28.6 mg calcium;
0.9 mg iron; 193.9 RE vitamin A;
50.2 mg vitamin C*

FAUX KIR

FAUX KIR

2 parts raspberry syrup (1 oz.)
White grape juice
Lemon twist, for garnish

Pour syrup over ice cubes in a chilled
wineglass. Fill with white grape juice
and stir well. Garnish with the lemon
twist. Serves one.

*164 calories; 0.2 gm fat; 1% calo-
ries from fat; 0 mg cholesterol; 5.7
mg sodium; 41.3 gm carbohydrate;
0.9 gm protein; 31.4 mg calcium;
1.4 mg iron; 2.1 RE vitamin A;
2.1 mg vitamin C*

FAUX KIR ROYALE

3 parts raspberry syrup (1½ oz.)
Sparkling white grape juice
Lemon twist, for garnish

Pour the syrup into a chilled wine-glass and fill the glass with cold sparkling grape juice. Stir gently and garnish with the lemon twist. Serves one.

202 calories; 0.2 gm fat; 1% calories from fat; 0 mg cholesterol; 6.4 mg sodium; 51 gm carbohydrate; 0.9 gm protein; 39.9 mg calcium; 1.9 mg iron; 2.1 RE vitamin A; 2.1 mg vitamin C

FERDINAND THE BULL

8 parts tomato juice (4 oz.)
8 parts beef bouillon, chilled (4 oz.)
2 parts fresh-squeezed lime juice (1 oz.)
Dash of Tabasco sauce
Dash of Worcestershire sauce
Freshly ground pepper, to taste
Lime wedge, for garnish

Combine all ingredients except pepper and lime wedge with cracked ice in a cocktail shaker and shake well. Strain over ice cubes into a chilled collins glass. Sprinkle with freshly ground pepper and taste to adjust Tabasco and Worcestershire sauce seasonings. Garnish with the lime wedge. Serves one.

39 calories; 0.3 gm fat; 7% calories from fat; 0 mg cholesterol; 849.4 mg sodium; 8.4 gm carbohydrate; 2.5 gm protein; 24.8 mg calcium; 1.2 mg iron; 68.2 RE vitamin A; 28.8 mg vitamin C

FEVER RELIEVER

8 parts pineapple juice (4 oz.)
6 parts fresh-squeezed orange juice (3 oz.)
2 parts fresh-squeezed lemon juice (1 oz.)
¼ tsp. cayenne pepper

Combine all ingredients in saucepan over medium heat. Heat until very hot, stirring occasionally. Pour into a warmed mug. Serves one.

110 calories; 0.3 gm fat; 3% calories from fat; 0 mg cholesterol; 2.2 mg sodium; 27.2 gm carbohydrate; 1.1 gm protein; 31.3 mg calcium; 0.5 mg iron; 36.9 RE vitamin A; 68 mg vitamin C

FERDINAND THE BULL

FILLMORE PUNCH

FILLMORE PUNCH

4 parts guava nectar (2 oz.)
4 parts fresh-squeezed
  lemon juice (2 oz.)
2 parts fresh-squeezed orange
  juice (1 oz.)
Lemon slice, for garnish

Combine all ingredients except lemon
slice with cracked ice in a blender and
blend until smooth. Pour into a
chilled margarita glass. Garnish with
the lemon slice. Serves one.

*56 calories; 0.4 gm fat; 5% calories
from fat; 0 mg cholesterol; 2.5 mg
sodium; 14.6 gm carbohydrate;
0.9 gm protein; 18.4 mg calcium;
0.3 mg iron; 51.7 RE vitamin A;
144.2 mg vitamin C*

FIVE EASY PIECES

6 parts tomato juice
  (3 oz.)
4 parts carrot juice (2 oz.)
4 parts beet juice (2 oz.)
4 parts celery juice (2 oz.)
4 parts red bell-pepper juice (2 oz.)
1 tbsp. fresh-squeezed lemon juice
Celery sticks, for garnish
Parsley sprigs, for garnish
Freshly ground black pepper, to taste

Combine all juices in a blender and
blend until smooth. Pour into chilled
old-fashioned glasses and garnish
with celery sticks and parsley sprigs.
Sprinkle with freshly ground black
pepper to taste. Serves two.

*47 calories; 0.2 gm fat; 3% calories
from fat; 0 mg cholesterol; 618.2
mg sodium; 11.1 gm carbohydrate;
1.4 gm protein; 29.7 mg calcium;
1.2 mg iron; 778.3 RE vitamin A;
20.8 mg vitamin C*

FIVE-FLOWER ICED TEA

16 parts chamomile tea, chilled (8 oz.)
16 parts hibiscus tea, chilled (8 oz.)
16 parts jasmine tea, chilled (8 oz.)
16 parts lemon-verbena tea,
  chilled (8 oz.)
16 parts rose-hip tea, chilled (8 oz.)
Fresh mint sprigs, for garnish
Lemon slices, for garnish

Combine teas in a large pitcher. Serve
over ice cubes in chilled collins glasses
and garnish with lemon slices and
mint sprigs. Serves four to six.

*2.3 calories; 0 gm fat; 0% calories
from fat; 0 mg cholesterol; 2.3 mg
sodium; 0.5 gm carbohydrate;
0 gm protein; 4.5 mg calcium;
0.2 mg iron; 0 RE vitamin A; 0 mg
vitamin C*

FLIGHT TO MARS

10 parts fresh-squeezed
  orange juice (5 oz.)
8 parts pineapple juice (4 oz.)
2 parts watermelon juice (1 oz.)
2 parts onion juice (1 oz.)
2 parts parsley juice (1 oz.)
1 part garlic juice (½ oz.)
1 part jalapeño pepper juice (½ oz.)
1 tsp. alcohol-free almond extract
Parsley sprigs, for garnish
Pineapple spears, for garnish

Combine all ingredients except parsley
sprigs and pineapple spears in a
blender and blend until smooth. Pour
over ice cubes into chilled highball
glasses and garnish with parsley sprigs
and pineapple spears. Serves two.

*102 calories; 0.4 gm fat; 4% calo-
ries from fat; 0 mg cholesterol;
114.7 mg sodium; 22.7 gm carbohydrate; 1.8 gm protein; 61.2 mg
calcium; 1.6 mg iron; 95.8 RE vitamin A; 67.2 mg vitamin C*

FLOODLIGHT

8 parts carrot juice (4 oz.)
4 parts alfalfa-sprout
  juice (2 oz.)
4 parts apple juice (2 oz.)
Carrot stick, for garnish

Combine juices with cracked ice in a
cocktail shaker and shake well. Strain
over ice cubes into a chilled highball
glass and garnish with the carrot stick.
Serves one.

*97 calories; 0.8 gm fat; 7% calories
from fat; 0 mg cholesterol; 39.7 mg
sodium; 20.4 gm carbohydrate; 4.5
gm protein; 58.5 mg calcium; 1.6
mg iron; 2,933 RE vitamin A; 39.9
mg vitamin C*

FOGTOWN COCKTAIL

10 parts clam juice (5 oz.)
1 part fresh-squeezed lemon
    juice (½ oz.)
3–5 dashes Tabasco sauce
3–5 dashes Worcestershire sauce
Lemon twist, for garnish

Combine all ingredients except lemon twist with cracked ice in a cocktail shaker and shake well. Strain into a chilled cocktail glass and garnish with lemon twist. Serves one.

71 calories; 0.1 gm fat; 2% calories from fat; 0 mg cholesterol; 600.9 mg sodium; 17.1 gm carbohydrate; 1 gm protein; 20.6 mg calcium; 1 mg iron; 33.8 RE vitamin A; 18.5 mg vitamin C

FORBIDDEN FRUIT

10 parts apple juice (5 oz.)
8 parts pomegranate
    juice (4 oz.)
½ tsp. ginger juice
Fresh ginger strips, for garnish

Combine juices with cracked ice in a cocktail shaker and shake well. Strain into chilled cocktail glasses and garnish with ginger strips. Serves one.

101 calories; 0.3 gm fat; 2% calories from fat; 0 mg cholesterol; 5.5 mg sodium; 25.8 gm carbohydrate; 0.7 gm protein; 7.1 mg calcium; 0.7 gm mg iron; 0 RE vitamin A; 33.8 mg vitamin C

FORMULA ONE

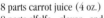

8 parts carrot juice (4 oz.)
8 parts alfalfa-, clover-, and
    radish-sprout juice (4 oz.)
6 parts fennel juice (3 oz.)
4 parts apple juice (2 oz.)
Apple slice, for garnish

Combine juices with cracked ice in a cocktail shaker and shake well. Strain into a chilled collins glass and garnish with the apple slice. Serves one.

148 calories; 1.4 gm fat; 8% calories from fat; 0 mg cholesterol; 101.7 mg sodium; 30.8 gm carbohydrate; 8.2 gm protein; 132.8 mg calcium; 2.1 mg iron; 2,942 RE vitamin A; 58.2 mg vitamin C

FORT ROSS BORSCHT

8 parts plain nonfat
    yogurt (4 oz.)
6 parts beet juice (3 oz.)
2 parts celery juice (1 oz.)
1 part fresh-squeezed lemon
    juice (½ oz.)
½ tsp. white horseradish
Salt, to taste
Fresh dill, for garnish

Combine all ingredients except salt and dill in a blender and blend until smooth. Pour into a chilled highball glass, add salt to taste and sprinkle with fresh. Serves one.

107 calories; 0.2 gm fat; 1% calories from fat; 2.5 mg cholesterol; 197.2 mg sodium; 19.9 gm carbohydrate; 8.2 gm protein; 252.7 mg calcium; 0.8 mg iron; 7 RE vitamin A; 12 mg vitamin C

FREE-ASSOCIATION

10 parts grapefruit
    juice (5 oz.)
6 parts cantaloupe juice (3 oz.)
6 parts kiwi juice (3 oz.)
Kiwi slice, for garnish

Combine juices with cracked ice in a cocktail shaker and shake well. Strain over ice cubes into a chilled collins glass and garnish with the kiwi slice. Serves one.

137 calories; 0.8 mg fat; 5% calories from fat; 0 mg cholesterol; 13.3 mg sodium; 32.8 gm carbohydrate; 2.3 gm protein; 44.3 mg calcium; 0.8 mg iron; 289.6 RE vitamin A; 173.1 mg vitamin C

FRESNO FIZZ

6 parts prune juice (3 oz.)
4 parts pineapple juice (2 oz.)
Sparkling mineral water

Combine juices with cracked ice in a cocktail shaker and shake well. Strain into a chilled highball glass and fill the glass with sparkling mineral water. Stir gently. Serves one.

92 calories; 0.1 gm fat; 1% calories from fat; 0 mg cholesterol; 3.4 mg sodium; 22.7 gm carbohydrate; 0.7 gm protein; 19.8 mg calcium; 1.2 mg iron; 0.6 RE vitamin A; 9.6 mg vitamin C

FROZEN HOT CHOCOLATE

32 parts hot chocolate,
   chilled (16 oz.)
3–5 scoops vanilla ice cream

Combine ingredients in a blender and blend until smooth. Pour into chilled highball glasses. Serves two.

337 calories; 16.6 gm fat; 43% calories from fat; 88.4 mg cholesterol; 8.2 mg sodium; 37.7 gm carbohydrate; 10.9 gm protein; 355.1 mg calcium; 0.8 mg iron; 186.4 RE vitamin A; 2.6 mg vitamin C

FROZEN PAPAYA

10 parts papaya juice (5 oz.)
8 parts fresh-squeezed
   orange juice (4 oz.)
1 tbsp. fresh-squeezed lemon juice

Combine all ingredients with cracked ice in a blender and blend until slushy. Pour into chilled highball glass. Serves one.

136 calories; 0.4 gm fat; 3% calories from fat; 0 mg cholesterol; 8.2 mg sodium; 33.7 gm carbohydrate; 1.1 gm protein; 27.6 mg calcium; 0.7 mg iron; 38.7 RE vitamin A; 68 mg vitamin C

FRUIT FLIRT

10 parts fresh-squeezed
   orange juice (5 oz.)
6 parts raspberry juice (3 oz.)
1 tbsp. fresh-squeezed lemon juice
Lemon slice, for garnish

Combine juices with cracked ice in a cocktail shaker and shake well. Strain over ice cubes into chilled highball glass and garnish with the lemon slice. Serves one.

109 calories; 0.8 gm fat; 6% calories from fat; 0 mg cholesterol; 1.3 mg sodium; 25.9 gm carbohydrate; 1.8 gm protein; 35.2 mg calcium; 0.8 mg iron; 39.7 RE vitamin A; 99.1 mg vitamin C

FRUIT FLOOD

8 parts strawberry puree
   (4 oz.)
8 parts apricot juice (4 oz.)
6 parts cantaloupe juice (3 oz.)
6 parts honeydew juice (3 oz.)
6 parts watermelon juice (3 oz.)
Whole strawberries, for garnish

Combine puree and juices with cracked ice in a blender and blend until slushy. Pour into chilled highball glasses and garnish with the whole strawberries. Serves two.

90.8 calories; 0.5 gm fat; 5% calories from fat; 0 mg cholesterol; 15.9 mg sodium; 22.5 gm carbohydrate; 1.4 gm protein; 23.4 mg calcium; 0.6 mg iron; 255.1 RE vitamin A; 81.6 mg vitamin C

FRUIT-JUICE SPRITZER

6 parts apple juice or fruit juice of
  your choice (3 oz.)
Sparkling mineral water
Lemon twist, for garnish

Pour juice over ice cubes into a chilled
wineglass. Fill with sparkling mineral
water and garnish with the lemon
twist. Serves one.

*40 calories; 0.1 gm fat; 2% calories
from fat; 0 mg cholesterol; 2.5 mg
sodium; 9.9 gm carbohydrate; 0.1
gm protein; 56 mg calcium; 0.3 mg
iron; 0 RE vitamin A; 2.6 mg vitamin C*

FRUITY YOGURT SHAKE

8 parts vanilla nonfat
  yogurt (4 oz.)
6 fresh strawberries, hulled and sliced
6 parts cantaloupe, chopped (3 oz.)
½ fresh papaya, peeled and chopped
1 tbsp. honey

Combine all ingredients in a blender
and blend until slushy. Pour into a
chilled collins glass. Serves one.

*253 calories; 0.7 gm fat; 2% calo-
ries from fat; 2.5 mg cholesterol;
91.7 mg sodium; 58.8 gm carbohydrate; 7.6 gm protein; 249.6 mg
calcium; 0.9 mg iron; 468.2 RE
vitamin A; 159.7 mg vitamin C*

FUNKY COLD VERBENA

10 parts strong brewed
  lemon-verbena tea, chilled (5 oz.)
4 parts white grape juice (2 oz.)
2 parts fresh-squeezed lime
  juice (1 oz.)
Lemon twist, for garnish

Combine tea and juices with cracked
ice in a cocktail shaker and shake
well. Strain over ice cubes into a
chilled highball glass and garnish
with the lemon twist. Serves one.

*44 calories; 0.1 gm fat; 1% calories
from fat; 0 mg cholesterol; 3.4 mg
sodium; 11.3 gm carbohydrate;
0.4 gm protein; 10.5 mg calcium;
0.3 mg iron; 0.7 RE vitamin A; 8.4
mg vitamin C*

FUNNY VALENTINE

16 parts pineapple juice (8 oz.)
10 parts strawberry puree (5 oz.)
1 banana, sliced
Whole strawberries, for garnish

Combine all ingredients except whole
strawberries in a blender and blend
until smooth. If mixture is too thick,
add more pineapple juice until desired
consistency is achieved. Pour into
chilled wineglasses and garnish with
the whole strawberries. Serves two.

*137 calories; 0.6 gm fat; 4% calo-
ries from fat; 0 mg cholesterol; 2.3
mg sodium; 34 gm carbohydrate;
1.4 gm protein; 32.7 mg calcium;
0.7 mg iron; 7.1 RE vitamin A;
57.5 mg vitamin C*

FUZZY PINK SPLASH

6 parts peach juice (3 oz.)
4 parts guava juice (2 oz.)
Sparkling mineral water
Fresh mint sprig, for garnish

Combine juices with cracked ice in a
cocktail shaker and shake well. Strain
into a chilled collins glass and fill
with sparkling mineral water. Stir gently and garnish with the mint sprig.
Serves one.

*75 calories; 0.4 gm fat; 4% calories
from fat; 0 mg cholesterol; 7.5 mg
sodium; 18.6 gm carbohydrate;
0.7 gm protein; 15.8 mg calcium;
0.3 mg iron; 66.9 RE vitamin A;
108.4 mg vitamin C*

G

GARDEN COOLER

8 parts carrot juice (4 oz.)
8 parts celery juice (4 oz.)
Lemon wedge, for garnish

Combine juices with cracked ice in a cocktail shaker and shake well. Strain into a chilled highball glass. Squeeze lemon wedge over the drink and drop it in. Serves one.

64 calories; 0.3 gm fat; 4% calories from fat; 0 mg cholesterol; 131.4 mg sodium; 14.7 gm carbohydrate; 1.9 gm protein; 72.6 mg calcium; 1 mg iron; 2,935 RE vitamin A; 17.6 mg vitamin C

GAZPACHO COCKTAIL

12 parts tomato juice (6 oz.)
2 parts fresh-squeezed lemon
    juice (1 oz.)
2 cucumber slices, chopped
1 scallion, white part only, sliced
Garlic clove, crushed
⅛ tsp. oregano
3–5 dashes tabasco sauce
Freshly ground black pepper, to taste
Salt, to taste
Cucumber slice, whole
Avocado slice, for garnish

Combine all ingredients except salt, pepper, whole cucumber slice, and avocado slice in a blender and blend until smooth. Pour mixture into a chilled collins glass, add salt and pepper to taste, and garnish with the cucumber and avocado slices. Serves one.

61 calories; 1.2 gm fat; 15% of calories from fat; 0 mg cholesterol; 627.0 mg sodium; 13.4 gm carbohydrate; 2.1 gm protein; 38.8 mg calcium; 1.4 mg iron; 104.6 RE vitamin A; 32.5 mg vitamin C

GESTALT CRANBERRY

1 scoop lemon sorbet
Sparkling cranberry juice
Fresh mint sprig, for garnish

Place lemon sorbet in a chilled highball glass and fill the glass with sparkling cranberry juice. Garnish with the fresh mint sprig. Serves one.

163 calories; 0.1 gm fat; 0% calories from fat; 0 mg cholesterol; 96 mg sodium; 59.1 gm carbohydrate; 3.9 gm protein; 6 mg calcium; .3 mg iron; 0 RE vitamin A; 81 mg vitamin C

GILDA COCKTAIL

8 parts carrot juice (4 oz.)
2 parts beet juice (1 oz.)
Lemon twist, for garnish

Combine all ingredients except lemon twist with cracked ice in a cocktail shaker and shake well. Strain into a chilled cocktail glass and garnish with the lemon twist. Serves one.

58 calories; 0.2 gm fat; 3% calories from fat; 0 mg cholesterol; 54.6 mg sodium; 13.4 gm carbohydrate; 1.6 gm protein; 31.9 mg calcium; 0.7 mg iron; 2,921 RE vitamin A; 10.7 mg vitamin C

GILROY TOMATO SPECIAL

16 parts tomato juice (8 oz.)
1 tbsp. fresh-squeezed lime juice
2 garlic cloves
Salt, to taste
Freshly ground black pepper, to taste
Parsley sprig, for garnish

Combine juices and garlic in a blender and blend until well-mixed. Pour into a chilled highball glass and add salt and pepper to taste. Garnish with the parsley sprigs. Serves one.

GAZPACHO COCKTAIL

52 calories; 0.2 gm fat; 3% calories from fat; 0 mg cholesterol; 818.4 mg sodium; 12.9 gm carbohdrate; 2.2 gm protein; 32.6 mg calcium; 1.4 mg iron; 126.5 RE vitamin A; 24.5 mg vitamin C

GINGER AND FRED

4 parts cranberry juice cocktail (2 oz.)
4 parts grapefruit juice (2 oz.)
4 parts fresh-squeezed orange juice (2 oz.)
2 parts ginger juice (1 oz.)
1 tsp. honey
Orange slice, for garnish

Combine all ingredients except orange slice with cracked ice in a cocktail shaker and shake well. Pour over ice cubes into a chilled highball glass. Garnish with the orange slice. Serves one.

180 calories; 0.3 gm fat; 1% calories from fat; 0 mg cholesterol; 8.6 mg sodium; 46.7 gm carbohydrate; 0.8 gm protein; 13.3 mg calcium; 1.1 mg iron; 11.9 RE vitamin A; 71.8 mg vitamin C

GINGER-ALE COCKTAIL

2 parts fresh-squeezed lemon
   juice (1 oz.)
2 parts maple syrup (1 oz.)
Ginger ale
Lemon twist, for garnish

Combine the lemon juice and maple syrup in a chilled cocktail glass. Fill the glass with ginger ale and stir gently. Garnish with the lemon twist. Serves one.

117 calories; 0 gm fat; 0% calories from fat; 0 mg cholesterol; 11.1 mg sodium; 30.7 mg carbohydrate; 0.1 gm protein; 34.9 mg calcium; 0.5 mg iron; 0.6 RE vitamin A; 13 mg vitamin C

GINGER-APPLE FIZZ

4 parts apple juice (2 oz.)
2 parts fresh-squeezed
   lemon juice (1 oz.)
1 tbsp. black-currant syrup
Ginger ale

Combine all ingredients except the ginger ale with cracked ice in a cocktail shaker and shake well. Strain over ice cubes into a chilled highball glass. Fill glass with the ginger ale and stir gently. Serves one.

104 calories; 0.1 gm fat; 1% calories from fat; 0 mg cholesterol; 6.9 mg sodium; 27.1 gm carbohydrate; 0.1 gm protein; 19.2 mg calcium; 1 mg iron; 0.6 RE vitamin A; 36.3 mg vitamin C

GINGER-MINT SPARKLER

4 parts fresh-squeezed
   lemon juice (2 oz.)
4 parts peppermint syrup (2 oz.)
Ginger ale
Fresh mint sprig, for garnish

Combine lemon juice and syrup with cracked ice in a cocktail shaker and shake well. Strain over ice cubes into a chilled collins glass. Fill the glass with ginger ale and stir gently. Garnish with the mint sprig. Serves one.

183 calories; 0 gm fat; 0% calories from fat; 0 mg cholesterol; 7.4 mg sodium; 48.4 gm carbohydrate; 0.2 gm protein; 39.6 mg calcium; 2.1 mg iron; 1.1 RE vitamin A; 26 mg vitamin C

GINGER-ORANGE SNAP

8 parts fresh-squeezed orange
   juice (4 oz.)
1 part ginger juice (½ oz.)
1 tsp. honey
Orange peel, for garnish

Combine juices and honey in a mixing glass with and stir until honey is dissolved. Strain into a chilled cocktail glass and garnish with the orange peel. Serves one.

88 calories; 0.2 gm fat; 2% calories from fat; 0 mg cholesterol; 2.3 mg sodium; 21.8 gm carbohydrate; 0.8 gm protein; 12.7 mg calcium; 0.4 mg iron; 22.7 RE vitamin A; 57.1 mg vitamin C

GINGER-PEACH SPARKLER

8 parts peach nectar (4 oz.)
Ginger ale
Lemon wedge, for garnish
Crystallized ginger, for garnish

Pour peach nectar over ice cubes into a chilled collins glass. Fill the glass with ginger ale and stir gently. Squeeze the lemon wedge into the drink and float crystallized ginger on top. Serves one.

103 calories; 0 gm fat; 0% calories from fat; 0 mg cholesterol; 16.3 mg sodium; 26.4 gm carbohydrate; 0.3 gm protein; 9.6 mg calcium; 0.4 mg iron; 28.3 RE vitamin A; 6 mg vitamin C

GINSENG BLITZ

10 parts strong-brewed
  ginseng tea, chilled (5 oz.)
8 parts apple juice (4 oz.)
2 parts ginger juice (1 oz.)
Honey, to taste

Combine tea and juices in a blender and blend until smooth. Add honey to taste. Pour over ice cubes into a chilled collins glass. Serves one.

155 calories; 0.2 gm fat; 1% calories from fat; 0 mg cholesterol; 10.2 mg sodium; 40.6 gm carbohydrate; 0.2 gm protein; 11.1 mg calcium; 1.3 mg iron; 0 RE vitamin A; 48.3 mg vitamin C

GIRAFFE HUNTER

8 parts fresh-squeezed
  orange juice (4 oz.)
2 parts unsweetened
  cherry juice (1 oz.)
6 parts ginger ale (3 oz.)
4 parts sparkling mineral water (2 oz.)
Lime slice, for garnish

Combine juices with cracked ice in a cocktail shaker and shake well. Strain over ice cubes into a chilled highball glass and add ginger ale and sparkling mineral water. Stir gently and garnish with the lime slice. Serves one.

91 calories; 0.5 gm fat; 5% calories from fat; 0 mg cholesterol; 4.9 mg sodium; 21.4 gm carbohydrate; 1.1 gm protein; 18.2 mg calcium; 0.4 mg iron; 28.8 RE vitamin A; 58.7 mg vitamin C

GLOBAL VILLAGE PUNCH

48 parts guava nectar (24 oz.)
48 parts pineapple juice (24 oz.)
16 parts fresh-squeezed orange
  juice (8 oz.)
6 parts fresh-squeezed lemon
  juice (3 oz.)
2 liters ginger ale
Orange slices, for garnish

Combine juices together in a large punch bowl. Just before serving, add ginger ale and stir gently. Add ice cubes and float orange slices on top. Serves ten.

231 calories; 1.4 gm fat; 5% calories from fat; 0 mg cholesterol; 21.9 mg sodium; 56.1 gm carbohydrate; 2.2 gm protein; 64 mg calcium; 1.2 mg iron; 176.2 RE vitamin A; 418.5 mg vitamin C

GLORY DAZE

8 parts plum juice (4 oz.)
6 parts carrot juice (3 oz.)
6 parts mango nectar (3 oz.)

Combine all ingredients with cracked ice in a blender and blend until slushy. Pour into a chilled collins glass. Serves one.

152 calories; 1.1 gm fat; 6% calories from fat; 0 mg cholesterol; 26.3 mg sodium; 37.1 gm carbohydrate; 2.1 gm protein; 33.6 mg calcium; 0.6 mg iron; 2,557 RE vitamin A; 41.6 mg vitamin C

GOLD RUSH CHOCOLATE

Unsweetened chocolate (1 solid oz.)
½ cup sugar
Dash of salt
16 parts water, heated to boiling (8 oz.)
16 parts half-and-half, heated (8 oz.)
24 parts strong-brewed coffee,
  hot (12 oz.)
1 tsp. alcohol-free vanilla extract
½ tsp. grated cinnamon
Chocolate shavings, for garnish

Using a microwave or double boiler combine chocolate, sugar, and salt and heat gently until chocolate has melted. Stir in boiling water and continue to heat until mixture is hot and well-blended. Add heated half-and-half and coffee and stir well. Add vanilla and cinnamon and stir again. Serve in warmed cups and sprinkle with chocolate shavings. Serves four.

183 calories 11.8 gm fat; 54% calories from fat; 22 mg cholesterol; 25.6 mg sodium; 20.1 gm carbohydrate; 2.6 gm protein; 71.2 mg calcium; 0.8 mg iron; 65.1 RE vitamin A; 0.6 mg vitamin C

GOLDEN COCONUT

10 parts papaya juice (5 oz.)
8 parts coconut milk (4 oz.)
4 parts fresh-squeezed orange
    juice (2 oz.)
1 tbsp. coconut syrup
½ tsp. alcohol-free almond extract
Orange slices, for garnish

Combine all ingredients except orange slices in a blender and blend until smooth. Pour into chilled old-fashioned glasses and garnish with the orange slices. Serves two.

227 calories; 16.2 gm fat; 64% calories from fat; 0 mg cholesterol; 10.8 mg sodium; 18.5 gm carbohydrate; 2.2 gm protein; 31 mg calcium; 1.2 mg iron; 148.4 RE vitamin A; 58 mg vitamin C

GOLDEN GATE

12 parts pineapple
    juice (6 oz.)
4 parts fresh-squeezed lemon
    juice (2 oz.)
Sparkling cider
Orange slices, for garnish

Combine juices with cracked ice in a cocktail shaker and shake well. Strain into chilled champagne flutes, filling each glass about two thirds full. Fill with the sparkling cider and stir gently. Garnish with the orange slices. Serves two.

70 calories; 0.1 gm fat; 1% calories from fat; 0 mg cholesterol; 2 mg sodium; 18.1 gm carbohydrate; 0.4 gm protein; 18.1 mg calcium; 0.4 mg iron; 0.9 RE vitamin A; 22.4 mg vitamin C

GOOD DAY SUNSHINE

12 parts fresh-squeezed
    orange juice (6 oz.)
6 parts grapefruit juice (3 oz.)
6 parts pineapple juice (3 oz.)
2 scoops strawberry sorbet

Combine all ingredients in a blender and blend until slushy. Pour into chilled highball glasses. Serves two.

228 calories; 0.5 gm fat; 2% calories from fat; 0 mg cholesterol; 3.4 mg sodium; 58.8 gm carbohydrate; 1.9 gm protein; 41.4 mg calcium; 1.3 mg iron; 27.9 RE vitamin A; 139 mg vitamin C

GRAFFITI LIMBO

8 parts apricot nectar
    (4 oz.)
6 parts fresh-squeezed orange
    juice (3 oz.)
2 parts pomegranate juice (1 oz.)
1 tsp. fresh-squeezed lemon juice
Orange slice, for garnish

Combine juices with cracked ice in a cocktail shaker and shake well. Strain over ice cubes into a chilled highball glass and garnish with the orange slice. Serves one.

142 calories; 0.4 gm fat; 3% calories from fat; 0 mg cholesterol; 5.8 mg sodium; 35.3 gm carbohydrate; 1.6 gm protein; 19.3 mg calcium; 0.8 mg iron; 166.7 RE vitamin A; 86.2 mg vitamin C

GRAND SLAM

8 parts apple juice (4 oz.)
6 parts celery juice (3 oz.)
6 parts green-leaf lettuce juice (3 oz.)
4 parts parsley juice (2 oz.)
Celery sticks, for garnish

Combine juices with cracked ice in a cocktail shaker and shake well. Strain over ice cubes into chilled old-fashioned glasses and garnish with the celery sticks. Serves two.

51 calories; 0.4 gm fat; 7% calories from fat; 0 mg cholesterol; 58.1 mg sodium; 11 gm carbohydrate; 1.9 gm protein; 75.1 mg calcium; 2.6 mg iron; 263.8 RE vitamin A; 74.1 mg vitamin C

GRAPEFRUIT AND FRIENDS

6 parts grapefruit juice (3 oz.)
6 parts apple juice (3 oz.)
2 parts fresh-squeezed orange
  juice (1 oz.)
Orange peel, for garnish

Combine juices with cracked ice in a cocktail shaker and shake well. Strain over ice cubes into a chilled old-fashioned glass and garnish with the orange peel. Serves one.

86 calories; 0.2 gm fat; 2% calories from fat; 0 mg cholesterol; 3.6 mg sodium; 20.7 gm carbohydrate; 0.7 gm protein; 16.7 mg calcium; 0.5 mg iron; 6.5 RE vitamin A; 81.4 mg vitamin C

GRAPEFRUIT FALL

10 parts grapefruit juice (5 oz.)
8 parts apple cider (4 oz.)
Ground nutmeg, for garnish

Combine juices with cracked ice in a cocktail shaker and shake well. Strain over ice cubes into a chilled collins glass and sprinkle with the nutmeg. Serves one.

120 calories; 0.3 gm fat; 2% calories from fat; 0 mg cholesterol; 15.7 mg sodium; 31.4 gm carbohydrate; 1.2 gm protein; 30.8 mg calcium; 0.9 mg iron; 0 RE vitamin A; 54 mg vitamin C

GRAPEFRUIT KIR

4 parts grapefruit juice (2 oz.)
1 tbsp. black-currant syrup
Sparkling white grape juice

In a chilled wineglass, combine grapefruit juice and syrup. Fill the glass with the sparkling grape juice and stir gently. Serves one.

107 calories; 0.1 gm fat; 1% calories from fat; 0 mg cholesterol; 3.2 mg sodium; 26.8 gm carbohydrate; 0.6 gm protein; 21.7 mg calcium; 0.9 mg iron; 1 RE vitamin A; 21.6 mg vitamin C

GRAPEVINE

12 parts sparkling white grape
  juice (6 oz.)
1 tsp. orgeat (almond) syrup
Lemon peel, for garnish

Pour the sparkling grape juice into a chilled wineglass and add the syrup. Stir gently and garnish with the lemon peel. Serves one.

86 calories; 0.1 gm fat; 1% calories from fat; 0 mg cholesterol; 3.7 mg sodium; 21.4 gm carbohydrate; 0.6 gm protein; 14.1 mg calcium; 0.5 mg iron; 0.9 RE vitamin A; 0.1 mg vitamin C

GRAPRICOT

8 parts apricot nectar (4 oz.)
4 parts red grape juice (2 oz.)

Pour apricot nectar over ice cubes into a chilled highball glass. Add the grape juice and stir gently. Serves one.

98.4 calories; 0.1 gm fat; 1% calories from fat; 0 mg cholesterol; 3.4 mg sodium; 24.7 gm carbohydrate; 0.8 mg protein; 8 mg calcium; 0.6 mg iron; 149.5 RE vitamin A; 37.9 mg vitamin C

GREAT GREEN SMOOTHIE

14 parts plain nonfat
    yogurt (7 oz.)
8 parts spinach juice (4 oz.)
4 parts celery juice (2 oz.)
4 parts parsley juice (2 oz.)
2 parts scallion juice (1 oz.)
Freshly ground black pepper, to taste
Celery stalks, for garnish

Combine all ingredients except pepper
and celery stalks in a blender and
blend until smooth. Add pepper to
taste. Pour into chilled highball glasses and garnish with the celery stalks.
Serves two.

*89 calories; 0.4 gm fat; 4% calories
from fat; 2.2 mg cholesterol; 152
mg sodium; 14.9 gm carbohydrate;
8.6 gm protein; 334.5 mg calcium;
4.1 mg iron; 615.4 RE vitamin A;
47 mg vitamin C*

GREEN COCONUT COCKTAIL

8 parts cucumber juice (4 oz.)
4 parts coconut milk (2 oz.)
2 parts onion juice (1 oz.)
5–7 dashes green Tabasco sauce
Freshly ground black pepper,
    for garnish

Combine all ingredients except black
pepper with cracked ice in a cocktail
shaker and shake well. Strain into a
chilled wineglass and sprinkle with
black pepper. Serves one.

*190 calories; 16.2 gm fat; 76%
calories from fat; 0 mg cholesterol;
24.6 mg sodium; 9.1 gm carbohydrate; 2.6 gm protein; 42.2 mg calcium; 1.4 mg iron; 7.2 RE vitamin
A; 10.6 mg vitamin C*

GREEN DAY

8 parts red or white grape
    juice (4 oz.)
4 parts fresh-squeezed lime
    juice (2 oz.)
Sparkling Cider
Lime slice, for garnish
Mint sprig, for garnish

Combine juices with cracked ice in a
cocktail shaker and shake well. Strain
over ice cubes into a chilled collins
glass and fill the glass with the
sparkling cider. Garnish with the lime
slice and the mint sprig. Serves one.

*107 calories; 0.1 gm fat; 0% calo-
ries from fat; 0 mg cholesterol; 0.6
mg sodium; 27.4 gm carbohydrate;
1 gm protein; 0.1 mg calcium;
0.5 mg iron; 0.6 RE vitamin A;
17.1 mg vitamin C*

GREEN HORNET

16 parts buttermilk (8 oz.)
8 parts cucumber juice
    (4 oz.)
4 parts celery juice (2 oz.)
4 parts scallion juice (2 oz.)
2 parts parsley juice (1 oz.)
1 Haas avocado, peeled and chopped
Freshly ground black pepper, to taste
Fresh parsley sprigs, for garnish

Combine all ingredients except pepper
and parsley sprigs in a blender and
blend until smooth. Add pepper to
taste. Pour into a chilled collins glasses and garnish with the parsley sprigs.
Serves two.

*234 calories; 16.2 gm fat; 58%
calories from fat; 4.2 mg cholesterol; 166.7 mg sodium; 19.1 gm
carbohydrate; 6.9 gm protein;
201.1 mg calcium; 2.5 mg iron;
144.5 RE vitamin A; 35 mg vitamin C*

GREEN SUMMER COOLER

6 parts pineapple juice (3 oz.)
4 parts fresh-squeezed lime juice (2 oz.)
2 parts green peppermint syrup (1 oz.)
Ginger ale
Cucumber slice, for garnish
Lime slice, for garnish

GREEN SUMMER COOLER

Combine juices and syrup with cracked ice in a cocktail shaker and shake well. Strain over ice cubes into a chilled collins glass. Fill the glass with the ginger ale and stir gently. Garnish with cucumber and lime slice. Serves one.

157 calories; 0.1 gm fat; 1% calories from fat; 0 mg cholesterol; 6.8 mg sodium; 41.1 gm carbohydrate; 0.5 gm protein; 38.2 mg calcium; 1.4 mg iron; 1 RE vitamin A; 25.7 mg vitamin C

GREENFIELD BROCCOLI BREW

8 parts broccoli juice (4 oz.)
6 parts carrot juice (3 oz.)
2 parts red bell-pepper juice (1 oz.)
Broccoli floret, for garnish

Combine juices in a blender and blend until frothy. Pour over ice cubes into a chilled collins glass and garnish with the broccoli floret. Serves one.

74 calories; 0.5 gm fat; 6% calories from fat; 0 mg cholesterol; 464.6 mg sodium; 15.9 gm carbohydrate; 4.2 gm protein; 74.8 mg calcium; 1.7 mg iron; 2,375 RE vitamin A; 118.9 mg vitamin C

GUACAMOLE SMOOTHIE

GUACAMOLE SMOOTHIE

1 Haas avocado, peeled,
    pitted, and diced
10 parts tomato juice (5 oz.)
4 parts fresh-squeezed lime
    juice (2 oz.)
1 small green chile, chopped
1 garlic clove, minced
Salt, to taste
Freshly ground black pepper, to taste
Lime wedge, for garnish

Combine all ingredients except salt, pepper, and lime wedge in a blender and blend until smooth. Chill the mixture for one hour. Pour into a chilled collins glass and add salt and pepper to taste. Garnish with the lime wedge. Serves one.

350 calories; 32.7 gm fat; 76% calories from fat; 0 mg cholesterol; 528.7 mg sodium; 16.6 gm carbohydrate; 7.1 gm protein; 62.8 mg calcium; 2.9 mg iron; 113.8 RE vitamin A; 138.1 mg vitamin C

GUAVA FRESCA

8 parts guava nectar (4 oz.)
5 fresh strawberries, hulled
  and sliced
1 whole strawberry, for garnish

Combine all ingredients except whole
strawberry with cracked ice in a
blender and blend until smooth. Pour
into a chilled wineglass and garnish
with the whole strawberry. Serves one.

*103 calories; 1.2 gm fat; 10% calo-
ries from fat; 0 mg cholesterol; 4.9
mg sodium; 24 gm carbohydrate;
1.8 gm protein; 43.6 mg calcium;
0.9 mg iron; 93.9 RE vitamin A;
292.4 mg vitamin C*

GUNGA DIN

8 parts pineapple
  juice (4 oz.)
4 parts guava nectar (2 oz.)
4 parts papaya juice (2 oz.)
1 tsp. fresh-squeezed lime juice
Lime slice, for garnish

Combine juices with cracked ice in a
cocktail shaker and shake well. Strain
over ice cubes into a chilled collins
glass and garnish with the lime slice.
Serves one.

*126 calories; 0.5 gm fat; 4% calo-
ries from fat; 0 mg cholesterol; 5.7
mg sodium; 31.1 gm carbohydrate;
0.9 gm protein; 36.8 mg calcium;
0.7 mg iron; 51.8 RE vitamin A;
119.3 mg vitamin C*

H

HAI WAHWEE

10 parts fresh-
squeezed orange
juice (5 oz.)
8 parts watermelon juice (4 oz.)
6 parts pineapple juice (3 oz.)
2 parts aloe-vera juice (1 oz.)
1 tsp. bee pollen

Combine all ingredients in a blender
and blend until smooth. Pour into
chilled old-fashioned glasses.
Serves two.

*74 calories; 0.4 gm fat; 5% calories
from fat; 0 mg cholesterol; 2.1 mg
sodium; 17.3 gm carbohydrate;
1 gm protein; 19.5 mg calcium;
0.4 mg iron; 35.1 RE vitamin A;
45.5 mg vitamin C*

*(Aloe vera juice and bee pollen not
included in nutritional analysis.)*

HAIGHT-
ASHBURY

8 parts cranberry juice cocktail (4 oz.)
8 parts fresh-squeezed orange
juice (4 oz.)
2 parts fresh-squeezed lemon
juice (1 oz.)
Lime slice, for garnish

Combine all ingredients except lime
slice with cracked ice in a mixing
glass and stir. Pour over ice cubes into
a chilled collins glass. Garnish with
the lime slice. Serves one.

*122 calories; 0.3 gm fat; 2% calo-
ries from fat; 0 mg cholesterol; 5.7
mg sodium; 30.6 gm sodium;
30.6 gm carbohydrate; 1 gm protein; 17.7 mg calcium; 0.4 mg
iron; 23.3 RE vitamin A; 110 mg
vitamin C*

HARVEST
MOON

10 parts apple juice
(5 oz.)
8 parts cranberry juice
cocktail (4 oz.)
8 parts pear juice (4 oz.)
6 parts unsweetened cranberry
juice (3 oz.)
6 parts pineapple juice (3 oz.)
4 parts fresh-squeezed orange
juice (2 oz.)
2 tbsp. honey
1 tsp. alcohol-free almond extract

Combine all ingredients with cracked
ice in a blender and blend until
slushy. Pour into chilled wineglasses.
Serves four.

*114 calories; 0.2 gm fat; 1% calo-
ries from fat; 0 mg cholesterol; 4.2
mg sodium; 28.8 gm carbohydrate;
0.3 gm protein; 11.8 mg calcium;
0.4 mg iron; 3.9 RE vitamin A;
37.2 mg vitamin C*

HAVE A NICE DAY

12 parts fresh-squeezed
orange juice (6 oz.)
8 parts papaya juice (4 oz.)
Orange slice, for garnish

Combine juices with cracked ice in a
cocktail shaker and shake well. Strain
into a chilled collins glass and garnish with the orange slice. Serves one.

*141 calories; 0.5 gm fat; 3% calo-
ries from fat; 0 mg cholesterol; 7 mg
sodium; 34.2 gm carbohydrate;
1.4 gm protein; 29.9 mg calcium;
0.7 mg iron; 46.6 RE vitamin A;
88.5 mg vitamin C*

HAYWARD FAULT COCKTAIL

8 parts pink-grapefruit juice (4 oz.)
4 parts pineapple juice (2 oz.)
1 tbsp. fresh-squeezed lemon juice
Lemon slice, for garnish

Combine juices with cracked ice in a cocktail shaker and shake well. Strain into chilled cocktail glass and garnish with the lemon slice. Serves one.

80 calories; 0.2 gm fat; 2% calories from fat; 0 mg cholesterol; 1.9 mg sodium; 19.6 gm carbohydrate; 0.8 gm protein; 20.9 mg calcium; 0.4 mg iron; 1.7 RE vitamin A; 56.2 mg vitamin C

HEART-SHAPED BOX

10 parts tomato juice
   (5 oz.)
2 parts scallion juice (1 oz.)
1 tbsp. cilantro juice
1 tbsp. fresh-squeezed lime juice
Fresh cilantro sprig, for garnish

Combine juices with cracked ice in a blender and blend until slushy. Pour into a chilled wineglass and garnish with the cilantro sprig. Serves one.

53 calories; 0.2 gm fat; 4% calories from fat; 0 mg cholesterol; 521.4 mg sodium; 11.5 gm carbohydrate; 2.1 gm protein; 63.5 mg calcium; 1.7 mg iron; 157.1 RE vitamin A; 22.2 mg vitamin C

HERBAL SMOOTHIE

12 parts plain nonfat yogurt
   (6 oz.)
2 parts dill juice (1 oz.)
2 parts parsley juice (1 oz.)
2 parts basil juice (1 oz.)
2 parts tarragon juice (1 oz.)
1 part thyme juice (½ oz.)
Apple juice
Fresh mint sprig, for garnish

Combine yogurt and herb juices in a
blender. While blender is running, add
apple juice until desired consistency is
achieved. Pour into a chilled collins
glass and garnish with the mint sprig.
Serves one.

*118 calories; 0.7 gm fat; 5% calo-
ries from fat; 3.7 mg cholesterol;
151.9 mg sodium; 18.5 gm carbohydrate; 12.3 gm protein; 476.1
mg calcium; 1.8 mg iron; 147.4 RE
vitamin A; 37.7 mg vitamin C*

HERMOSA BEACH COOLER

6 parts grapefruit
   juice (3 oz.)
4 parts fresh-squeezed orange
   juice (2 oz.)
1 tbsp. fresh-squeezed lemon juice
1 tsp. honey
Sparkling mineral water
Orange slice, for garnish

Combine all ingredients except
sparkling mineral water and orange
slice in a blender and blend until
smooth. Pour over ice cubes into a
chilled collins glass and fill the glass
with the sparkling mineral water. Stir
gently and garnish with the orange
slice. Serves one.

*84 calories; 0.2 gm fat; 2% calories
from fat; 0 mg cholesterol; 1.8 mg
sodium; 20.8 gm carbohydrate;
0.9 gm protein; 15.2 mg calcium;
0.3 mg iron; 12.5 RE vitamin A;
67.8 mg vitamin C*

HETCH HETCHY HOOTCH

8 parts fresh-squeezed
   orange juice (4 oz.)
1 tsp. alcohol-free brandy extract
Sparkling cranberry juice
Orange twist, for garnish

Combine orange juice and brandy
extract with cracked ice in a cocktail
shaker and shake well. Strain into
chilled wineglass and fill the glass
with the sparkling cranberry juice.
Garnish with the orange twist. Serves
one.

*82 calories; 0.3 gm fat; 3% calories
from fat; 0 mg cholesterol; 1.5 mg
sodium; 17.9 gm carbohydrate;
0.8 gm protein; 13.2 mg calcium;
0.3 mg iron; 22.7 RE vitamin A;
63.1 mg vitamin C*

HIBISCUS WIND

8 parts hibiscus tea, chilled
   (4 oz.)
8 parts pomegranate juice (4 oz.)
6 parts fresh-squeezed orange
   juice (3 oz.)
Orange slices, for garnish

Combine tea and juices with cracked
ice in a cocktail shaker and shake
well. Strain over crushed ice into
chilled wineglasses and garnish with
the orange slices. Serves two.

*68 calories; 0.3 gm fat; 4% calories
from fat; 0 mg cholesterol; 3 mg
sodium; 16.7 gm carbohydrate; 1
gm protein; 1.9 mg calcium; 0.3
mg iron; 8.5 RE vitamin A; 25.6
mg vitamin C*

HIGH AND DRY

10 parts tomato juice (5 oz.)
4 parts carrot juice (2 oz.)
4 parts celery juice (2 oz.)
3–5 dashes green Tabasco sauce
Freshly ground black pepper,
   for garnish
Celery stick, for garnish
Lime wedge, for garnish

Combine juices and Tabasco sauce with cracked ice in a cocktail shaker and shake well. Strain into a chilled highball glass. Sprinkle with black pepper and garnish with the celery stick and lime slice. Serves one.

56 calories; 0.2 gm fat; 4% calories from fat; 0 mg cholesterol; 580.9 mg sodium; 13.4 gm carbohydrate; 2.1 gm protein; 49.1 mg calcium; 1.3 mg iron; 1,547 RE vitamin A; 20.8 mg vitamin C

HIGH HEELS

8 parts de-alcoholized white wine (4 oz.)
2 parts fresh-squeezed lemon juice (1 oz.)
1 tbsp. cherry syrup
Bing cherry, for garnish

Combine all ingredients except bing cherry with cracked ice in a cocktail shaker and shake well. Strain into a chilled cocktail glass and garnish with a the bing cherry. Serves one.

150 calories; 0.2 mg fat; 1% calories from fat; 0 mg cholesterol; 6.9 mg sodium; 19.9 gm carbohydrate; 0.5 gm protein; 26.8 mg calcium; 1.1 mg iron; 4.9 RE vitamin A; 14.5 mg vitamin C

HIGH SIERRA HOT-VEGGIE HEATER

20 parts carrot juice (10 oz.)
10 parts celery juice (5 oz.)
3 scallions, white part only, chopped fine
2 garlic cloves, chopped
1 tsp. chopped parsley
½ jalapeño pepper, seeded and chopped
½ tsp. dried oregano
½ tsp. dried thyme
Freshly ground pepper, to taste
Salt, to taste

Combine all ingredients except salt and pepper in a saucepan and bring to a boil over medium heat. Immediately reduce heat to low and simmer for at least an hour, stirring occasionally. Add salt and pepper to taste. Serve in warmed mugs. Serves two.

86 calories; 0.4 gm fat; 4% calories from fat; 0 mg cholesterol; 312.8 mg sodium; 19.5 gm carbohydrate; 2.3 gm protein; 87.9 mg calcium; 1.9 mg iron; 3,676 RE vitamin A; 22.6 mg vitamin C

HIGH-TIDE COCKTAIL

6 parts tomato juice (3 oz.)
2 parts clam juice (1 oz.)
½ tsp. fresh-squeezed lime juice
5–7 dashes Worcestershire sauce
Lime slice, for garnish

Combine all ingredients except lime slice with cracked ice in a cocktail shaker and shake well. Strain into a cocktail glass and garnish with the lime slice. Serves one.

30 calories; 0.1 gm fat; 2% calories from fat; 0 mg cholesterol; 444 mg sodium; 7.4 gm carbohydrate; 0.9 gm protein; 13.8 mg calcium; 0.8 mg iron; 54.5 RE vitamin A; 13.2 mg vitamin C

HIGHWAY PATROL

10 parts pineapple juice (5 oz.)
8 parts guava juice (4 oz.)
4 parts fresh-squeezed orange juice (2 oz.)
Orange twists, for garnish

Combine juices in a blender and blend until smooth. Pour into chilled old-fashioned glasses over ice cubes and garnish with orange twists. Serves two.

81 calories; 0.5 gm fat; 5% fat from calories; 0 mg cholesterol; 2.6 mg sodium; 19.5 gm carbohydrate; 0.9 gm protein; 26.5 mg calcium; 0.4 mg iron; 50.9 RE vitamin A; 125.7 mg vitamin C

HOLIDAY DEFROSTER

8 parts apple cider (4 oz.)
6 parts pear juice (3 oz.)
2 parts fresh-squeezed lemon
    juice (1 oz.)

Combine all ingredients in a saucepan over medium heat. Heat until very hot but not boiling. Pour into a warmed mug. Serves one.

115 calories; 0.5 gm fat; 5% calories from fat; 0 mg cholesterol; 6.7 mg sodium; 31.5 gm carbohydrate; 0.3 gm protein; 12.5 mg calcium; 0.8 mg iron; 0.6 RE vitamin A; 15.1 mg vitamin C

HOLIDAY ON ICE

8 parts cantaloupe
    juice (4 oz.)
8 parts pineapple juice (4 oz.)
4 parts watermelon juice (2 oz.)
4 fresh strawberries, hulled and sliced
2 scoops vanilla frozen yogurt
Pineapple spears, for garnish

Combine all ingredients except the pineapple spear in a blender and blend until smooth. (If mixture is too thick, add more watermelon juice.) Pour into chilled highball glasses and garnish with the pineapple. Serves two.

184 calories; 4.4 gm fat; 20% calories from fat; 2 mg cholesterol; 75.9 mg sodium; 34.4 gm carbohydrate; 3.9 gm protein; 128 mg calcium; 0.7 mg iron; 268.1 RE vitamin A; 51.7 mg vitamin C

HOLLYWOOD AND VINE

8 parts fresh-squeezed
    orange juice (4 oz.)
6 parts red grape juice (3 oz.)
4 parts peach juice (2 oz.)
Orange slice, for garnish

Combine juices with cracked ice in a cocktail shaker and shake well. Pour over ice cubes into a chilled collins glass and garnish with the orange slice. Serves one.

133 calories; 0.2 gm fat; 2% calories from fat; 0 mg cholesterol; 4.8 mg sodium; 32.2 gm carbohydrate; 1.4 gm protein; 15.3 mg calcium; 0.5 mg iron; 37.3 RE vitamin A; 59.7 mg vitamin C

HONEYDEW FIZZ

8 parts honeydew
    melon juice (4 oz.)
4 parts kiwi juice (2 oz.)
Ginger ale
Honeydew melon slice, for garnish

Combine juices with cracked ice in a cocktail shaker and shake well. Strain over ice cubes into a a chilled collins glass and fill the glass with the ginger ale. Stir gently and garnish with the melon slice. Serves one.

94 calories; 0.4 gm fat; 3% calories from fat; 0 mg cholesterol; 18.2 mg sodium; 23.8 mg carbohydrate; 1.1 gm protein; 23.3 mg calcium; 0.4 mg iron; 14.5 RE vitamin A; 83.7 mg vitamin C

HONEYDEW FREEZE

8 parts honeydew
    melon juice (4 oz.)
4 parts raspberry puree (2 oz.)
2 parts strawberry puree (1 oz.)
1 tbsp. fresh-squeezed lime juice
1 tbsp. honey
Fresh mint sprig, for garnish

Combine ingredients with cracked ice in a blender and blend until slushy. Pour into a chilled collins glass and garnish with the fresh mint sprig. Serves one.

166 calories; 0.8 gm fat; 4% calories from fat; 0 mg cholesterol; 13.1 mg sodium; 42.8 gm carbohydrate; 1.8 gm protein; 35.9 mg calcium; 0.9 mg iron; 17.3 RE vitamin A; 86.3 mg vitamin C

HONEY DON'T

10 parts grapefruit
   juice (5 oz.)
8 parts honeydew melon juice (4 oz.)
2 parts white grape juice (1 oz.)
Fresh mint sprig, for garnish

Combine juices in a blender and
blend until smooth. Pour into a
chilled collins glass and garnish with
the mint sprig. Serves one.

112 calories; 0.3 gm fat; 2% calories from fat; 0 mg cholesterol; 13.6 mg sodium; 27.7 gm carbohydrate; 1.4 gm protein; 22.1 mg calcium; 0.4 mg iron; 6.2 RE vitamin A; 82.1 mg vitamin C

HOT APPLE PIE

10 parts apple cider (5 oz.)
2 tsp. maple syrup
1 tsp. fresh-squeezed lemon juice
3 whole cloves
½ tsp. ground cinnamon
¼ tsp. ground nutmeg
Whipped cream, for garnish
Cinnamon stick, for garnish

Combine apple cider, maple syrup,
lemon juice, and spices in a saucepan
over medium heat until mixture is
well-heated but not boiling. Pour into
a warmed mug and top with a dollop
of whipped cream and garnish with
the cinnamon stick. Serves one.

121 calories; 1.2 gm fat; 8% calories from fat; 2.9 mg cholesterol; 10.9 mg sodium; 30.4 gm carbohydrate; 0.4 gm protein; 41.3 mg calcium; 1.3 mg iron; 10.9 RE vitamin A; 6.4 mg vitamin C

HOT CARROT COCKTAIL

8 parts carrot juice (4 oz.)
8 parts vegetable bouillon (4 oz.)
8 parts nonfat milk (4 oz.)
1 tbsp. onion, finely chopped
Freshly ground black pepper, to taste
Celery stick, for garnish

Combine liquids and onion in a
saucepan over medium heat. Stir constantly until mixture is hot but not
boiling. Pour into warmed mugs and

add pepper to taste. Garnish with the
celery stick. Serves two.

68 calories; 0.2 gm fat; 3% calories form fat; 0.9 mg cholesterol; 54.8 mg sodium; 11.9 gm carbohydrate; 3.1 gm protein; 89 mg calcium; 0.5 mg iron; 1,582 RE vitamin A; 6.5 mg vitamin C

HOT FOOT

8 parts carrot juice
   (4 oz.)
6 parts fresh-squeezed
   orange juice (3 oz.)
5–7 dashes Tabasco sauce
Celery stick, for garnish

Combine all ingredients except celery
stick with cracked ice in a cocktail
shaker and shake well. Strain over ice
cubes into a chilled highball glass
and garnish with the celery stick.
Serves one.

83 calories; 0.3 gm fat; 4% calories from fat; 0 mg cholesterol; 44.6 mg sodium; 19.5 gm carbohydrate; 1.7 gm protein; 36.6 mg calcium; 0.7 mg iron; 2,938 RE vitamin A; 53.9 mg vitamin C

HOT PIE AND COFFEE

16 parts apple cider (6 oz.)
2 tbsp. brown sugar
1 tbsp. fresh-squeezed lemon juice
½ tsp. ground cinnamon
½ tsp. ground nutmeg
16 parts black coffee, heated (8 oz)
Whipped cream, for garnish
Cinnamon sticks, for garnish

Combine apple cider, brown sugar,
lemon juice, and spices in a saucepan
over medium heat until the mixture is
well-heated but not boiling. Fill
warmed mugs half-full. Add hot coffee
and stir gently. Top with a dollop of
whipped cream and garnish with cinnamon sticks. Serves two.

111 calories; 1.1 gm fat; 8% calories from fat; 2.9 mg cholesterol; 15.3 mg sodium; 27.3 gm carbohydrate; 0.4 gm protein; 30.9 mg calcium; 1 mg iron; 10.6 RE vitamin A; 4.5 mg vitamin C

HOT-TOT TODDY

HOT TOMATO

10 parts tomato juice (5 oz.)
2 parts fresh-squeezed lime
   juice (1 oz.)
½ tsp. white horseradish
½ tsp. Worcestershire sauce
3–5 dashes Tabasco sauce
Celery salt, to taste
Freshly ground pepper, to taste
Celery stick, for garnish

Combine all ingredients except celery salt, black pepper, and celery stick in a saucepan over medium heat, stirring until mixture is very hot but not boiling. Pour into warmed mug and add celery salt and pepper to taste. Garnish with the celery stick. Serves one.

34 calories; 0.1 gm fat; 2% calories from fat; 0 mg cholesterol; 576.2 mg sodium; 9 gm carbohydrate; 1.4 gm protein; 17.9 mg calcium; 0.9 mg iron; 80.5 RE vitamin A; 21.8 mg vitamin C

HOT-TOT TODDY

2 parts fresh-squeezed lemon
  juice (1 oz.)
2 tbsp. honey
5 whole cloves
Lemon slice
Hot tea
Ground cinnamon, to taste
Cinnamon stick, for garnish
Freshly ground nutmeg, for garnish

Muddle all ingredients except cinnamon, tea, nutmeg, and cinnamon stick in the bottom of a warmed mug. Fill with hot tea and stir. Add cinnamon to taste. Garnish with the cinnamon stick and sprinkle with nutmeg. Serves one.

156 calories; 1 gm fat; 6% calories from fat; 0 mg cholesterol; 9.5 mg sodium; 39.1 gm carbohydrate; 0.3 gm protein; 22 mg calcium; 0.6 mg iron; 1.4 RE vitamin A; 14 mg vitamin C

HUCK FINN

4 parts carrot juice (2 oz.)
4 parts tomato juice (2 oz.)
4 parts bell-pepper juice (2 oz.)
4 parts cucumber juice (2 oz.)
4 parts celery juice (2 oz.)
Carrot stick, for garnish

Combine juices with cracked ice in a cocktail shaker. Shake well and strain over ice cubes into a chilled collins glass. Garnish with carrot stick. Serves one.

57 calories; 0.2 gm fat; 3% calories from fat; 0 mg cholesterol; 1,088 mg sodium; 13.7 gm carbohydrate; 1.4 gm protein; 41.4 mg calcium; 1.5 mg iron; 1,519 RE vitamin A; 25.3 mg vitamin C

HUMBOLDT HANGOVER CURE

10 parts grapefruit juice
  (5 oz.)
4 parts fresh-squeezed lemon
  juice (2 oz.)
2 garlic cloves, peeled and chopped
1 tbsp. olive oil
½ tsp. cayenne pepper

Combine all ingredients in a blender and mix well. Strain into a chilled highball glass. Serves one.

199 calories; 13.8 gm fat; 59% calories from fat; 0 mg cholesterol; 3.1 mg sodium; 20.2 gm carbohydrate; 1.4 gm protein; 28.3 mg calcium; 0.5 mg iron; 21.3 RE vitamin A; 82.1 mg vitamin C

I LOVE JUICY

8 parts carrot juice
 (4 oz.)
8 parts fresh-squeezed orange
 juice (4 oz.)
8 parts nonfat milk (4 oz.)
Paprika (hot or sweet), for garnish

Combine juices and milk in a blender
with cracked ice and blend until
slushy. Pour into chilled old-fashioned
glasses and sprinkle with paprika.
Serves two.

*68 calories; 0.3 gm fat; 4% calories
from fat; 0.9 mg cholesterol; 46.1
mg sodium; 13.9 gm carbohydrate;
2.9 gm protein; 89.7 mg calcium;
0.4 mg iron; 1,506 RE vitamin A;
33.8 mg vitamin C.*

IMPERIAL VALLEY
PUNCH

64 parts fresh-squeezed orange
 juice (32 oz.)
16 parts pink-grapefruit juice (8 oz.)
8 parts fresh-squeezed lime
 juice (4 oz.)
4 parts orgeat (almond) syrup (2 oz.)
4 parts raspberry syrup (2 oz.)
1 liter ginger ale
Orange slices, for garnish

Combine all ingredients except ginger
ale and orange slices in a large punch
bowl and stir well. Chill thoroughly.
Just before serving, add a cake of ice
and the ginger ale. Stir gently and
float orange slices on top. Serves
twelve to fourteen.

*98 calories; 0.2 gm fat; 2% calories
from fat; 0 mg cholesterol; 7.4 mg
sodium; 24.3 gm carbohydrate; 0.7
gm protein; 19 mg calcium; 0.7 mg
iron; 15.4 RE vitamin A; 47.8 mg
vitamin C.*

IN THE PINK

8 parts pink-grapefruit
 juice (4 oz.)
4 parts pineapple juice (2 oz.)
4 parts unsweetened cherry
 cider (2 oz.)

Combine juices with cracked ice in a
blender and blend until slushy. Pour
into chilled old-fashioned glasses.
Serves two.

*58 calories; 0.4 gm fat; 5% calories
from fat; 0 mg cholesterol; 0.9 mg
sodium; 13.8 gm carbohydrate;
0.7 gm protein; 14.1 mg calcium;
0.3 mg iron; 6.8 RE vitamin A;
26.6 mg vitamin C.*

INFAMOUS ANGEL

8 parts cantaloupe
 juice (4 oz.)
6 parts pineapple juice (3 oz.)
4 parts white grape juice (2 oz.)
Pineapple spear, for garnish

Combine juices with cracked ice in a
cocktail shaker and shake well. Strain
over ice cubes into a chilled collins
glass and garnish with the pineapple
spear. Serves one.

*122 calories; 0.4 gm fat; 3% calo-
ries from fat; 0 mg cholesterol; 12.8
mg sodium; 29.7 gm carbohydrate;
1.6 gm protein; 32.1 mg calcium;
0.6 mg iron; 365.3 RE vitamin A;
57 mg vitamin C.*

ITALIAN SODA

ITALIAN SODA

2 parts Italian syrup of your
    choice (1 oz.)
Sparkling mineral water
Lemon or lime slice, for garnish

Add syrup to a chilled collins glass
filled with ice cubes. Add sparkling
water and stir gently. Garnish with
slice of lemon or lime. If you prefer
a sweeter soda, use more syrup.
Serves one.

*75 calories; 0 gm fat; 0% calories
from fat; 0 mg cholesterol; 1.4 mg
sodium; 19.4 gm carbohydrate; 0
gm protein; 17.1 mg calcium; 1 mg
iron; 0 RE vitamin A; 0.3 mg vitamin C.*

*Note: Italian syrups come in a vari-
ety of flavors and are available at
specialty food stores and Italian grocery stores. Flavors vary from
orgeat (almond) and hazelnut to
nearly all fruits, as well as peppermint and other unusual choices.*

115

JABBERWOCKY

12 parts carrot juice (6 oz.)
10 parts apple juice (5 oz.)
4 parts red bell-pepper juice (2 oz.)
4 parts cucumber juice (2 oz.)
Carrot sticks, for garnish

Combine juices with cracked ice in a cocktail shaker. Shake well and strain over ice cubes into chilled highball glasses. Garnish with the carrot sticks. Serves two.

68 calories; 0.2 gm fat; 4% calories from fat; 0 mg cholesterol; 428.4 mg sodium; 16.4 gm carbohydrate; 0.7 gm protein; 22.5 mg calcium; 1 mg iron; 1,471 RE vitamin A; 41.3 mg vitamin C

JACK LONDON SPECIAL

8 parts pineapple juice (4 oz.)
6 parts broccoli juice (3 oz.)
Broccoli floret, for garnish

Combine juices with cracked ice in a cocktail shaker and shake well. Strain over ice cubes into a chilled highball glass and garnish with the broccoli floret. Serves one.

95 calories; 0.5 gm fat; 4% calories from fat; 0 mg cholesterol; 31.8 mg sodium; 21.6 gm carbohydrate; 3.7 gm protein; 73.7 mg calcium; 1.3 mg iron; 175.8 RE vitamin A; 117.8 mg vitamin C

JASMINE SPARKLER

10 parts jasmine tea, chilled (5 oz.)
1 tbsp. ginger juice
Ginger ale
Lemon twist, for garnish

Combine tea and juice in a mixing glass. Strain over ice cubes into a chilled collins glass and fill with ginger ale. Stir gently and garnish with the lemon twist. Serves one.

37 calories; 0 gm fat; 0% calories from fat; 0 mg cholesterol; 9.2 mg sodium; 9.6 gm carbohydrate; 0 gm protein; 1.7 mg calcium; 0.3 mg iron; 0 RE vitamin A; 0.3 mg vitamin C

JASON'S FROZEN MELON MISHMASH

8 parts cantaloupe juice (4 oz.)
6 parts fresh-squeezed orange juice (3 oz.)
6 parts white grape juice (3 oz.)
4 parts papaya nectar (2 oz.)
4 parts strawberry puree (2 oz.)
4 parts fresh-squeezed lime juice (2 oz.)
Fresh mint sprigs, for garnish

Combine all ingredients except mint sprigs with cracked ice in a blender and blend until slushy. Pour into chilled highball glasses and garnish with the mint sprigs. Serves three to four.

64 calories; 0.2 mg fat; 3% calories from fat; 0 mg cholesterol; 10 mg sodium; 16 gm carbohydrate; 0.9 gm protein; 16.8 mg calcium; 0.3 mg iron; 152.3 RE vitamin A; 45.1 mg vitamin C

JESSE JAMES

8 parts tomato juice (4 oz.)
4 parts broccoli juice (2 oz.)
1 tsp. garlic puree
Freshly ground pepper, to taste
Broccoli floret, for garnish

Combine all ingredients except broccoli floret with cracked ice in a cocktail shaker and shake well. Strain into a chilled old-fashioned glass, add pepper to taste, and garnish with the broccoli floret. Serves one.

40 calories; 0.3 gm fat; 5% calories from fat; 0 mg cholesterol; 424.5 mg sodium; 8.7 gm carbohydrate; 2.7 gm protein; 42.8 mg calcium; 1.2 mg iron; 150.8 RE vitamin A; 62.8 mg vitamin C

JET-FRESH LEMONADE

JET-FRESH LEMONADE

6 parts pineapple juice (3 oz.)
1 recipe for Traditional Lemonade
(page 207)
Pineapple spear, for garnish

Prepare recipe for Traditional
Lemonade. Pour pineapple juice over
ice cubes into a chilled collins glass.
Fill the glass with lemonade and stir.
Garnish with the pineapple spear.
Serves one.

165 calories; 0.1 gm fat; 1% calories from fat; 0 mg cholesterol; 11.8 mg sodium; 31.8 gm carbohydratel 1 gm protein; 28.6 mg calcium; 0.4 mg iron; 2.9 RE vitamin A; 66.1 mg vitamin C

JEZEBEL

10 parts fresh-squeezed
orange juice (5 oz.)
1 scoop vanilla frozen yogurt
1 tsp. honey
½ tsp. alcohol-free vanilla extract

Combine all ingredients in a blender
and blend until smooth. Pour into a
chilled collins glass. Serves one.

309 calories; 8.2 gm fat; 23% calories from fat; 0 mg cholesterol; 125.5 mg sodium; 54.7 gm carbohydrate; 6.5 gm protein; 218.6 mg calcium; 0.8 mg iron; 109.1 RE vitamin A; 72.1 mg vitamin C

JOHN'S PINEAPPLE PICK-ME-UP

8 parts pineapple
    juice (4 oz.)
6 parts peach nectar (3 oz.)
2 parts fresh-squeezed lime
    juice (1 oz.)
½ tsp. dried rosemary, crushed
Fresh rosemary sprigs, for garnish

Combine all ingredients except fresh
rosemary sprigs in blender and blend
until well-mixed. Pour over ice cubes
into chilled old-fashioned glasses.
Garnish with the rosemary sprigs.
Serves one.

*59 calories; 0.1 gm fat; 2% calories
from fat; 0 mg cholesterol; 125.5
mg sodium; 54.7 gm carbohydrate;
0.4 gm protein; 16.9 mg calcium;
0.3 mg iron; 12.4 RE vitamin A;
12.7 mg vitamin C*

JOSHUA TREE JUBILEE

10 parts apple juice (5
    oz.)
8 parts coconut milk (4 oz.)
8 parts pear juice (4 oz.)
4 parts fresh-squeezed orange
    juice (2 oz.)
1 tbsp. fresh-squeezed lemon juice
Orange twists, for garnish

Combine all ingredients except orange
twists in a blender and blend until
smooth. Pour into chilled wineglasses
and garnish with the orange twists.
Serves two.

*240 calories; 16.2 gm fat; 60%
calories from fat; 0 mg cholesterol;
12.4 mg sodium; 22.5 gm carbohydrate; 1.9 gm protein; 16.2 mg calcium; 1.2 mg iron; 5.8 RE vitamin
A; 47.4 mg vitamin C*

JUICY JULEP

2 parts fresh-squeezed lime
    juice (1 oz.)
2 parts fresh-squeezed orange
    juice (1 oz.)
2 parts pineapple juice (1 oz.)
1 part raspberry syrup (½ oz.)
Fresh crushed mint leaves
Ginger ale
Fresh mint sprig, for garnish

Combine all ingredients except ginger
ale and mint sprig with cracked ice
in a cocktail shaker and shake well.
Pour into a chilled collins glass. Fill
the glass with ginger ale and stir
gently. Garnish with the mint sprig.
Serves one.

*121 calories; 0.1 gm fat; 1% calo-
ries from fat; 0 mg cholesterol; 4.5
mg sodium; 31.3 gm carbohydrate;
0.5 gm protein; 34.4 mg calcium;
1.3 mg iron; 22.1 RE vitamin A;
29.1 mg vitamin C*

JULY SMASH

8 parts nectarine
    juice (4 oz.)
3 parts fresh-squeezed orange
    juice (1½ oz.)
Nectarine slice with skin, for garnish

Combine juices with cracked ice in
a cocktail shaker and shake well.
Strain into a chilled cocktail glass and
garnish with the nectarine slice.
Serves one.

*75 calories; 0.6 gm fat; 7% calories
from fat; 0 mg cholesterol; 0.3 mg
sodium; 17.8 gm carbohydrate;
1.4 gm protein; 10.3 mg calcium;
0.3 mg iron; 91.9 RE vitamin A;
27.4 mg vitamin C*

JUICY JULEP

JUMP-START

10 parts carrot juice (5 oz.)
1 tsp. ginger juice
Ground nutmeg, for garnish

Combine juices with cracked ice in a cocktail shaker and shake well. Strain into a chilled old-fashioned glass and sprinkle with nutmeg. Serves one.

72 calories; 0.2 gm fat; 3% calories from fat; 0 mg cholesterol; 42.1 mg sodium; 17.5 gm carbohydrate; 1.4 gm protein; 34 mg calcium; 0.8 mg iron; 3,650 RE vitamin A; 12.4 mg vitamin C

K

KID GALAHAD

16 parts strong-brewed coffee,
  chilled (8 oz.)
2 scoops vanilla frozen yogurt
1 Haas avocado, peeled, pitted,
  and chopped
1 tbsp. honey
½ tsp. alcohol-free mint extract

Combine all ingredients in a blender
and blend until smooth. If mixture is
too thick, add more coffee until
desired consistency is achieved. Pour
into a chilled collins glass. Serves one.

*602 calories; 38 gm fat; 53% calo-
ries from fat; 4 mg cholesterol;
152.6 mg sodium; 64.9 gm carbohydrate; 9.5 gm protein; 230.6 mg
calcium; 2.7 mg iron; 188 RE vitamin A; 15.1 mg vitamin C*

KING'S CANYON
CREAMY
COOLER

8 parts peach juice (4 oz.)
8 parts coconut milk (4 oz.)
6 parts pineapple juice (3 oz.)
4 parts rehydrated raisins, chopped
  (2 oz.)
1 banana, sliced
Pineapple spears, for garnish

Combine all ingredients except
pineapple spears with cracked ice in a
blender and blend until smooth. If
mixture is too thick, add more peach
juice until desired consistency is
achieved. Pour into chilled highball
glasses and garnish with the pineapple
spears. Serves two.

*350 calories; 16.5 gm fat; 41%
calories from fat; 0 mg cholesterol;
16.2 mg sodium; 50.7 gm carbohydrate; 3.4 gm protein; 35.8 mg
calcium; 1.7 mg iron; 19.9 RE vitamin A; 13.6 mg vitamin C*

KIR ABSOLUTE

3 parts black-currant syrup (1½ oz.)
De-alcoholized sparkling wine
Lime twist, for garnish

Pour syrup into a chilled champagne
flute. Fill with the sparkling wine and
stir gently. Garnish with the lime twist.
Serves one.

*189 calories; 0 gm fat; 0% calories
from fat; 0 mg cholesterol; 7.8 mg
sodium; 29.8 gm carbohydrate;
0.1 gm protein; 35.7 mg calcium;
1.9 mg iron; 0 RE vitamin A; 0 mg
vitamin C*

KIR EXTREME

3 parts black-currant syrup (1½ oz.)
De-alcoholized white wine
Lemon twist, for garnish

Pour syrup into a chilled wineglass.
Fill the glass with wine and stir.
Garnish with the lemon twist.
Serves one.

*208 calories; 0 gm fat; 0% calories
from fat; 0 mg cholesterol; 9.2 mg
sodium; 30 gm carbohydrate;
0.1 gm protein; 38.2 mg calcium;
2 mg iron; 0 RE vitamin A; 0 mg
vitamin C*

KISS KISS

10 parts cucumber
  juice (5 oz.)
6 parts apple juice (3 oz.)
6 parts carrot juice (3 oz.)
1 tbsp. fresh-squeezed lemon juice
Lemon slices, for garnish

Combine juices with cracked ice in a
cocktail shaker and shake well. Strain
over ice cubes into chilled old-
fashioned glasses and garnish with the
lemon slices. Serves two.

*48 calories; 0.2 gm fat; 4% calories
from fat; 0 mg cholesterol; 15.1 mg
sodium; 11.7 gm carbohydrate; 0.8*

gm protein; 23.6 mg calcium; 0.6 mg iron; 1,098 RE vitamin A; 27.9 mg vitamin C

KIWI COCKTAIL

8 parts kiwi juice
(4 oz.)
2 parts fresh-squeezed lemon
juice (1 oz.)
Lemon twist, for garnish

Combine juices with cracked ice in a cocktail shaker and shake well. Strain into a chilled cocktail glass and garnish with the lemon twist. Serves one.

94 calories; 0.6 gm fat; 5% calories from fat; 0 mg cholesterol; 7.4 mg sodium; 23.5 gm carbohydrate; 1.5 gm protein; 38.9 mg calcium; 0.6 mg iron; 25.4 RE vitamin A; 152 mg vitamin C

KIWI FREEZE

8 parts kiwi juice
(4 oz.)
4 parts fresh-squeezed orange
juice (2 oz.)
4 parts white grape juice (2 oz.)

Combine all ingredients with cracked ice in a blender and blend until slushy. Pour into a chilled highball glass. Serves one.

147 calories; 0.7 gm fat; 4% calories from fat; 0 mg cholesterol; 7.5 mg sodium; 35.3 gm carbohydrate; 2.1 gm protein; 43.1 mg calcium; 0.8 mg iron; 36.2 RE vitamin A; 167.3 mg vitamin C

KIWI KISS

8 parts kiwi juice
(4 oz.)
4 parts pineapple juice (2 oz.)
1 tsp. fresh-squeezed lemon juice
1 tsp. fresh-squeezed lime juice
Lemon twist, for garnish
Lime twist, for garnish

Combine juices with cracked ice in a cocktail shaker and shake well. Strain into a chilled wineglass and garnish with the lemon and lime twists. Serves one.

160 calories; 5.2 gm fat; 27% calories from fat; 0 mg cholesterol; 7.7 mg sodium; 29.3 gm carbohydrate; 1.6 gm protein; 46.9 mg calcium; 0.7 mg iron; 25.2 RE vitamin A; 147.4 mg vitamin C

KIWI KOOLER

8 parts kiwi juice
(4 oz.)
8 parts raspberry juice (4 oz.)
2 parts fresh-squeezed lime
juice (1 oz.)
Sparkling mineral water
Kiwi slice, for garnish
Lime slice, for garnish

Combine juices with cracked ice in a cocktail shaker and shake well. Strain over ice cubes into a chilled collins glass. Slowly fill the glass with sparkling mineral water and stir gently. Garnish with the kiwi and lime slices. Serves one.

164 calories; 1.4 gm fat; 7% calories from fat; 0 mg cholesterol; 7.4 mg sodium; 40 gm carbohydrate; 2.8 gm protein; 70.7 mg calcium; 1.4 mg iron; 45.5 RE vitamin A; 182.8 mg vitamin C

KIWI QUENCHER

8 parts kiwi juice (4 oz.)
8 parts watermelon
juice (4 oz.)
4 parts white grape juice (2 oz.)
Sparkling mineral water
Kiwi slices, for garnish

Combine juices with cracked ice in a cocktail shaker and shake well. Pour over ice cubes into chilled collins glasses. Fill the glasses with sparkling mineral water and stir gently. Garnish with the kiwi slices. Serves two.

79 calories; 0.6 gm fat; 6% calories from fat; 0 mg cholesterol; 5.5 mg sodium; 18.9 gm carbohydrate; 1.2 gm protein; 25.6 mg calcium; 0.5 mg iron; 33.4 RE vitamin A; 75 mg vitamin C

KIWI SPARKLER

8 parts kiwi juice
(4 oz.)
2 parts fresh-squeezed lemon
juice (1 oz.)
Ginger ale
Lemon slice, for garnish

Combine juices with cracked ice in a
cocktail shaker and shake well. Strain
over ice cubes into a chilled collins
glass and slowly fill the glass with ginger ale. Stir gently and garnish with
the lemon slice. Serves one.

*103 calories; 0.6 gm fat; 5% calo-
ries from fat; 5% calories from fat;
0 mg cholesterol; 9.4 mg sodium;
26 gm carbohydrate; 1.5 gm protein; 39.8 mg calcium; 0.6 mg
iron; 25.4 RE vitamin A; 152 mg
vitamin C*

KIWI ZAPPER

4 parts kiwi juice (2 oz.)
4 parts pineapple juice (2 oz.)
1 part ginger juice (½ oz.)
½ tsp. alcohol-free mint extract
Sparkling mineral water
Fresh mint sprig, for garnish

Combine juices and mint extract with
cracked ice in a cocktail shaker and
shake well. Strain over ice cubes into
a chilled collins glass. Fill the glass
with sparkling mineral water and stir
gently. Garnish with the mint sprig.
Serves one.

*99 calories; 0.4 gm fat; 4% calories
from fat; 0 mg cholesterol; 5.8 mg
sodium; 24.7 gm carbohydrate;
1 gm protein; 31.8 mg calcium;
0.6 mg iron; 15.2 RE vitamin A;
89.8 mg vitamin C*

KLAMATH FALLS

8 parts apple juice (4 oz.)
8 parts pear juice (4 oz.)
8 parts strawberry puree (4 oz.)
1 banana, sliced

Combine all ingredients in a blender
and blend until a frappe-like consistency is achieved. Pour into chilled
highball glasses. Serves two.

*130 calories; 0.6 gm fat; 4% calo-
ries from fat; 0 mg cholesterol; 4.8
mg sodium; 32.5 gm carbohydrate;
1 gm protein; 12.5 mg calcium;
0.7 mg iron; 6.2 RE vitamin A;
61.2 mg vitamin C*

KLONDIKE ANNIE

10 parts coconut milk (5 oz.)
10 parts pineapple juice (5 oz.)
2 pineapple spears, for garnish

Combine liquid ingredients with
cracked ice in a blender and blend
until slushy. Pour into chilled wineglasses and garnish with the pineapple
spears. Serves two.

*237 calories; 20.1 gm fat; 76%
calories from fat; 0 mg cholesterol;
10.7 mg sodium; 11.8 gm carbohydrate; 2.2 gm protein; 18.4 mg
calcium; 1.1 mg iron; 0.3 RE vitamin A; 7.6 mg vitamin C*

KOSMIC KIWI
KOOLER

8 parts kiwi juice
(4 oz.)
6 parts mango juice (3 oz.)
1 tbsp. fresh-squeezed lime juice
Sparkling mineral water
Lime slice, for garnish

Combine juices in a blender and
blend until smooth. Pour into a
chilled collins glass and slowly fill the
glass with sparkling mineral water.
Stir gently and garnish with the lime
slice. Serves one.

*146 calories; 0.8 gm fat; 5% calo-
ries from fat; 0 mg cholesterol; 8.9
mg sodium; 36.9 gm carbohydrate;
1.9 gm protein; 146.2 calcium;
0.7 mg iron; 356.1 RE vitamin A;
167 mg vitamin C*

L

LADY BE GOOD

4 parts fresh-squeezed
  orange juice (2 oz.)
4 parts pineapple juice (2 oz.)
4 parts red grape juice (2 oz.)
4 parts strawberry puree (2 oz.)
Fresh mint sprig, for garnish

Combine juices with cracked ice in a
blender and blend until slushy. Pour
into a chilled collins glass and garnish the with mint sprig. Serves one.

*109 calories; 0.4 gm fat; 3% calo-
ries from fat; 0 mg cholesterol; 3.3
mg sodium; 26.2 gm carbohydrate;
1.2 gm protein; 28.9 mg calcium;
0.6 mg iron; 13.6 RE vitamin A;
66.6 mg vitamin C*

LAGUNA LIFT

4 parts apple juice (2 oz.)
4 parts pineapple juice (2 oz.)
Tonic water
Pineapple spear, for garnish

Combine juices with cracked ice in a
cocktail shaker and shake well. Strain
over ice cubes into a chilled collins
glass and fill with tonic water. Stir
gently and garnish with the pineapple
spear. Serves one.

*77.7 calories; 0.1 mg fat; 1% calo-
ries from fat; 0 mg cholesterol; 4.5
mg sodium; 19.4 gm carbohydrate;
0.2 gm protein; 14.2 mg calcium;
0.4 mg iron; 0.3 RE vitamin A;
29.4 mg vitamin C*

LA JOLLA LIME SPECIAL

4 parts fresh-squeezed lime
  juice (2 oz.)
2 scoops vanilla frozen yogurt
Natural lemon-lime soda
Lime slice, for garnish

Combine lime juice and frozen yogurt
in a blender and blend until smooth.
Pour into a chilled collins glass and
slowly fill the glass with the lemon-
lime soda. Stir gently and garnish
with the lime slice. Serves one.

*266 calories; 8.1 gm fat; 26% calo-
ries from fat; 4 mg cholesterol;
132.8 mg sodium; 19.4 gm carbohydrate; 5.8 gm protein; 212.2 mg
calcium; 0.5 mg iron; 82.6 RE vitamin A; 17.3 mg vitamin C*

LAKE MERRITT FESTIVAL TEA

16 parts black tea, hot (8 oz.)
16 parts chamomile tea, hot (8 oz.)
4 parts fresh-squeezed lemon
  juice (2 oz.)
2 tbsp. honey
½ tsp. alcohol-free almond extract
Lemon slices, for garnish

Combine ingredients except lemon
slices in a saucepan over low heat and
stir until honey is dissolved. Serve in
warmed mugs and garnish with the
lemon slices. Serves two.

*49 calories; 0 gm fat; 0% calories
from fat; 0 mg cholesterol; 2.4 mg
sodium; 13.4 gm carbohydrate;
0.1 gm protein; 5 mg calcium; 0.2
mg iron; 0.4 RE vitamin A; 8.8 mg
vitamin C*

LASSEN STEAMER

2 tsp. unsweetened cocoa powder
2 tbsp. sugar
16 parts hot milk (8 oz.)
½ tsp. alcohol-free mint extract
Whipped cream, for garnish
Peppermint candy stick, for garnish

Combine the cocoa powder and sugar
in a warmed mug. Add the hot milk
and mint extract and stir until completely blended. Top with a dollop of
whipped cream and garnish with the
peppermint candy stick. Serves one.

*274 calories; 14.2 gm fat; 47%
calories from fat; 33.9 mg cholesterol; 140.1 mg sodium; 25.1 gm
carbohydrate; 11.7 gm protein; 295
mg calcium; 2.6 mg iron; 141.6 RE
vitamin A; 2.1 mg vitamin C*

LAST COWBOY

10 parts tomato juice (5 oz.)
4 parts celery juice (2 oz.)
4 parts cucumber juice (2 oz.)
3–5 dashes Tabasco sauce
½ tsp. tarragon
Celery stick, for garnish
Freshly ground black pepper,
   for garnish

Combine all ingredients except celery
stick and black pepper in a blender
and blend until smooth. Strain over
ice cubes into a chilled collins glass.
Sprinkle with black pepper and garnish with the celery stick. Serves one.

*41 calories; 0.2 gm fat; 4% calories
from fat; 0 mg cholesterol; 567.8
mg sodium; 9.7 gm carbohydrate;
1.8 gm protein; 43.5 mg calcium;
1.2 mg iron; 90.1 RE vitamin A;
19 mg vitamin C*

LATE-SUMMER TREAT

10 parts apple juice (5 oz.)
8 parts fresh figs, chopped (4 oz.)
4 parts unsweetened cranberry
   juice (2 oz.)
4 parts fresh-squeezed orange
   juice (2 oz.)
1 tbsp. honey
½ tsp. alcohol-free almond extract
Orange twists, for garnish

Combine all ingredients except orange
twists in a blender and blend until
smooth. Pour into chilled wineglasses
and garnish with the orange twists.
Serves two.

*134 calories; 0.4 gm fat; 2% calo-
ries from fat; 0 mg cholesterol;
4.3 mg sodium; 34.3 gm carbohydrate; 0.8 gm protein; 31.1 mg calcium; 0.6 mg iron; 15 RE vitamin
A; 48.3 mg vitamin C*

LAVENDER LIBERTY

8 parts blueberry juice
   (4 oz.)
8 parts nonfat milk (4 oz.)
2 parts fresh-squeezed lemon
   juice (1 oz.)
1 tbsp. honey
Fresh blueberries, for garnish

Combine all ingredients except the
fresh blueberries with cracked ice in
a blender and blend until slushy. Pour
into chilled wineglasses. Float
fresh blueberries on top for garnish.
Serves two.

*95 calories; 0.4 gm fat; 3% calories
from fat; 0.9 mg cholesterol; 34.1
mg sodium; 22.6 gm carbohydrate;
2.5 gm protein; 75.7 mg calcium;
0.2 mg iron; 42.1 RE vitamin A;
16.4 mg vitamin C*

LEFT-COAST EGG CREAM

7 parts milk, chilled (3½ oz.)
2 parts chocolate syrup (1 oz.)
1 tbsp. coconut syrup
Sparkling mineral water

Add the syrups and the milk in the bottom of a chilled collins glass and stir. Add the sparkling mineral water and stir vigorously until a foamy head appears. Serves one.

174 calories; 3.6 gm fat; 17% calories from fat; 13.4 mg cholesterol; 64.7 mg sodium; 34.5 gm carbohydrate; 3.8 gm protein; 134.4 mg calcium; 1.2 mg iron; 37.5 RE vitamin A; 0.9 mg vitamin C

LEMON SOUR

4 parts fresh-squeezed
   lemon juice (2 oz.)
1 part fresh-squeezed lime
   juice (½ oz.)
1 tbsp. bar sugar (or more to taste)
8 parts ice-water (4 oz.)
Orange slice, for garnish

Combine all ingredients except orange with cracked ice in a cocktail shaker and shake vigorously. Strain into a chilled sour glass and garnish with the orange slice. Serves one.

29 calories; 0 gm fat; 0% calories from fat; 0 gm cholesterol; 0.7 mg sodium; 9 gm carbohydrate; 0.3 gm protein; 5.3 mg calcium; 0 mg iron; 1.3 RE vitamin A; 30.2 mg vitamin C

LEMON VELVET FIZZ

8 parts apricot nectar (4 oz.)
Bitter-lemon soda
Lemon slice, for garnish

Pour apricot nectar over ice cubes into a chilled highball glass. Fill the glass with bitter lemon and stir gently. Garnish with the lemon slice. Serves one.

75 calories; 0.1 gm fat; 1% calories from fat; 0 mg cholesterol; 6.5 mg sodium; 19.3 gm carbohydrate; 0.4 gm protein; 8.5 mg calcium; 0.5 mg iron; 149.5 RE vitamin A; 37.9 mg vitamin C

LEMON YELLOW SKY

12 parts pineapple
   juice (6 oz.)
6 parts papaya juice (3 oz.)
4 parts fresh-squeezed lemon
   juice (2 oz.)
Pineapple spear, for garnish
Lemon slice, for garnish

Combine juices with cracked ice in a cocktail shaker. Shake well and pour into a chilled collins glass. Garnish with the lemon slice and pineapple spear. Serves one.

158 calories; 0.3 gm fat; 1% calories from fat; 0 mg cholesterol; 6.5 mg sodium; 40.7 gm carbohydrate; 0.9 gm protein; 41.4 mg calcium; 0.7 mg iron; 11.4 RE vitamin A; 46.8 mg vitamin C

LEMONADE ICED TEA

1 recipe Traditional Lemonade
   (see page 207)
1 recipe Classic Iced Tea (see page 63)

Combine recipes for Traditional Lemonade and Classic Iced Tea and chill well. Serves twenty.

11 calories; 0 gm fat; 0% calories from fat; 0 mg cholesterol; 1.3 mg sodium; 3.3 gm carbohydrate; 0.1 gm protein; 1.8 mg calcium; 0 mg iron; 0.5 RE vitamin A; 11.2 mg vitamin C

LEMON-BERRY FREEZE

8 parts mixed bush berries (4 oz.)
2 scoops lemon sorbet
White grape juice

Combine sorbet and berries in a blender. While running the blender at its lowest speed, slowly add grape juice through the top of blender until desired consistency is achieved. Pour into a chilled highball glass. Serves one.

170 calories; l 0.4 gm fat; 2% calories from fat; 0 mg cholesterol; 8.1 mg sodium; 43.5 gm carbohydrate; 1.2 gm protein; 16.8 mg calcium; 0.5 mg iron; 8.8 RE vitamin A; 18 mg vitamin C

125

LIME SOUR

6 parts ice-water (3 oz.)
4 parts fresh-squeezed lime
   juice (2 oz.)
1 part fresh-squeezed lemon
   juice (½ oz.)
1 tbsp. bar sugar
Orange slice, for garnish

Combine all ingredients except orange
slice with cracked ice in a cocktail
shaker and shake well. Strain into a
chilled sour glass and garnish with
the orange slice. Serves one.

*67 calories; 0.1 gm fat; 1% calories
from fat; 0 mg cholesterol; 0.9 mg
sodium; 18.9 gm carbohydrate;
0.3 gm protein; 6.5 mg calcium;
0 gm iron; 0.7 RE vitamin C; 20.7
mg vitamin C*

LIMEADE

40 parts cold water
   (80 oz. / 10 cups)
32 parts fresh-squeezed lime
   juice (16 oz. / 2 cups)
32 parts sugar syrup (16 oz. / 2 cups)
10 fresh mint sprigs
Lime slices, for garnish

Combine cold water and lime juice in
a large pitcher. Add one-half cup of
the sugar syrup and mint sprigs and
stir. Add more sugar syrup to taste. Stir
well and add ice. Float lime slices on
top for garnish. Serves ten.

*176 calories; 0 gm fat; 0% calories
from fat; 0 mg cholesterol; 3.6 mg
sodium; 46 gm carbohydrate;
0.2 gm protein; 41.4 mg calcium;
2.2 mg iron; 0.5 RE vitamin A;
14.4 mg vitamin C*

LIMEADE PUNCH

40 parts cold water
   (80 oz. / 10 cups)
32 parts fresh-squeezed lime juice
   (16 oz. / 2 cups)
32 parts sugar syrup (16 oz. / 2 cups)
16 parts fresh-squeezed lemon
   juice (8 oz.)
8 parts grenadine (4 oz.)
10 fresh mint sprigs
2 liters ginger ale
Lime slices, for garnish

Combine the cold water and lime- and
lemon juices in large pitcher. Add one-
half cup of the sugar syrup and mint
sprigs and stir. Add the grenadine, and
add more sugar syrup to taste. Stir
well and add ice. When ready to serve,
pour mixture into a large punch bowl
and add ice. Add ginger ale and stir
gently. Float several lime slices on top.
Serves twenty.

*141 calories; 0 gm fat; 0% calories
from fat; 0 mg cholesterol; 9.4 mg
sodium; 37.1 gm carbohydrate;
0.2 gm protein; 28.1 mg calcium;
1.5 mg iron; 0.5 RE vitamin A;
12.8 mg vitamin C*

LIMONATA EROTICA

4 parts guava nectar (2 oz.)
4 parts plum juice (2 oz.)
Lemonade (see Traditional
   Lemonade, page 207)

Combine guava nectar and plum juice
with cracked ice in a cocktail shaker
and shake well. Strain over ice cubes
into a a chilled collins glass and fill
the glass with lemonade. Stir gently.
Serves one.

*132 calories; 0 gm fat; 0% calories
from fat; 0 mg cholesterol; 15.9 mg
sodium; 36.1 gm carbohydrate;
1 gm protein; 22.2 mg calcium;
0.4 mg iron; 82 RE vitamin A;
61 mg vitamin C*

LIQUID SKY

4 parts passion-fruit juice (2 oz.)
2 parts peppermint syrup (1 oz.)
Sparkling mineral water
Fresh mint sprig, for garnish

Combine juice and syrup in a mixing
glass and stir well. Pour over ice cubes
into a chilled highball glass and fill
the glass with sparkling mineral water.
Stir gently and garnish with the mint
sprig. Serves one.

*108 calories; 0.1 gm fat; 1% calo-
ries from fat; 0 mg cholesterol; 4.8
mg sodium; 27.5 gm carbohydrate;
0.4 gm protein; 19.2 mg calcium;
1.2 mg iron; 135.6 RE vitamin A;
10.3 mg vitamin C*

LITTLE GREEN

4 parts fresh-squeezed
   orange juice (2 oz.)
1 tbsp. parsley juice
Bitter-lemon soda
Parsley sprig, for garnish

Combine juices in a mixing glass and
stir well. Pour over ice cubes into a
chilled highball glass. Fill the glass
with bitter-lemon soda and stir gently.
Garnish with the parsley sprig.
Serves one.

*49 calories; 0.1 gm fat; 3% calories
from fat; 0 mg cholesterol; 8.8 mg
sodium; 12 gm carbohydrate;
0.5 gm protein; 12.4 mg calcium;
0.4 mg iron; 30.8 RE vitamin A;
33.3 mg vitamin C*

LONG-LIFE VEGGIE DRINK

10 parts apple juice (5 oz.)
8 parts carrot juice (4 oz.)
4 parts celery juice (2 oz.)
4 parts wheatgrass juice (2 oz.)
2 parts parsley juice (1 oz.)
Parsley sprigs, for garnish

Combine all ingredients with cracked
ice in a cocktail shaker and shake
well. Strain over ice cubes into chilled
highball glasses and garnish with the
parsley sprigs. Serves two.

*73 calories; 0.5 gm fat; 5% calories
from fat; 0 mg cholesterol; 71.6 mg
sodium; 16.9 gm carbohydrate;
1.7 gm protein; 74.3 mg calcium;
2.5 mg iron; 1,613 RE vitamin A;
74.6 mg vitamin C*

LOOK SHARP

10 parts apple juice (5 oz.)
8 parts carrot juice (4 oz.)
6 parts red-radish juice (3 oz.)
Carrot sticks, for garnish

Combine juices in a blender and
blend until smooth. Pour over ice
cubes into chilled old-fashioned
glasses and garnish with carrot sticks.
Serves two.

*66 calories; 0.5 gm fat; 6% calories
from fat; 0 mg cholesterol; 32.2 mg
sodium; 15.6 gm carbohydrate;
0.9 gm protein; 30.5 mg calcium;
0.7 mg iron; 1,460 RE vitamin A;
46.9 mg vitamin C*

LOW-TIDE COCKTAIL

6 parts clam juice (3 oz.)
2 parts tomato juice (1 oz.)
½ tsp. fresh-squeezed lime juice
½ tsp. curry powder
Lime slice, for garnish

Combine all ingredients except lime
slice with cracked ice in a cocktail
shaker and shake well. Strain into a
cocktail glass and garnish with the
lime slice. Serves one.

*10 calories; 0.1 mg fat; 8% calories
from fat; 0 mg cholesterol; 346.2
mg sodium; 2 gm carbohydrate;
0.7 gm protein; 19.7 mg calcium;
18.1 mg iron; 131.1 RE vitamin A;
17.8 mg vitamin C*

M

MACHO GRANDE

8 parts carrot juice (4 oz.)
4 parts beet juice (2 oz.)
4 parts spinach juice (2 oz.)
2 parts cabbage juice (1 oz.)

Combine juices with cracked ice in a
cocktail shaker and shake well. Strain
into chilled old-fashioned glasses.
Serves two.

*48 calories; 0.3 gm fat; 4% calories
from fat; 0 mg cholesterol; 160.7
mg sodium; 10.4 gm carbohydrate;
2.3 gm protein; 82.1 mg calcium;
2.1 mg iron; 1,810 RE vitamin A;
14.1 mg vitamin C*

MAGIC APPLE

10 parts apple cider (5 oz.)
4 parts beet juice (2 oz.)
Lemon slice, for garnish

Combine juices with cracked ice in a
cocktail shaker and shake well. Strain
over ice cubes into a chilled highball
glass. Garnish with the lemon slice.
Serves one.

*96 calories; 0.2 gm fat; 2% calories
from fat; 0 mg cholesterol; 227.9
mg sodium; 25.3 gm carbohydrate;
0.9 gm protein; 20.4 mg calcium;
1.3 mg iron; 0.9 RE vitamin A; 4.7
mg vitamin C*

MALIBU MUDSLIDE

12 parts papaya juice (6 oz.)
8 parts fresh-squeezed
   orange juice (4 oz.)
2 scoops vanilla frozen yogurt
1 banana, sliced
1 tsp. fresh-squeezed lemon juice
½ tsp. alcohol-free coconut extract

Combine all ingredients in a blender
and blend until smooth. If mixture is
too thick, add more fruit juice until
desired consistency is achieved.
Pour into chilled highball glasses.
Serves two.

*241 calories; 4.5 gm fat; 16% calo-
ries from fat; 2 mg cholesterol; 68.2
mg sodium; 49.2 gm carbohydrate;
3.9 gm protein; 121.4 mg calcium;
0.8 mg iron; 66.4 RE vitamin A;
37.8 mg vitamin C*

MANGO CRAZY

8 parts white grape
   juice (4 oz.)
8 parts apple cider (4 oz.)
6 parts mango juice (3 oz.)

Combine all ingredients in a cocktail
shaker and shake vigorously. Pour
into chilled highball glasses.
Serves two.

*91 calories; 0.2 gm fat; 2% calories
from fat; 0 mg cholesterol; 4.2 mg
sodium; 23.5 gm carbohydrate;
0.6 gm protein; 12.8 mg calcium;
0.9 mg iron; 166 RE vitamin A;
12.4 mg vitamin C*

MANGO DELIGHT

4 parts ripe mango,
   chopped (2 oz.)
3 large fresh strawberries
2 parts fresh-squeezed lime juice (1 oz.)
Lime slice, for garnish

Combine all ingredients except one
whole strawberry and the lime slice
with cracked ice in a blender. Blend
until slushy. Pour into a chilled wineglass and garnish with the whole
strawberry and lime slice. Serves one.

*58 calories; 0.4 gm fat; 5% calories
from fat; 0 mg cholesterol; 1.9 mg
sodium; 15.6 gm carbohydrate;
0.8 gm protein; 16.2 mg calcium;
0.3 mg iron; 203.4 RE vitamin A;
56.4 mg vitamin C*

MANGO MORNING

8 parts mango juice
   (4 oz.)
8 parts fresh-squeezed orange
   juice (4 oz.)
4 parts raspberry puree (2 oz.)

MANGO DELIGHT

Combine all ingredients in a blender and blend until smooth. Pour into chilled old-fashioned glasses. Serves two.

83 calories; 0.5 gm fat; 5% calories from fat; 32.7 mg cholesterol; 181.2 mg sodium; 20.5 gm carbohydrate; 1.1 gm protein; 21.3 mg calcium; 0.4 mg iron; 237.6 RE vitamin A; 54.7 mg vitamin C

MANGO-CHILE FREEZE

12 parts mango juice
  (6 oz.)
2 parts fresh-squeezed lime
  juice (2 oz.)
1 tsp. jalapeño pepper juice
Lime slice, for garnish

Combine juices with cracked ice in a blender and blend until slushy. Pour into a chilled collins glass and garnish with the lime slice. Serves one.

128 calories; 0.5 gm fat; 3% calories from fat; 0 mg cholesterol; 79.7 mg sodium; 34.4 gm carbohydrate; 1.1 gm protein; 22.4 mg calcium; 0.3 mg iron; 664.9 RE vitamin A; 63.7 mg vitamin C

MANGO-CITRUS FREEZE

8 parts fresh-squeezed
  orange juice (4 oz.)
2 parts fresh Meyer lemon juice (1 oz.)
1 mango, peeled, pitted, and chopped

Combine ingredients with cracked ice in a blender and blend until slushy. If mixture is too thick, add more orange juice until desired consistency is achieved. Pour into a chilled collins glass. Serves one.

35 calories; 0.8 gm fat; 3% calories from fat; 0 mg cholesterol; 5.2 mg sodium; 49.5 gm carbohydrate; 2 gm protein; 35.3 mg calcium; 0.5 mg iron; 829.2 RE vitamin A; 127 mg vitamin C

MAPLE SMOOTHIE

16 parts milk (8 oz.)
4 parts maple syrup (2 oz.)
1 banana, sliced
1 scoop vanilla frozen yogurt

Combine all ingredients in a blender and blend until smooth. Pour into a chilled collins glass. Serves one.

501 calories; 12.1 gm fat; 21% calories from fat; 32.7 mg cholesterol; 181.2 mg sodium; 91.5 gm carbohydrate; 11.4 gm protein; 439.4 mg calcium; 1.4 mg iron; 135.9 RE vitamin A; 13 mg vitamin C

MARK TWAIN'S STRAWBERRY SHAKE

16 parts buttermilk (8 oz.)
10 parts fresh strawberries,
  hulled and sliced (5 oz.)
1 tbsp. honey
Whole strawberries, for garnish

Combine all ingredients except whole strawberries in a blender and blend until smooth. Pour into chilled highball glasses and garnish with the whole strawberries. Serves two.

99 calories; 1.3 gm fat; 11% calories from fat; 4.2 mg cholesterol; 120.2 mg sodium; 19 gm carbohydrate; 4.2 gm protein; 142.4 mg calcium; 0.4 mg iron; 13.2 RE vitamin A; 41.4 mg vitamin C

129

MARY'S CREAMY CARROT

10 parts carrot juice (5 oz.)
4 parts red bell-pepper juice (2 oz.)
10 parts milk (5 oz.)
½ tsp. dried thyme, crushed
3–5 dashes Tabasco sauce
Salt, to taste
Freshly ground black pepper, to taste

Combine all ingredients except salt and pepper in a blender and blend until well-mixed. Pour over ice cubes into chilled highball glasses and add salt and pepper to taste. Serves two.

80 calories; 2.5 gm fat; 27% calories from fat; 9.6 mg cholesterol; 469.2 mg sodium; 12 gm carbohydrate; 3 gm protein; 104.2 mg calcium; 0.9 mg iron; 1,839 RE vitamin A; 13.4 mg vitamin C

MAXIMUM VEG

10 parts carrot juice (5 oz.)
8 parts celery juice (4 oz.)
6 parts cucumber juice (3 oz.)
4 parts spinach juice (2 oz.)
4 parts beet juice (2 oz.)
2 parts cabbage juice (1 oz.)
2 parts green-pepper juice (1 oz.)
Carrot sticks, for garnish
Celery sticks, for garnish

Combine all juices in a blender and blend until well-mixed. Pour into chilled old-fashioned glasses and garnish with the carrot and celery sticks. Serves four.

37 calories; 0.2 gm fat; 5% calories from fat; 0 mg cholesterol; 104 mg sodium; 8.5 gm carbohydrate; 1.5 gm protein; 51.1 mg calcium; 1.1 mg iron; 1,043 RE vitamin A; 24.3 mg vitamin C

MELLOW YELLOW

8 parts fresh-squeezed
   lemon juice (4 oz.)
8 parts cucumber juice (4 oz.)
6 parts fresh-squeezed lime
   juice (3 oz.)
2–5 tsp. sugar, to taste
Lemon slices, for garnish

Combine all ingredients except lemon slices in a cocktail shaker and shake well. Add sugar to taste. Pour over ice cubes into chilled old-fashioned glasses and garnish with the lemon slices. Serves two.

57 calories; 0.1 gm fat; 1% calories from fat; 0 mg cholesterol; 2.2 mg sodium; 16.6 gm carbohydrate; 0.7 gm protein; 15.8 mg calcium; 0.2 mg iron; 4.4 RE vitamin A; 41.2 mg vitamin C

MELON MEDLEY

8 parts fresh-squeezed
   orange juice (4 oz.)
8 parts cantaloupe, cubed (4 oz.)
1 part fresh-squeezed lemon
   juice (½ oz.)

Combine all ingredients with cracked ice in a blender and blend until slushy. Pour into a chilled collins glass. Serves one.

90 calories; 0.4 gm fat; 3% calories from fat; 0 mg cholesterol; 23.9 mg sodium; 22 gm carbohydrate; 1.9 gm protein; 28 mg calcium; 0.5 mg iron; 453.8 RE vitamin A; 105.5 mg vitamin C

MELON MELANGE

8 parts fresh-squeezed
   orange juice (4 oz.)
4 parts cantaloupe juice (2 oz.)
4 parts honeydew melon juice (2 oz.)
1 tbsp. fresh-squeezed lime juice

Combine all ingredients with cracked ice in a blender and blend until slushy. Pour into chilled wineglasses. Serves two.

46 calories; 0.2 gm fat; 3% calories from fat; 0 mg cholesterol; 9.1 mg sodium; 11.4 gm carbohydrate; 0.8 gm protein; 12.2 mg calcium; 0.2 mg iron; 120.3 RE vitamin A; 48.2 mg vitamin C

MELON MEDLEY

MELON SMOOTHIE

10 parts cantaloupe juice
 (5 oz.)
8 parts nonfat yogurt (4 oz.)
1 tbsp. honey
1 banana, sliced

Combine all ingredients in a blender
and blend until smooth. If drink is too
thick, add more cantaloupe juice until
desired consistency is achieved. Pour
into a chilled collins glass. Serves one.

*273 calories; 0.7 gm fat; 2% calo-
ries from fat; 2.5 mg cholesterol;
110.5 mg sodium; 64.1 gm carbohydrate; 9 gm protein; 251 mg
calcium; 0.8 mg iron; 547.8 RE
vitamin A; 63.4 mg vitamin C*

MELON-BERRY QUENCHER

10 parts cantaloupe or
 honeydew melon juice (5 oz.)
6 parts blueberry juice (3 oz.)
2 parts white grape juice (1 oz.)
5 fresh mint sprigs
Melon balls, for garnish

Combine the juices and mint sprigs
with cracked ice in a blender and
blend until slushy. Pour into a
chilled highball glass and garnish
with melon balls on a toothpick.
Serves one.

*110 calories; 0.5 gm fat; 4% calo-
ries from fat; 0 mg cholesterol; 34.5
mg sodium; 27.5 gm carbohydrate;*

2 gm protein; 26 mg calcium;
0.5 mg iron; 547.3 RE vitamin A;
63.9 mg vitamin C

MELON-CARROT BABY

8 parts cantaloupe juice
   (4 oz.)
6 parts carrot juice (3 oz.)
3 parts fresh-squeezed lime
   juice (1½ oz.)
Carrot stick, for garnish

Combine juices with cracked ice in a
cocktail shaker and shake well. Strain
over ice cubes into a chilled highball
glass and garnish with the carrot stick.
Serves one.

81.5 calories; 0.3 mg fat; 3% calories from fat; 0 mg cholesterol; 47.9
mg sodium; 20.7 gm carbohydrate;
2 gm protein; 38.9 mg calcium;
0.6 mg iron; 2,621 RE vitamin A;
62 mg vitamin C

MELONUS MAJORES

8 parts strawberry
   puree (4 oz.)
4 parts cantaloupe juice (2 oz.)
4 parts honeydew melon juice (2 oz.)
4 parts pineapple juice (2 oz.)
4 parts watermelon juice (2 oz.)
2 parts fresh-squeezed lemon
   juice (1 oz.)

132

Combine all ingredients in a blender and blend until smooth. Pour into chilled wineglasses. Serves two.

64 calories; 0.4 gm fat; 5% fat from calories; 0 mg cholesterol; 10.1 mg sodium; 16 gm carbohydrate; 1 gm protein; 21.4 mg calcium; 0.4 mg iron; 121.2 RE vitamin A; 62 mg vitamin C

MELROSE AVENUE SMOOTHIE

8 parts cantaloupe
  juice (4 oz.)
8 parts pineapple juice (4 oz.)
6 parts watermelon juice (3 oz.)
1 banana, sliced
Cantaloupe slices, for garnish

Combine all ingredients in a blender and blend until smooth. If mixture is too thick, add more juice of your choice until desired consistency is achieved. Pour into chilled highball glasses and garnish with the cantaloupe slices. Serves two.

120 calories; 0.6 gm fat; 4% calories from fat; 0 mg cholesterol; 13.6 mg sodium; 29.7 gm carbohydrate; 1.6 gm protein; 25 mg calcium; 0.5 mg iron; 241 RE vitamin A; 37.8 mg vitamin C

MERMAID'S SONG

4 parts fresh-squeezed
  orange juice (2 oz.)
2 parts passion-fruit juice (1 oz.)
2 parts coconut milk (1 oz.)
2 parts pineapple juice (1 oz.)
1 part fresh-squeezed lime
  juice (½ oz.)
Pineapple spear, for garnish

Combine all ingredients except the pineapple spear with cracked ice in a cocktail shaker. Shake well and strain into chilled wineglass and garnish with the pineapple spear. Serves one.

141 calories; 8.2 gm fat; 51% calories from fat; 0 mg cholesterol; 6.6 mg sodium; 16 gm carbohydrate; 1.5 gm protein; 16 mg calcium; 0.7 mg iron; 80 RE vitamin A; 40.7 mg vitamin C

MEXICALI SPRITZER

MEXICALI SPRITZER

5 parts pineapple juice
  (2½ oz.)
3 parts fresh-squeezed lime
  juice (1½ oz.)
½ banana, sliced
Bitter-lemon soda

Combine all ingredients except bitter-lemon soda with cracked ice in a blender and blend until smooth. Pour into a chilled highball glass, fill the glass with the bitter-lemon soda, and stir. Serves one.

179 calories; 0.6 gm fat; 3% calories from fat; 0 mg cholesterol; 8.4 mg sodium; 46.2 gm carbohydrate; 1.6 gm protein; 24 mg calcium; 0.6 mg iron; 10 RE vitamin A; 30.4 mg vitamin C

MEXICAN CITRUS COOLER

8 parts cilantro tea, chilled
  (4 oz.) (see Mexican Cooler, below)
8 parts fresh-squeezed orange
  juice (4 oz.)
8 parts pineapple juice (4 oz.)
Fresh cilantro sprigs, for garnish

Combine cilantro tea and juices in a cocktail shaker and shake well. Strain over ice cubes into two highball glasses and garnish with the cilantro sprigs. Serves two.

133

43 calories; 0.2 gm fat; 3% calories from fat; 0 mg cholesterol; 11.4 mg sodium; 10.2 mg carbohydrate; 0.6 gm protein; 17.7 mg calcium; 0.5 mg iron; 25.4 RE vitamin A; 7.5 mg vitamin C

MEXICAN COOLER

16 parts water, heated to boiling (8 oz.)
2 tbsp. fresh cilantro, chopped
Bitter-lemon soda
Fresh cilantro sprigs, for garnish

Place the cilantro in a heat-proof glass and fill the glass with boiling water. Let the mixture steep for at least twenty minutes. Strain the liquid and chill. To make the cooler, pour 8 parts (4 oz.) of the cilantro tea over ice cubes into a a chilled collins glass. Fill the glass with bitter-lemon soda and stir gently. Garnish with a fresh cilantro sprig. Serves one.

47 calories; 0 gm fat; 0% fat from calories; 0 mg cholesterol; 13.9 mg sodium; 11.8 gm carbohydrate; 0.1 gm protein; 7.9 mg calcium; 0.2 mg iron; 15.6 RE vitamin A; 0.6 mg vitamin C

MID-LIFE CRISIS

12 parts tomato juice (6 oz.)
2 parts beet juice (1 oz.)
2 parts celery juice (1 oz.)
1 part parsley juice (½ oz.)
1 tsp. pureed garlic
1 tsp. fresh dill, chopped fine
Freshly ground black pepper, to taste
Fresh dill sprigs, for garnish
Lemon twists, for garnish

Combine all ingredients except pepper, dill sprigs, and lemon twists in a blender and blend until smooth. Pour over ice cubes into chilled old-fashioned glasses, add pepper to taste, and garnish with the dill sprigs and lemon twists. Serves two.

28 calories; 0.2 gm fat; 5% calories from fat; 0 mg cholesterol; 364.3 mg sodium; 6.5 gm carbohydrate; 1.4 gm protein; 37.4 mg calcium; 1.5 mg iron; 123.1 RE vitamin A; 27.7 mg vitamin C

MILAGRO

12 parts apple juice (6 oz.)
4 parts rehydrated raisins, chopped fine (2 oz.)
4 parts coconut milk (2 oz.)
1 tbsp. honey
½ tsp. alcohol-free almond extract

Combine all ingredients with cracked ice in a blender and blend until slushy. Pour into chilled wineglasses. Serves two.

236 calories; 0.3 mg fat; 30% calories from fat; 0 mg cholesterol; 10.5 mg sodium; 41.3 gm carbohydrate; 1.8 gm protein; 26.1 mg calcium; 1.3 mg iron; 0.5 RE vitamin A; 36 mg vitamin C

MIMOSA

Sparkling white grape juice, chilled
Fresh-squeezed orange juice
Fresh mint sprig, for garnish

Fill a chilled champagne flute half-full of orange juice. Fill the glass with the sparkling grape juice and stir gently. Garnish with the mint sprig. Serves one.

73 calories; 0.2 gm fat; 3% calories from fat; 0 mg cholesterol; 2.4 mg sodium; 17.3 gm carbohydrate; 0.9 gm protein; 14.4 mg calcium; 0.3 mg iron; 17.5 RE vitamin A; 42.6 mg vitamin C

MINT REFRESHER

12 parts strong-brewed mint tea, chilled (6 oz.)
Lemon-flavored sparkling mineral water
Fresh mint sprig, for garnish
Lemon slice, for garnish

Pour mint tea over ice cubes into a chilled collins glass. Fill the glass with the sparkling mineral water and stir gently. Garnish with the mint sprig and lemon slice. Serves one.

1.8 calories; 0 gm fat; 0% calories from fat; 0 mg cholesterol; 1.7 mg sodium; 0.4 gm carbohydrate;

MIMOSA

0 gm protein; 3.4 mg calcium;
0.1 mg iron; 0 RE vitamin A;
0.2 mg vitamin C

MINTY GINGER ALE

1 tsp. alcohol-free mint extract
Ginger ale
Fresh mint sprig, for garnish

Pour ginger ale over ice cubes into a
chilled highball glass and add mint
extract. Stir gently and garnish with
the mint sprig. Serves one.

58 calories; 0 gm fat; 0% calories
from fat; 0 mg cholesterol; 11.9 mg
sodium; 14.8 gm carbohydrate; 0
gm protein; 5.1 mg calcium; 0.3
mg iron; 0 RE vitamin A; 0 mg vitamin C

MINTY MELONADE

10 parts honeydew melon juice (5 oz.)
4 parts coconut milk (2 oz.)
4 parts fresh-squeezed orange
   juice (2 oz.)
1 tsp. alcohol-free mint extract
Fresh mint sprigs, for garnish

Combine all ingredients except mint
sprigs in a blender and blend until
smooth. Pour over ice cubes into a
chilled collins glass and garnish with
the mint sprigs. Serves one.

*233 calories; 16.3 gm fat; 61% fat
from calories; 0 mg cholesterol;
22.6 mg sodium; 20.6 gm carbohydrate; 2.6 gm protein; 19.8 mg calcium; 1 mg iron; 17 RE vitamin A;
63.5 mg vitamin C*

MR. LUCKY

Ginger beer
1 tsp. fresh-squeezed lime juice
1 tsp. fresh-squeezed lemon juice
1 tsp. fresh-squeezed orange juice
Orange twist, for garnish

Pour ginger beer into a chilled pilsner
glass and add the juices. Stir gently
and garnish with the orange twist.
Serves one.

*82 calories; 0.5 gm fat; 6% calories
from fat; 0 mg cholesterol; 15.1 mg
sodium; 18.9 gm carbohydrate;
0.6 gm protein; 6.5 mg calcium;
0.3 mg iron; 1.2 RE vitamin A; 6.4
mg vitamin C*

MR. MACGREGOR'S GARDEN

10 parts carrot juice (5 oz.)
8 parts celery juice (4 oz.)
4 parts spinach juice (2 oz.)
2 parts parsley juice (1 oz.)
Carrot stick, for garnish

Combine juices with cracked ice in a
cocktail shaker and shake well. Strain
over ice cubes into a chilled collins
glass. Garnish with the carrot stick.
Serves one.

*98 calories; 0.7 gm fat; 6% calories
from fat; 0 mg cholesterol; 195.3
mg sodium; 21.3 gm carbohydrate;
4.7 gm protein; 195.3 mg calcium;
4.9 mg iron; 4,276 RE vitamin A;
63.3 mg vitamin C*

MR. SANDMAN

10 parts milk (5 oz.)
2 parts maple syrup (1 oz.)
3–5 dashes alcohol-free almond extract
Ground nutmeg, for garnish

Combine milk, maple syrup, and
extract in a saucepan over medium
heat until very hot but not boiling.
Pour into a warmed mug and sprinkle
with nutmeg. Serves one.

*162 calories; 4.9 gm fat; 27% calo-
ries from fat; 19.2 mg cholesterol;
72.6 mg sodium; 25.4 gm carbohydrate; 4.7 gm protein; 199.3 mg
calcium; 0.4 mg iron; 53.6 RE vitamin C; 1.3 mg vitamin C*

MOBY GRAPE

10 parts red grape juice
   (5 oz.)
8 parts strawberry puree (4 oz.)
1 tbsp. fresh-squeezed lemon juice
1 whole strawberry, for garnish

Combine puree and juices with
cracked ice in a blender and blend
until slushy. Pour into a chilled highball glass and garnish with the whole
strawberry. Serves one.

*124 calories; 0.5 gm fat; 4% calo-
ries from fat; 0 mg cholesterol; 5.5
mg sodium; 30.5 gm carbohydrate;
1.5 gm protein; 29.8 mg calcium;
0.8 mg iron; 4.5 RE vitamin A;
71.5 mg vitamin C*

MOCHA SLUSH

MOCHA SLUSH

8 parts milk (4 oz.)
4 parts coffee syrup (2 oz.)
2 parts chocolate syrup (1 oz.)
Chocolate shavings, for garnish

Combine all ingredients except chocolate shavings with cracked ice in a
blender. Blend until slushy and pour
into chilled wineglass. Sprinkle with
chocolate shavings. Serves one.

*281 calories; 9 gm fat; 12% calories
from fat; 15.3 mg cholesterol; 73.5
mg sodium; 60.5 gm carbohydrate;
4.3 gm protein; 173.7 mg calcium;
2.5 mg iron; 42.9 RE vitamin A;
1.1 mg vitamin C*

MODESTO MALTED

16 parts milk (8 oz.)
4 parts chocolate syrup (2 oz.)
3 tbsp. malted-milk powder
2 scoops chocolate ice cream
1 tsp. alcohol-free almond extract

Combine all ingredients in a blender
and blend until smooth. Pour into
chilled highball glasses. Serves two.

*203 calories; 7.7 gm fat; 26% calo-
ries from fat; 256.3 mg cholesterol;
107.2 mg sodium; 43.8 gm carbohydrate; 6.4 gm protein; 182.7 mg
calcium; 2.1 mg iron; 81.9 RE vitamin A; 1.3 mg vitamin C*

137

MONTECITO COOLER

MONTECITO COOLER

6 parts fresh-squeezed lime
   juice (3 oz.)
1 part sugar syrup (½ oz.)
Bitter-lemon soda
Lime slice, for garnish

Combine lime juice and sugar syrup
with cracked ice in a cocktail shaker
and shake well. Strain over ice cubes
into a chilled collins glass. Fill the
glass with the bitter-lemon soda. Stir
gently and garnish with the lime slice.
Serves one.

*83 calories; 0.1 gm fat; 1% calories
from fat; 0 mg cholesterol; 7.8 mg
sodium; 23.2 carbohydrate; 0.4 gm
protein; 17 mg calcium; 0.6 mg
iron; 0.9 RE vitamin A; 24.9 mg
vitamin C*

MONTEREY MINT TEA

Iced tea, unsweetened
4 parts peppermint syrup (2 oz.)
Lime wedge, for garnish
Fresh mint sprig, for garnish

Combine iced tea and syrup in a
chilled collins glass filled with ice
cubes. Squeeze the lime wedge over
the drink and drop it in. Stir and garnish with the mint sprig. Serves one.

*150 calories; 0 gm fat; 0% calories
from fat; 0 mg cholesterol; 6.2 mg
sodium; 38.9 gm carbohydrate;
0 gm protein; 33.6 mg calcium;
2.1 mg iron; 0 RE vitamin A; 0 mg
vitamin C*

138

MORNING DEW

10 parts grapefruit juice (5 oz.)
6 parts cherry juice (3 oz.)
4 parts fresh-squeezed orange
   juice (2 oz.)
Orange slice, for garnish

Combine the juices in a chilled collins glass and stir well. Garnish with the orange slice. Serves one.

142 calories; 1.1 mg fat; 6% calories from fat; 0 mg cholesterol; 1.9 mg sodium; 33.1 gm carbohydrate; 2.1 gm protein; 21.4 mg calcium; 0.7 mg iron; 31 RE vitamin A; 88.2 mg vitamin C

MORNING SHAKE

1 banana, frozen
16 parts fresh-squeezed
   orange juice (8 oz.)
4 parts unsweetened cherry
   juice (2 oz.)

Combine frozen banana and orange juice in a blender and blend until frothy. Add cherry juice and blend again. Pour into a chilled collins glasses. Serves two.

134 calories; 0.9 gm fat; 6% calories from fat; 0 mg cholesterol; 1.4 mg sodium; 32.2 gm carbohydrate;

MONTEREY MINT TEA

*1.9 gm protein; 22.1 mg calcium;
0.6 mg iron; 36.4 RE vitamin A;
64.8 mg vitamin C*

*Note: see chapter on ingredients for
frozen banana instructions.*

MORNING SUN

8 parts fresh-squeezed
    orange juice (4 oz.)
4 parts guava nectar (2 oz.)
4 parts raspberry puree (2 oz.)
Fresh raspberries, for garnish

Combine all ingredients except fresh
raspberries with cracked ice in a cocktail shaker and shake well. Pour into a
chilled collins glass and garnish with
the fresh raspberries. Serves one.

*121 calories; 1 gm fat; 7% calories
from fat; 0 mg cholesterol; 2.6 mg
sodium; 28.4 gm carbohydrate;
2 gm protein; 42.4 mg calcium;
0.9 mg iron; 78.7 RE vitamin A;
181.9 mg vitamin C*

MOTHER LODE

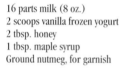

16 parts milk (8 oz.)
2 scoops vanilla frozen yogurt
2 tbsp. honey
1 tbsp. maple syrup
Ground nutmeg, for garnish

Combine all ingredients except nutmeg in a blender and blend until
smooth. Pour into a chilled collins
glass and sprinkle with nutmeg.
Serves one.

*543 calories; 15.6 gm fat; 25%
calories from fat; 34.7 mg cholesterol; 241.5 mg sodium; 92.2 gm
carbohydrate; 13.2 gm protein;
498.5 mg calcium; 1 mg iron;
167.7 RE vitamin A; 3.7 vitamin C*

MOTHER'S MILK

MOTHER'S MILK

8 parts milk (4 oz.)
1 part honey (½ oz.)
½ tsp. alcohol-free vanilla extract
Ground nutmeg, for garnish

Combine all ingredients except the
nutmeg with cracked ice in a cocktail
shaker and shake well. Strain into a
chilled old-fashioned glass and sprinkle with the nutmeg. Serves one.

*123 calories; 3.9 gm fat; 29% calo-
ries from fat; 15.3 mg cholesterol;
56.6 mg sodium; 17.9 gm carbohydrate; 3.8 gm protein; 136.8 mg
calcium; 0.1 mg iron; 42.9 RE vitamin A; 1.2 mg vitamin C*

MOUNTAIN
GREENERY

10 parts apple juice (5 oz.)
8 parts carrot juice (4 oz.)
4 parts wheatgrass juice (2 oz.)
4 parts alfalfa-sprout juice (2 oz.)
2 parts parsley juice (1 oz.)
2 parts beet juice (1 oz.)
Parsley sprigs, for garnish

Combine juices in a blender and
blend until smooth. Strain over ice
cubes into a chilled highball glasses
and garnish with the parsley sprigs.
Serves two.

*74 calories; 0.5 gm fat; 5% calories
from fat; 0 mg cholesterol; 65.6 mg*

MULLED CIDER

sodium; 16.5 gm carbohydrate; 2.3 gm protein; 40 mg calcium; 1.8 mg iron; 1,538 RE vitamin A; 55.7 mg vitamin C

MULLED CIDER

64 parts Apple cider
(32 oz. / 1 quart)
6 parts honey (3 oz.)
1 tbsp. dried orange peel
1 tsp. freshly ground cinnamon
½ tsp. ground ginger
½ tsp. freshly ground nutmeg
¼ tsp. ground allspice
5 cardamom seeds
8 whole cloves
Cinnamon sticks, for garnish

Combine all ingredients except cinnamon sticks in a saucepan over high heat. Stir until the honey dissolves. Reduce heat and simmer for about fifteen minutes. Strain into warmed mugs and garnish with the cinnamon sticks. Serves six.

129 calories; 0.2 gm fat; 2% calories from fat; 0 mg cholesterol; 6.2 mg sodium; 35.3 gm carbohydrate; 0.3 gm protein; 18.4 mg calcium; 1.1 mg iron; 0.7 RE vitamin A; 3.4 mg vitamin C

MULLED CRANBERRY JUICE

12 parts cranberry juice
   cocktail (6 oz.)
3 whole cloves
2 lemon slices
¼ tsp. freshly grated nutmeg
Honey, to taste
Cinnamon stick, for garnish

Combine all ingredients except honey
and cinnamon stick in a saucepan
over low heat until hot but not boiling. Add honey to taste. Strain into a
warmed mug and garnish with the
cinnamon stick. Serves one.

*164 calories; 0.4 gm fat; 2% calo-
ries from fat; 0 mg cholesterol; 8.8
mg sodium; 42.1 gm carbohydrate;
0.1 gm protein; 9.7 mg calcium;
0.4 mg iron; 0.2 RE vitamin A;
60.8 mg vitamin C*

MULLED PINEAPPLE JUICE

12 parts pineapple juice (6 oz.)
2 parts fresh-squeezed lemon
   juice (1 oz.)
1 tbsp. honey
2 whole cloves
½ tsp. allspice
Cinnamon stick, for garnish
Ground nutmeg, for garnish

Combine all ingredients except cinnamon stick and nutmeg in a saucepan
low heat until hot but not boiling. Stir
well and pour into a warmed mug.
Garnish with the cinnamon stick and
sprinkle with nutmeg. Serves one.

*168 calories; 0.3 gm fat; 2% calo-
ries from fat; 0 mg cholesterol; 4.1
mg sodium; 43.5 gm carbohydrate;
0.8 gm protein; 35.2 mg calcium;
0.6 mg iron; 1.6 RE vitamin A;
31.8 mg vitamin C*

MY BRILLIANT CAREER

10 parts apple juice (5 oz.)
8 parts kiwi juice (4 oz.)
4 parts coconut milk (2 oz.)
1 banana, sliced

Combine ingredients with cracked ice
in a blender and blend until slushy. If
mixture is too thick, add more apple
juice until desired consistency is
achieved. Pour into chilled highball
glasses. Serves two.

*199 calories; 8.6 gm fat; 37% calo-
ries from fat; 0 mg cholesterol; 9.4
mg sodium; 30.9 gm carbohydrate;
2 gm protein; 25.8 mg calcium;
1 mg iron; 14.5 RE vitamin A;
89.8 mg vitamin C*

MY GREEN TANGERINE

10 parts fresh-squeezed
   tangerine juice (5 oz.)
4 parts cucumber juice (2 oz.)
1 tbsp. parsley juice

Combine juices with cracked ice in a
cocktail shaker and shake well. Strain
over ice cubes into a chilled highball
glass. Serves one.

*70 calories; 0.4 gm fat; 5% calories
from fat; 0 mg cholesterol; 4.4 mg
sodium; 16.2 gm carbohydrate;
1.1 gm protein; 38.3 mg calcium;
0.7 mg iron; 82 RE vitamin A;
51.6 mg vitamin C*

MYSTERY DATE

8 parts cantaloupe juice
   (4 oz.)
8 parts pineapple juice (4 oz.)
4 parts rehydrated dates,
   chopped (2 oz.)
1 banana, sliced

Combine all ingredients in a blender
and blend until smooth. If mixture is
too thick, add more cantaloupe juice
until desired consistency is achieved.
Pour into a chilled collins glass.
Serves one.

*376 calories; 1 gm fat; 2% calories
from fat; 0 mg cholesterol; 14 mg
sodium; 92.5 gm carbohydrate;
4 gm protein; 70 mg calcium;
1.3 mg iron; 387.3 RE vitamin A;
70.2 mg vitamin C*

N

NAFTA FRAPPE

10 parts apple cider (5 oz.)
10 parts mango nectar (5 oz.)
8 parts unsweetened cranberry
    juice (4 oz.)
8 parts pineapple juice (4 oz.)
2 pineapple spears, for garnish

Combine all ingredients except
pineapple spears in a blender. Blend
until smooth. Pour into a chilled
collins glasses and garnish with the
pineapple spears. Serves two.

148 calories; 0.5 gm fat; 3% calories from fat; 0 mg cholesterol; 4.7 mg sodium; 38.7 gm carbohydrate; 0.9 gm protein; 26.2 mg calcium; 0.7 mg iron; 279.5 RE vitamin A; 35.9 mg vitamin C

NECTAR OF THE GODS

8 parts pineapple juice
    (4 oz.)
8 parts tangerine juice (4 oz.)
6 parts coconut milk (3 oz.)
1 banana, sliced
Shredded coconut, for garnish

Combine juices, coconut milk, and
banana in a blender and blend until
smooth. Pour into chilled wineglasses
and sprinkle with shredded coconut.
Serves two.

227 calories; 12.5 gm fat; 48% calories from fat; 0 mg cholesterol; 7.5 mg sodium; 28.2 gm carbohydrate; 2.2 gm protein; 27.1 mg calcium; 1 mg iron; 28.8 RE vitamin A; 28.8 mg vitamin C

NECTARINE A DAY

16 parts nectarine,
    peeled, pitted, and
    chopped (8 oz. / 1 cup)
8 parts blueberries (4 oz. / ½ cup)
Fresh-squeezed orange juice

Combine the nectarine and blueberries in a blender until liquified.
Pour into two chilled old-fashioned
glasses. Add enough orange juice to
thin the drink to desired consistency.
Serves two.

100 calories; 0.8 gm fat; 7% calories from fat; 0 mg cholesterol; 2.4 mg sodium; 24.1 gm carbohydrate; 1.7 gm protein; 12.1 mg calcium; 0.3 mg iron; 109.3 RE vitamin A; 26.2 mg vitamin C

NECTARINE NIRVANA

4 parts nectarine juice (2 oz.)
2 parts fresh-squeezed lemon
    juice (1 oz.)
2 parts fresh-squeezed lime
    juice (1 oz.)
2 parts sugar syrup (1 oz.)
2 parts cold water (1 oz.)
Lime slice, for garnish

Combine all ingredients except lime
slice with cracked ice in a cocktail
shaker and shake well. Strain into a
chilled cocktail glass and garnish with
the lime slice. Serves one.

117 calories; 0.3 gm fat; 2% calories from fat; 0 mg cholesterol; 2 mg sodium; 31 gm carbohydrate; 0.8 gm protein; 24.3 mg calcium; 1.1 mg iron; 42.6 RE vitamin A; 24.4 mg vitamin C

NEON MELON

8 parts honeydew
    melon or cantaloupe
    juice (4 oz.)
4 parts fresh-squeezed orange
    juice (2 oz.)
Lime-flavored sparkling mineral water
Lime slice, for garnish

Combine juices with cracked ice in a
cocktail shaker and shake well. Strain
over ice cubes into a chilled collins
glass. Fill the glass with sparkling
water and stir gently. Garnish with
the lime slice. Serves one.

66 calories; 0.2 gm fat; 3% calories from fat; 0 mg cholesterol; 11.9 mg sodium; 16.8 gm carbohydrate; 0.9 gm protein; 13.4 mg calcium; 0.2 mg iron; 15.9 RE vitamin A; 58 mg vitamin C

'NINERS VICTORY SPARKLER

4 parts fresh-squeezed orange juice (2 oz.)
2 parts fresh-squeezed lemon juice (1 oz.)
1 tsp. ginger juice
1 tsp. honey
Tonic water
Lemon slice, for garnish

Combine juices and honey in a chilled collins glass and stir until honey is dissolved. Fill the glass with tonic water until the glass is about two-thirds full. Stir gently and add ice cubes. Garnish the with lemon slice. Serves one.

91 calories; 0.1 gm fat; 1% calories from fat; 0 mg cholesterol; 5 gm sodium; 23.7 gm carbohydrate; 0.5 gm protein; 9.4 mg calcium; 0.2 mg iron; 11.9 RE vitamin A; 41.6 mg vitamin C

NO STRINGS

6 parts passion-fruit juice (3 oz.)
Sparkling white grape juice

Pour passion-fruit juice into a chilled wineglass. Fill the glasses with sparkling grape juice and stir gently. serves one.

85 calories; 0.2 gm fat; 2% calories from fat; 0 mg cholesterol; 6.8 mg sodium; 20.8 gm carbohydrate; 0.9 gm protein; 8.5 mg calcium; 0.4 mg iron; 205.3 RE vitamin A; 15.6 mg vitamin C

NONTOXIC PRAIRIE OYSTER

8 parts egg substitute (4 oz.)
1 part Worcestershire sauce (½ oz.)
1 part catsup (½ oz.)
1 part vinegar of your choice (½ oz.)
3–5 dashes Tabasco sauce
Salt, to taste
Cayenne pepper to taste

Combine all ingredients except salt and cayenne pepper in a cocktail shaker and shake well. Strain into a chilled old-fashioned glass. Add salt and cayenne pepper to taste, and ice if desired. Serves one.

147 calories; 3.9 gm fat; 24% calories from fat; 1.1 mg cholesterol; 717 mg sodium; 12.7 gm carbohydrate; 15.3 gm protein; 68.3 mg calcium; 3.5 mg iron; 274.7 RE vitamin A; 7.3 mg vitamin C

NORTH AND SOUTH

8 parts strawberry juice (4 oz.)
6 parts raspberry juice (3 oz.)
1 tbsp. fresh-squeezed lemon juice
Sparkling mineral water
Lemon slices, for garnish

Combine juices with cracked ice in a cocktail shaker and shake well. Strain mixture over ice cubes into highball glasses and slowly fill the glasses with sparkling mineral water. Garnish with the lemon slices. Serves two.

80 calories; 0.9 gm fat; 9% calories from fat; 0 mg cholesterol; 1.3 mg sodium; 19.1 gm carbohydrate; 1.5 gm protein; 35.7 mg calcium; 0.9 mg iron; 14.5 RE vitamin A; 92.6 mg vitamin C

NOTHING SACRED

8 parts cranberry juice cocktail (4 oz.)
6 parts fresh-squeezed orange juice (3 oz.)
1 part fresh-squeezed lemon juice (½ oz.)
Ginger ale
Orange slice, for garnish

Combine juices with cracked ice in a cocktail shaker and shake well. Strain over ice cubes into a chilled collins glass. Fill with ginger ale and stir gently. Garnish with the orange slice. Serves one.

126 calories; 0.3 gm fat; 2% calories from fat; 0 mg cholesterol; 9.3 mg sodium; 31.3 gm carbohydrate; 0.7 gm protein; 15.4 mg calcium; 0.4 mg iron; 17.3 RE vitamin A; 89.2 mg vitamin C

NOVEMBER CIDER

6 parts apple cider (3 oz.)
6 parts fresh-squeezed orange
    juice (3 oz.)
6 parts black tea, chilled (3 oz.)
3 parts fresh-squeezed lemon
    juice (1½ oz.)
Lemon slice

Combine all ingredients with ice cubes in a mixing glass and stir well. Pour into a chilled collins glass and garnish with the lemon slice. Serves one.

92 calories; 0.3 gm fat; 2% calories from fat; 0 mg cholesterol; 6.2 mg sodium; 24.5 gm carbohydrate; 0.8 gm protein; 17.4 mg calcium; 0.6 mg iron; 17.9 RE vitamin A; 62.9 mg vitamin C

145

NUTTY COLA

NUTTY COLA

4 parts hazelnut or orgeat
  (almond) syrup (2 oz.)
4 parts fresh-squeezed lime
  juice (2 oz.)
Natural cola

Combine syrup and lime juice in a
cocktail shaker and shake well. Pour
over ice cubes into a chilled collins
glass. Fill the glass with the cola and
stir gently. Serves one.

*199 calories; 0.1 gm fat; 0% calo-
ries from fat; 0 mg cholesterol; 6.8
mg sodium; 52.5 gm carbohydrate;
0.2 gm protein; 41.6 mg calcium;
2.1 mg iron; 0.6 RE vitamin A;
16.6 mg vitamin C*

NUTTY PEACH FREEZE

16 parts peach juice (8 oz.)
12 parts nonfat milk (6 oz.)
½ tsp. alcohol-free almond extract
Toasted almonds, chopped fine,
  for garnish

Combine all ingredients except toasted
almonds with cracked ice in a blender
and blend until slushy. Pour into
chilled highball glasses and sprinkle
with the toasted almonds. Serves two.

*136 calories; 0.9 gm fat; 6% calo-
ries from fat; 9.2 mg cholesterol;
69.1 mg sodium; 7 gm carbohydrate; 23 gm protein; 146.8 mg
calcium; 0.4 mg iron; 62.4 RE vitamin A; 0.8 mg vitamin C*

O

OAKLAND EGG CREAM

4 parts peppermint syrup (2 oz.)
2 parts chocolate syrup (1 oz.)
Sparkling mineral water
Fresh mint sprig, for garnish

Combine syrups in a chilled highball glass. Fill the glass with ice cubes and top off with the sparkling mineral water. Stir gently and garnish with the mint sprig. Serves one

211 calories; 0.3 gm fat; 1% calories from fat; 0 mg cholesterol; 17.8 sodium; 55.3 gm carbohydrate; 0.5 gm protein; 38.4 mg calcium; 2.5 mg iron; 0 RE vitamin A; 0 mg vitamin C

OAKLAND EGG CREAM

OCCIDENTAL IRISH COFFEE

14 parts coffee, hot (7 oz.)
1 tbsp. honey
1 tsp. alcohol-free brandy extract
Whipped cream, for garnish
Ground nutmeg, for garnish

Pour coffee into a warmed mug. Add honey and brandy extract and stir well. Top with a dollop of whipped cream and sprinkle with ground nutmeg. Serves one.

72 calories; 0.4 gm fat; 4% calories from fat; 0.9 mg cholesterol; 6.7 mg sodium; 18.2 gm carbohydrate; 0.3 gm protein; 6.7 mg calcium; 0.2 mg iron; 3.5 RE vitamin A; 0.2 mg vitamin C

OCTOBER'S BOUNTY

6 parts apple juice
  (3 oz.)
6 parts fuyu persimmon juice (3 oz.)
6 parts pomegranate juice (3 oz.)
1 part fresh-squeezed lime
  juice (½ oz.)
1 tbsp. honey
Ground nutmeg, for garnish

Combine all ingredients except nutmeg in a blender and mix well. Pour into a chilled highball glass and sprinkle with nutmeg. Serves one.

275 calories; 0.8 gm fat; 2% calories from fat; 0 mg cholesterol; 270 mg sodium; 71.6 gm carbohydrate; 1.7 gm protein; 34.2 mg calcium; 2.8 mg iron; 186.6 RE vitamin A; 100.6 mg vitamin C

OJAI SMOOTHIE

12 parts apple juice (6 oz.)
8 parts fresh strawberries,
  hulled and sliced (4 oz.)
1 tbsp. fresh-squeezed lemon juice
1 ripe Haas avocado, peeled, pitted,
  and chopped

Combine all ingredients in a blender and blend until smooth. If drink is too thick, add more apple juice until desired consistency is achieved. Pour into chilled collins glasses. Serves two.

458 calories; 27.6 gm fat; 50% calories from fat; 0 mg cholesterol; 21.6 mg sodium; 56.3 gm carbohydrate; 5.7 gm protein; 62.3 mg calcium; 2.7 mg iron; 189.4 RE vitamin A; 165.1 mg vitamin C

OLD-FASHIONED ICE CREAM SODA

2–3 scoops vanilla ice cream
Sarsaparilla soda

Place ice cream in a a chilled collins glass. Slowly fill the glass with sarsaparilla soda. Do not stir. Serves one.

324 calories; 16.8 gm fat; 45% calories from fat; 117 mg cholesterol; 92.7 mg sodium; 40.7 gm carbohydrate; 5.3 gm protein; 175.2 mg calcium; 0.3 mg iron; 199.5 RE vitamin A; 0.9 mg vitamin C

OLIVE COCKTAIL

8 parts tomato juice (4 oz.)
4 parts black-olive juice (2 oz.)
Celery salt, to taste
Black olive, for garnish

Combine all ingredients except black olive with cracked ice in a cocktail shaker and shake well. Strain into a chilled cocktail glass. Garnish with the black olive. Serves one.

519 calories; 56.8 gm fat; 96% calories from fat; 0 mg cholesterol;

408.6 mg sodium; 4.8 gm carbohydrate; 0.7 gm protein; 18.3 mg calcium; 0.9 mg iron; 63.2 RE vitamin A; 9 mg vitamin C

Note: Olive juice is the liquid in which black olives are packed.

ON THE BEACH

6 parts clam juice (3 oz.)
6 parts vegetable bouillon,
   chilled (3 oz.)
1 tbsp. fresh-squeezed lime juice
½ tsp. white horseradish
3–5 dashes Worcestershire sauce
Cocktail olive, for garnish
Celery stick, for garnish

Combine all ingredients except celery stick and cocktail olive with cracked ice in a cocktail shaker and shake well. Strain into a chilled highball glass. Garnish with the cocktail olive and celery stick. Serves one.

7 calories; 0.3 gm fat; 3% calories from fat; 0 mg cholesterol; 214.9 mg sodium; 1.7 gm carbohydrate; 0.5 gm protein; 13.9 mg calcium; 13.4 mg iron; 86.8 RE vitamin A; 16.8 mg vitamin C

ORANGE AND TONIC

8 parts fresh-squeezed orange
   juice (4 oz.)
Tonic water
Lime wedge, for garnish

Pour orange juice over ice cubes into a chilled collins glass. Fill the glass with the tonic water and stir gently. Squeeze the lime wedge over the drink and drop it in. Serves one.

70 calories; 0.2 gm fat; 3% calories from fat; 0 mg cholesterol; 3.2 mg sodium; 16.8 gm carbohydrate; 0.8 gm protein; 12.9 mg calcium; 0.2 mg iron; 22.7 RE vitamin A; 56.7 mg vitamin C

ORANGE BLOSSOM SPECIAL

10 parts fresh-squeezed
   orange juice (5 oz.)
6 parts rose-hips tea, chilled (3 oz.)
6 parts hibiscus tea, chilled (3 oz.)
4 parts white grape juice (2 oz.)
Orange slices, for garnish
Nasturtiums or other edible flowers,
   for garnish

Combine juices and teas with cracked ice in a cocktail shaker and shake well. Strain over ice cubes into chilled highball glasses and garnish with the orange slices and flowers. Serves two.

50 calories; 0.2 gm fat; 3% calories from fat; 0 mg cholesterol; 2.3 mg sodium; 11.8 gm carbohydrate; 0.7 gm protein; 12 mg calcium; 0.3 mg iron; 14.4 RE vitamin A; 35.5 mg vitamin C

ORANGE COUNTY BLUES

8 parts pineapple
   juice (4 oz.)
8 parts fresh-squeezed orange
   juice (4 oz.)
4 parts fresh-squeezed lime
   juice (2 oz.)
1 banana, sliced

Combine juices and banana in a blender and blend until smooth. Pour into chilled highball glasses. Serves two.

117 calories; 0.5 gm fat; 3% calories from fat; 0 mg cholesterol; 1.8 mg sodium; 29.6 gm carbohydrate; 1.3 gm protein; 22.9 mg calcium; 0.4 mg iron; 16.5 RE vitamin A; 47.9 mg vitamin C

ORANGE JOEY

8 parts fresh-squeezed
   orange juice (4 oz.)
6 parts half-and-half (3 oz.)
4 parts vanilla syrup (2 oz.)
Orange slice, for garnish

Combine all ingredients except orange
slice with cracked ice in a blender and
blend until smooth. Pour into a
chilled highball glass. Garnish with
the orange slice. Serves one.

*310 calories; 10 gm fat; 28% calo-
ries from fat; 31.3 mg cholesterol;
38.2 mg sodium; 54 gm carbohydrate; 3.3 gm protein; 135.6 mg
calcium; 2.3 mg iron; 133.4 RE
vitamin A; 57.4 mg vitamin C*

ORANGE SALSA

8 parts fresh-squeezed
   orange juice (4 oz.)
8 parts tomato juice (4 oz.)
4 parts fresh-squeezed lime
   juice (2 oz.)
1 part garlic juice (½ oz.)
1 part jalapeño-pepper juice (½ oz.)
1 part scallion juice (½ oz.)
1 tsp. cilantro juice
Cilantro sprigs, for garnish
Orange slices, for garnish

Combine all ingredients except
cilantro sprigs and orange slices in a
blender and blend until smooth.
Strain over ice cubes into chilled double old-fashioned glasses and garnish
with cilantro sprigs and orange slices.
Serves two.

*60 calories; 0.3 gm fat; 4% calories
from fat; 0 mg cholesterol; 311.2
mg sodium; 14.3 gm carbohydrate;
1.6 gm protein; 35.2 mg calcium;
0.9 mg iron; 59.2 RE vitamin A;
45.3 mg vitamin C*

ORANGE VELVET

8 parts fresh-squeezed
   orange juice (4 oz.)
6 parts apricot juice (3 oz.)
1 tbsp. fresh-squeezed lime juice

Combine ingredients with cracked ice
in a cocktail shaker and shake well.

Strain over ice cubes into a chilled
highball glass. Serves one.

*71 calories; 0.2 gm fat; 2% calories
from fat; 0 mg cholesterol; 14.5 mg
sodium; 18.4 gm carbohydrate;
1.2 gm protein; 17.4 mg calcium;
0.9 mg iron; 175.6 RE vitamin A;
25.8 mg vitamin C*

ORANGE-CREAM COCKTAIL

6 parts half-and-half (3 oz.)
4 parts fresh-squeezed orange
   juice (2 oz.)
2 parts pineapple juice (1 oz.)
Orange slice, for garnish

Combine all ingredients except orange
slice with cracked ice in a cocktail
shaker and shake vigorously. Pour
into a chilled wineglass filled with
crushed ice and garnish with the
orange slice. Serves one.

*136 calories; 9.8 gm fat; 63% calo-
ries from fat; 31.3 mg cholesterol;
10.4 mg sodium; 10 gm carbohydrate; 3 gm protein; 99.2 mg
calcium; 0.5 mg iron; 142.7 RE
vitamin A; 14.16 mg vitamin C*

ORANGE-FENNEL SPARKLER

10 parts fresh-squeezed
   orange juice (5 oz.)
4 parts fennel juice (2 oz.)
Sparkling mineral water
Dill sprig, for garnish

Combine juices with cracked ice in a
cocktail shaker and shake well. Strain
over ice cubes into a chilled collins
glass and fill the glass with the
sparkling mineral water. Stir gently
and garnish with the dill sprig.
Serves one.

*81 calories; 0.4 gm fat; 4% calories
from fat; 0 mg cholesterol; 30.5 mg
sodium; 18.9 gm carbohydrate;
1.7 gm protein; 43.5 mg calcium;
0.3 mg iron; 28.4 RE vitamin A;
77.7 mg vitamin C*

ORANGE JOEY

ORANGE-LICORICE ICED TEA

12 parts licorice-root tea, hot (6 oz.)
1 tbsp. orange peel, chopped
1 tbsp. lemon peel, chopped
4 parts fresh-squeezed orange
  juice (2 oz.)
Cinnamon stick, for garnish

Combine the licorice-root tea and the citrus peels in a heat-proof glass and let steep for at least twenty minutes. Add the orange juice and stir.

Refrigerate for at least one hour. Pour mixture over ice cubes into a chilled highball glass and garnish with the cinnamon stick. Serves one.

37 calories; 0.1 gm fat; 3% calories from fat; 0 mg cholesterol; 2.2 mg sodium; 8.7 gm carbohydrate; 0.6 gm protein; 27.6 mg calcium; 0.4 mg iron; 14.6 RE vitamin A; 44.3 mg vitamin C

151

ORANGE-SPICED COFFEE

2 parts orange juice (1 oz.)
Peel of ½ orange
½ tsp. ground ginger
½ tsp. ground cinnamon
Dash ground cardamom
2 tsp. honey
12 parts strong black coffee, hot
    (6 oz.)
½ tsp. alcohol-free anise extract
Hot milk (optional)
Whipped cream, for garnish
Grated orange peel, for garnish
Cinnamon sticks, for garnish

In a heat-proof bowl, combine the orange juice, orange peel, spices, and honey. Add the hot coffee and stir. Pour into warmed mugs and add hot milk if desired. Top with a dollop of whipped cream, sprinkle with grated orange peel, and garnish with the cinnamon sticks. Serves two. *79 calories; 5.3 gm fat; 58% calories from fat; 19.13 mg cholesterol; 7.6 mg sodium; 8.1 gm carbohydrate; 0.7 gm protein; 34.8 mg calcium; 0.4 mg iron; 64 RE vitamin A; 19.6 vitamin C*

(Milk not included in nutritional analysis.)

P-Q

Ps 'N' CARROTS

1 bunch fresh parsley,
  well-rinsed
8 parts fresh carrot juice (4 oz.)
Fresh parsley sprig, for garnish
Carrot stick, for garnish
Freshly ground black pepper,
  for garnish

Puree or juice the parsley and combine its juice with the carrot juice in a cocktail shaker and shake well. Pour into a chilled old-fashioned glass. Garnish with parsley sprig and carrot stick and freshly ground black pepper. Serves one.

213 calories; 5.7 gm fat; 23% calories from fat; 39 mg cholesterol; 32.8 mg sodium; 39.3 gm carbohydrate; 2.8 gm protein; 76.9 mg calcium; 2.1 mg iron; 67.1 RE vitamin A; 7.3 mg vitamin C

PACIFIC SUNSET

8 parts fresh-squeezed
  orange juice (4 oz.)
8 parts pineapple juice (4 oz.)
2 tsp. grenadine
1 tsp. fresh-squeezed lemon juice
Orange slices, for garnish

Combine juices with cracked ice in a cocktail shaker and shake well. Pour over ice cubes into chilled old-fashioned glasses and slowly pour one teaspoon of the grenadine over each drink. Do not stir. Garnish with the orange slices. Serves two.

59 calories; 0.1 gm fat; 1% calories from fat; 0 mg cholesterol; 6.6 mg sodium; 14.8 carbohydrate; 0.6 gm protein; 18.8 mg calcium; 0.7 mg iron; 32.2 RE vitamin A; 17.6 mg vitamin C

PALE RIDER

10 parts grapefruit juice
  (5 oz.)
8 parts fresh-squeezed orange
  juice (4 oz.)
1 tbsp. blackberry syrup
Orange slice, for garnish

Combine ingredients in a blender and blend until smooth. Pour over ice cubes into a chilled collins glass and garnish with orange slice. Serves one.

137 calories; 0.4 gm fat; 2% calories from fat; 0 mg cholesterol; 9 mg sodium; 33.7 gm carbohydrate; 1.5 gm protein; 26.7 mg calcium; 1.5 mg iron; 82.1 RE vitamin A; 62.4 mg vitamin C

PALM DESERT COOLER

10 parts grapefruit juice (5 oz.)
8 parts peach juice (4 oz.)
6 parts coconut milk (3 oz.)
2 parts aloe-vera juice (1 oz.)

Combine ingredients in a blender and blend until well-mixed. Pour over ice cubes into chilled highball glasses. Serves two.

177 calories; 12.1 gm fat; 61% calories from fat; 0 mg cholesterol; 10.6 mg sodium; 15.7 gm carbohydrate; 1.7 gm protein; 13.2 mg calcium; 0.8 mg iron; 15.4 RE vitamin A; 29.9 mg vitamin C

(Aloe-vera juice not included in nutritional analysis.)

PAPAYA QUEEN

8 parts papaya juice (4 oz.)
6 parts raspberry juice (3 oz.)
1 scoop lemon sorbet
Fresh raspberries, for garnish

Combine all ingredients except fresh raspberries in a blender and blend until smooth. Pour into a chilled collins glass and garnish with fresh raspberries. Serves one.

160 calories; 2 gm fat; 3% calories from fat; 0 mg cholesterol; 7 mg sodium; 25 gm carbohydrate; 4 gm protein; 40.2 mg calcium; 2 mg iron; 60.4 RE vitamin A; 132.2 mg vitamin C

PAPAYA SMOOTHIE

12 parts fresh-squeezed
   orange juice (6 oz.)
1 part honey (½ oz.)
1 banana, sliced
½ papaya, cubed
¼ tsp. alcohol-free vanilla extract

Combine all ingredients in a blender and blend until smooth. Pour into a chilled collins glass. Serves one.

338 calories; 1.4 gm fat; 3% calories from fat; 0 mg cholesterol; 6.4 mg sodium; 85.3 gm carbohydrate; 3.3 gm protein; 43.5 mg calcium; 1 mg iron; 705.5 RE vitamin A; 142.6 mg vitamin C

PAPAYA-MANGO FREEZE

10 parts papaya juice (5 oz.)
4 parts fresh-squeezed lime
   juice (2 oz.)
½ mango, peeled, pitted, and chopped
1 tbsp. honey

Combine ingredients with cracked ice in a blender and blend until slushy. Pour into a chilled collins glass. Serves one.

295 calories; 0.8 gm fat; 2% fat; 0 mg cholesterol; 12.7 mg sodium; 78.1 gm carbohydrate; 1.6 gm protein; 41.3 mg calcium; 0.9 mg iron; 822.3 RE vitamin A; 78.4 mg vitamin C

PARADISE PUNCH

8 parts tangerine juice
   (4 oz.)
4 parts cranberry juice cocktail (2 oz.)
4 parts grapefruit juice (2 oz.)
2 parts orgeat (almond) syrup (1 oz.)
Tangerine slices, for garnish

PAPAYA SMOOTHIE

Combine all ingredients except the tangerine slices with cracked ice in a cocktail shaker and shake well. Strain over ice cubes into chilled old-fashioned glasses. Garnish with the tangerine slices. Serves two.

89 calories; 0.2 gm fat; 2% calories from fat; 0 mg cholesterol; 2.6 mg sodium; 22.1 gm carbohydrate; 0.4 gm protein; 22 mg calcium; 0.7 mg iron; 24.2 RE vitamin A; 38.4 mg vitamin C

PARK VIEW TERRACE

4 parts fresh-squeezed lime
   juice (2 oz.)
4 parts fresh-squeezed orange
   juice (2 oz.)
4 parts pineapple juice (2 oz.)
4 parts guava nectar (2 oz.)
2 parts grenadine (1 oz.)
1 part orgeat (almond) syrup (½ oz.)
Fresh mint sprig, for garnish
Pineapple spear, for garnish

Combine all ingredients except mint sprig and pineapple spear with cracked ice in a blender and blend until smooth. Pour into a chilled collins glass and garnish with the mint sprig and pineapple spear. Serves one.

175 calories; 0.5 gm fat; 2% calories from fat; 0 mg cholesterol; 4.7 mg sodium; 44.6 gm carbohydrate; 1.3 gm protein; 48.1 mg calcium; 1.5 mg iron; 57.7 RE vitamin A; 164.4 mg vitamin C

113 calories; 0.8 gm fat; 6% calories from fat; 0 mg cholesterol; 9.4 mg sodium; 26.6 gm carbohydrate; 1.5 gm protein; 22 mg calcium; 0.8 mg iron; 340.6 RE vitamin A; 176.6 mg vitamin C

PASSION PLAY

8 parts passion-fruit juice (4 oz.)
6 parts guava nectar (3 oz.)
3–5 drops alcohol-free almond extract
Ground nutmeg, for garnish

Combine all ingredients except nutmeg with cracked ice in a cocktail shaker and shake well. Strain over ice cubes into a chilled highball glass and sprinkle with nutmeg. serves one.

PASSIONATE APE

4 parts apricot juice (2 oz.)
4 parts passion-fruit juice (2 oz.)
Sparkling mineral water

Combine juices with cracked ice in a cocktail shaker and shake well. Strain over ice cubes into a chilled highball glass and fill the glass with the sparkling mineral water. Stir gently. Serves one.

155

66 calories; 0.2 gm fat; 2% calories from fat; 0 mg cholesterol; 5.4 mg sodium; 16.4 gm carbohydrate; 0.6 gm protein; 6.1 mg calcium; 0.4 mg iron; 24.1 RE vitamin A; 10.7 mg vitamin C

PASSIONATE KISSES

4 parts passion-fruit juice (2 oz.)
1 tbsp. raspberry syrup
Sparkling mineral water
Orange slice, for garnish

Combine juice and syrup in a chilled highball glass. Fill the glass about two-thirds full with the sparkling mineral water and stir gently. Add ice cubes and garnish with the orange slice. Serves one.

85 calories; 0.1 gm fat; 1% calories from fat; 0 mg cholesterol; 4.4 mg sodium; 21.3 gm carbohydrate; 0.4 gm protein; 13.8 mg calcium; 0.9 mg iron; 136.6 RE vitamin A; 10.3 mg vitamin C

P.C. SMOOTHIE

12 parts peach nectar (6 oz.)
6 parts coconut milk (3 oz.)
1 banana, sliced
1 tsp. bee pollen
½ tsp. alcohol-free almond extract

Combine all ingredients in a blender and blend until smooth. Pour into chilled highball glasses. Serves two.

217 calories; 12.3 gm fat; 49% calories from fat; 0 mg cholesterol; 12.3 mg sodium; 26.4 gm carbohydrate; 2 gm protein; 11.8 mg calcium; 0.9 mg iron; 26.6 RE vitamin A; 9.2 mg vitamin C

(Bee pollen not included in nutritional analysis.)

PEACH BLUSH

8 parts peach nectar (4 oz.)
4 parts pomegranate juice (2 oz.)
Fresh peach slice, for garnish

Combine juices in a chilled highball glass. Do not blend completely. Add ice if desired. Garnish with the peach slice. Serves one.

119 calories; 0.3 gm fat; 2% calories from fat; 0 mg cholesterol; 10.6 mg sodium; 30.4 gm carbohydrate; 1.1 gm protein; 8.5 mg calcium; 0.5 mg iron; 29.3 RE vitamin A; 11.2 mg vitamin C

PEACH FRAPPE

12 parts peach juice (6 oz.)
8 parts fresh peaches, peeled, pitted, and chopped (4 oz.)
2 scoops vanilla frozen yogurt
1 tbsp. unsweetened peach preserves
3–5 dashes alcohol-free almond extract
Nonfat milk

Combine all ingredients except milk in a blender and blend until smooth but not watery. For a thinner consistency, add milk as needed. Pour into chilled highball glasses. Serves two.

319 calories; 4.4 gm fat; 12% calories from fat; 2.5 mg cholesterol; 38.5 mg sodium; 69.3 gm carbohydrate; 6.4 gm protein; 160 mg calcium; 0.8 mg iron; 266.3 RE vitamin A; 28.3 mg vitamin C

PEACH FUZZ

4 parts fresh-squeezed lemon juice (2 oz.)
4 parts peach juice (2 oz.)
4 parts half-and-half (2 oz.)
1 tsp. sugar syrup
5 fresh strawberries, mashed
Sparkling mineral water
Fresh peach slice, for garnish

PEACH FUZZ

PEACHY CREAM

PEACHY MELBA

Combine all ingredients except sparkling mineral water and peach slice with cracked ice in a cocktail shaker and shake well. Pour into a chilled highball glass. Fill the glass with the sparkling mineral water and stir gently. Garnish with the peach slice. Serves one.

158 calories; 6.8 gm fat; 36% calories from fat; 20.9 mg cholesterol; 28.5 mg sodium; 24.9 gm carbohydrate; 2.5 gm protein; 80.8 mg calcium; 0.7 mg iron; 91.6 RE vitamin A; 71.8 mg vitamin C

PEACH SMOOTHIE

10 parts peach juice (5 oz.)
6 parts fresh grapefruit juice (3 oz.)
2 parts cherry juice (1 oz.)
1 banana, sliced

Combine ingredients in a blender and blend until smooth. Pour into a chilled collins glass. Serves one.

235 calories; 0.9 gm fat; 3% calories from fat; 0 mg cholesterol; 11.5 mg sodium; 59 gm carbohydrate; 2.3 gm protein; 26.2 mg calcium; 0.9 mg iron; 52.7 RE vitamin A; 52.1 mg vitamin C

PEACHES AND CREAM

16 parts milk (8 oz.)
8 parts fresh peaches, peeled, pitted, and chopped (4 oz.)
2 scoops vanilla ice cream
1 tbsp. ginger juice
1 tbsp. orgeat (almond) syrup

Combine all ingredients in a blender and blend until smooth. Pour into chilled highball glasses. Serves two.

346 calories; 9.7 gm fat; 24% calories from fat; 54.3 mg cholesterol; 82.8 mg sodium; 62.2 gm carbohydrate; 7.9 gm protein; 214.9 mg calcium; 0.9 mg iron; 295.4 RE vitamin A; 24.5 mg vitamin C

PEACHY CREAM

4 parts peach juice (2 oz.)
4 parts half-and-half (2 oz.)

Combine ingredients with cracked ice in a cocktail shaker and shake well. Strain over ice cubes into a chilled old-fashioned glass. Serves one.

106 calories; 7 gm fat; 57% calories from fat; 22.3 mg cholesterol; 27.3 mg sodium; 9.8 gm carbohydrate; 2.2 gm protein; 67.3 mg calcium; 0.2 mg iron; 102.5 RE vitamin A; 2.7 mg vitamin C

PEACHY MELBA

6 parts peach juice (3 oz.)
2 parts grenadine (1 oz.)
2 parts fresh-squeezed lemon juice (1 oz.)
2 parts fresh-squeezed lime juice (1 oz.)
Fresh peach slice, for garnish

Combine all ingredients except peach slice with cracked ice in a cocktail shaker and shake well. Pour into a chilled old-fashioned glass. Garnish with the peach slice. Serves one.

157

104 calories; 6.5 gm fat; 55% calories from fat; 20.9 mg cholesterol; 26.8 mg sodium; 10.3 gm carbohydrate; 1.8 gm protein; 62.5 mg calcium; 0.1 mg iron; 88.5 RE vitamin A; 6.7 mg vitamin C

PEAR COMFORTER

14 parts pear juice (7 oz.)
1 tbsp. maple syrup
1 tsp. fresh-squeezed lemon juice
½ tsp. alcohol-free almond extract
3 whole cloves
½ tsp. ground cinnamon
½ tsp. ground nutmeg
½ tsp. ground ginger
Whipped cream, for garnish
Cinnamon stick, for garnish

Combine pear juice, maple syrup, lemon juice, almond extract and spices in a saucepan over medium heat. When mixture is well heated but not boiling, pour into a warmed mug. Top with a dollop of whipped cream and garnish with the cinnamon stick. Serves one.

224 calories; 5.7 gm fat; 22% calories from fat: 20.4 mg cholesterol; 15 mg sodium; 45.4 gm carbohydrate; 0.6 gm protein; 45.5 mg calcium; 0.9 mg iron; 66 RE vitamin A; 4.7 mg vitamin C

PEAR SOUR

8 parts pear juice (4 oz.)
3 parts unsweetened cranberry juice (1½ oz.)
1 parts fresh-squeezed lemon juice (½ oz.)
Lime slice, for garnish

Combine juices with cracked ice in a cocktail shaker and shake well. Strain into a chilled sour glass and garnish with the lime slice. Serves one.

99 calories; 0.1 gm fat; 1% calories from fat; 0 mg cholesterol; 4.7 mg sodium; 26.3 gm carbohydrate; 0.4 gm protein; 10.1 mg calcium; 0.4 mg iron; 2.9 RE vitamin A; 15.4 mg vitamin C

PECHE À LA FROG

12 parts peach juice (6 oz.)
1 part fresh-squeezed lemon juice (½ oz.)
1 part fresh-squeezed lime juice (½ oz.)
Lime slice, for garnish

Combine juices with cracked ice in a blender and blend until slushy. Pour into a chilled margarita glass and garnish with the lime slice. Serves one.

99 calories; 0 gm fat; 0% calories from fat; 0 mg cholesterol; 11.9 mg sodium; 26.2 gm carbohydrate; 0.6 gm protein; 11.1 mg calcium; 0.3 mg iron; 44.4 RE vitamin A; 19.6 mg vitamin C

PEPPER POT

8 parts pineapple juice (4 oz.)
2 parts orgeat (almond) syrup (1 oz.)
2 parts fresh-squeezed lemon juice (1 oz.)
3–5 dashes Tabasco sauce
Cayenne pepper, to taste
Curry powder, for garnish

Combine all ingredients except the curry powder with cracked ice in a cocktail shaker. Shake well and pour into a chilled highball glass. Sprinkle with curry powder. Serves one.

146 calories; 0.1 gm fat; 1% calories from fat; 0 mg cholesterol; 14 mg sodium; 37.7 gm carbohydrate; 0.6 gm protein; 40.4 mg calcium; 1.5 mg iron; 3 RE vitamin A; 26.9 mg vitamin C

PEPPER POT

PERSEPHONE'S SLIP

8 parts pear juice (4 oz.)
8 parts pomegranate
  juice (4 oz.)
4 parts fresh-squeezed orange
  juice (2 oz.)
4 parts white grape juice (2 oz.)
Orange slice, for garnish

Combine juices with cracked ice in a cocktail shaker and shake well. Strain into a chilled highball glass and garnish with the orange slice. Serves one.

186 calories; 0.4 gm fat; 2% calories from fat; 0 mg cholesterol; 8.8 mg sodium; 37.7 gm carbohydrate; 1.6 gm protein; 18.8 mg calcium; 0.8 mg iron; 11.8 RE vitamin A; 26.9 mg vitamin C

PETER PIPER

8 parts bell-pepper juice
  (4 oz.)
6 parts apple juice (3 oz.)
4 parts carrot juice (2 oz.)
Carrot stick, for garnish

Combine juices with cracked ice in a cocktail shaker and shake well. Strain over ice cubes into a chilled collins glass and garnish with the carrot stick. Serves one.

95 calories; 0.2 gm fat; 2% calories from fat; 0 mg cholesterol; 16.6 mg sodium; 23.2 gm carbohydrate; 0.6 gm protein; 19.6 mg calcium; 2 mg iron; 1,500 RE vitamin A; 63.7 mg vitamin C

PINEAPPLE DREAM

6 parts coconut milk (3 oz.)
6 parts crushed pineapple (3 oz.)
1 tbsp. honey
Pineapple spear, for garnish

Combine all ingredients except
pineapple spear with cracked ice in a
blender and blend until slushy. Pour
into a chilled wineglass and garnish
with the pineapple spear. Serves one.

*328 calcium; 24.2 gm fat; 65%
calories from fat; 0 mg cholesterol;
13.8 mg sodium; 26.7 gm carbohydrate; 2.8 gm protein; 21.5 mg calcium; 1.6 mg iron; 1.3 RE vitamin
A; 6.7 mg vitamin C*

PINEAPPLE SPARKLER

PINEAPPLE PASSION

8 parts pineapple juice
   (4 oz.)
6 parts passion-fruit juice (3 oz.)
4 parts fresh-squeezed orange
   juice (2 oz.)
Pineapple spear, for garnish

Combine juices with cracked ice in a
cocktail shaker and shake well. Strain
over ice cubes into a chilled collins
glass and garnish with the pineapple
spear. Serves one.

*132 calories; 0.2 gm fat; 2% calo-
ries from fat; 0 mg cholesterol; 6.7
mg sodium; 33.1 gm carbohydrate;
1.1 gm protein; 28.6 mg calcium;
0.6 mg iron; 72.8 RE vitamin A;
65.9 mg vitamin C*

PINEAPPLE SPARKLER

8 parts pineapple juice (4 oz.)
1 part sugar syrup (½ oz.)
Sparkling mineral water
Lime slice, for garnish

Combine ingredients except the
sparkling mineral water and the lime
slice with cracked ice in a cocktail
shaker and shake well. Pour over ice
cubes into a chilled collins glass. Fill
the glass with the sparkling mineral
water and stir gently. Garnish with the
lime slice. Serves one.

*101 calories; 0.1 gm fat; 1% calo-
ries from fat; 0 mg cholesterol; 2.3
mg sodium; 23.6 gm carbohydrate;
0.4 gm protein; 27.8 mg calcium;
0.8 mg iron; 0.5 RE vitamin A;
12.2 mg vitamin C*

PINEAPPLE ZAP

8 parts pineapple juice
   (4 oz.)
4 parts carrot juice (2 oz.)
4 parts fresh-squeezed orange
   juice (2 oz.)
1 tsp. ginger juice

Combine juices with cracked ice in a
cocktail shaker and shake well. Strain
over ice cubes into a chilled highball
glass. Serves one.

*118 calcium; 1 gm fat; 3 % calories
from fat; 0 mg cholesterol; 18.6 mg
sodium; 28.2 gm carbohydrate;
1.5 gm protein; 41.1 mg calcium;
0.9 mg iron; 1,472 RE vitamin A;
45.4 mg vitamin C*

PINEAPPLE-CHERRY SPARKLER

8 parts pineapple juice (4 oz.)
Natural cherry soda
Pineapple spear, for garnish

Pour pineapple juice over ice cube into a chilled collins glass. Fill the glass with the cherry soda and stir gently. Garnish with the pineapple spear. Serves one.

87 calories; 0.3 gm fat; 3% calories from fat; 0 mg cholesterol; 5.6 mg sodium; 21.1 gm carbohydrate; 0.5 gm protein; 19.3 mg calcium; 0.3 mg iron; 0.5 RE vitamin A; 12.1 mg vitamin C

PINEAPPLE-GRAPEFRUIT SWIRL

6 parts grapefruit juice (3 oz.)
6 parts pineapple juice (3 oz.)
2 parts grenadine (1 oz.)
Fresh mint sprig, for garnish

Combine juices with cracked ice in a cocktail shaker and shake well. Strain into a chilled highball glass. Slowly pour grenadine into drink, creating a swirling effect. Do not stir. Garnish with the fresh mint sprig. Serves one.

155 calories; 0.2 gm fat; 1% calories from fat; 0 mg cholesterol; 3.1 mg sodium; 38.8 gm carbohydrate; 0.7 gm protein; 39 mg calcium; 1.4 mg iron; 1.3 RE vitamin A; 41.5 mg vitamin C

PINEAPPLE-MANGO WHITE-OUT

10 parts pineapple juice
   (5 oz.)
6 parts mango juice (3 oz.)
2 parts fresh-squeezed lime
   juice (1 oz.)
2 scoops vanilla frozen yogurt

Combine all ingredients in a blender and blend until smooth. Pour into chilled wineglasses. Serves two.

185 calcium; 4.1 gm fat; 19% calories from fat; 2 mg cholesterol; 64.7 mg sodium; 35.7 gm carbohydrate; 3.3 gm protein; 120.6 mg calcium; 0.5 mg iron; 207.1 RE vitamin A; 24.1 mg vitamin C

PINEAPPLE-MINT SOUR

6 fresh mint leaves
8 parts pineapple juice (4 oz.)
Bitter-lemon soda
Fresh mint sprig, for garnish

Mash the mint leaves in the bottom of a chilled collins glass. Add the pineapple juice and stir. Add a few ice cubes and fill with the bitter-lemon soda. Stir gently and garnish with the mint sprig. Serves one.

86 calories; 0.1 gm fat; 1% calories from fat; 0 mg cholesterol; 7.4 mg sodium; 21.5 gm carbohydrate; 0.4 gm protein; 20.4 mg calcium; 0.3 mg iron; 0.5 RE vitamin A; 12.2 mg vitamin C

PINEAPPLE-ORANGE PUNCH

1 quart strong, unsweetened
   black tea (32 oz.)
32 parts fresh-squeezed orange
   juice (16 oz.)
32 parts pineapple juice (16 oz.)
8 parts fresh-squeezed lemon
   juice (4 oz.)
2 liters ginger ale
Orange slices, for garnish

Combine the tea and juices in a large punch bowl and add ice. Just before serving, add ginger ale and float orange slices on top. Serves twenty-five.

48 calories; 0.1 gm fat; 1% calories from fat; 0 mg cholesterol; 7.2 mg sodium; 12 gm carbohydrate; 0.2 gm protein; 7.9 mg calcium; 0.2 mg iron; 3.8 RE vitamin A; 13.1 mg vitamin C

PINEAPPLE-RASPBERRY FRAPPE

12 parts pineapple juice (6 oz.)
8 parts fresh raspberries (4 oz.)
1 banana, peeled and sliced
Pineapple spear, for garnish

Combine all ingredients except the pineapple spear in a blender and blend until smooth. If drink is too thick, add more pineapple juice until desired consistency is achieved. Pour into a chilled collins glass and garnish with the pineapple spear. Serves one.

228 calories; 1 gm fat; 4% calories from fat; 0 mg cholesterol; 2.7 mg sodium; 56.7 gm carbohydrate; 2.2 gm protein; 48.4 mg calcium; 1.1 mg iron; 17.4 RE vitamin A; 42.7 mg vitamin C

PINEAPPLE-STRAWBERRY SODA

8 parts pineapple juice (4 oz.)
6 parts strawberry puree (3 oz.)
Sparkling mineral water
Pineapple spear, for garnish
1 whole strawberry, for garnish

Combine pineapple juice and puree with cracked ice in a cocktail shaker and shake well. Pour over ice cubes into a chilled collins glass and fill the glass with the sparkling mineral water. Stir gently and garnish with the pineapple spear and the whole strawberry. Serves one.

98 calories; 0.5 gm fat; 4% calories from fat; 0 mg cholesterol; 2.3 mg sodium; 23.6 gm carbohydrate; 1.1 gm protein; 35.2 mg calcium; 0.7 mg iron; 3.7 RE vitamin A; 76.5 mg vitamin C

PINK GRAPEFRUIT

8 parts grapefruit juice
    (4 oz.)
8 parts guava juice (4 oz.)

Combine juice with cracked ices in a cocktail shaker and shake well. Strain into a chilled highball glass. Serves one.

117 calories; 1 gm fat; 7% calories from fat; 0 mg cholesterol; 5.4 mg sodium; 27.3 gm carbohydrate; 1.7 gm protein; 38.5 mg calcium; 0.7 mg iron; 113.4 RE vitamin A; 303 mg vitamin C

PINK PEACH

8 parts peach juice (4 oz.)
4 parts unsweetened cherry
    juice (2 oz.)
½ tsp. alcohol-free almond extract

Combine ingredients with cracked ice in a cocktail shaker and shake well. Strain into a chilled wineglass, and add ice if desired. Serves one.

122 calories; 0.8 gm fat; 6% calories from fat; 0 mg cholesterol; 7.7 mg sodium; 30 gm carbohydrate; 1.3 gm protein; 18.4 mg calcium; 0.5 mg iron; 47.5 RE vitamin A; 12 mg vitamin C

PINK PEAR TREAT

10 parts pear juice (5 oz.)
4 parts unsweetened cherry cider (2 oz.)

Combine juices in a mixing glass and stir well. Pour over ice cubes into a chilled highball glass. Serves one.

146 calories; 0.8 gm fat; 5% calories from fat; 0 mg cholesterol; 5.1 mg sodium; 36.5 gm carbohydrate; 1.2 gm protein; 18.7 mg calcium; 0.7 mg iron; 18.3 RE vitamin A; 7.5 mg vitamin C

PINK PINEAPPLE

12 parts pineapple juice (6 oz.)
6 parts cranberry juice
    cocktail (3 oz.)
½ tsp. alcohol-free almond extract
Pineapple spear, for garnish

Combine all ingredients except pineapple spear over ice cubes in a cocktail shaker and shake well. Strain over ice cubes into a chilled highball glass and garnish with the pineapple spear. Serves one.

144 calories; 0.2 gm fat; 1% calories from fat; 0 mg cholesterol; 5.1 mg sodium; 35.7 gm carbohydrate; 0.5 gm protein; 31.5 mg calcium; 0.6 mg iron; 0.8 RE vitamin A; 7.5 mg vitamin C

PIXIE

8 parts apricot juice (4 oz.)
8 parts honeydew melon
   juice (4 oz.)
Sparkling white grape juice

Combine apricot and melon juices with cracked ice in a cocktail shaker and shake well. Pour mixture into chilled wineglasses and fill the glasses with the sparkling grape juice. Stir gently. Serves two.

65 calories; 0.1 gm fat; 2% calories from fat; 0 mg cholesterol; 9.2 mg sodium; 16.8 gm carbohydrate; 0.6 gm protein; 9.5 mg calcium; 0.3 mg iron; 77.7 RE vitamin A; 36.5 mg vitamin C

POKER-FLAT FRAPPE

12 parts Limeade (6 oz.) (see Limeade, page 126)
1 tsp. alcohol-free almond extract
1 scoop lemon sorbet
Lime-flavored sparkling mineral water
Lime twist, for garnish

Combine all ingredients except the sparkling mineral water and the lime twist in a blender and blend until smooth. Pour into a a chilled collins glass and fill the glass with the sparkling mineral water. Stir gently and garnish with the lime twist. Serves one.

130 calories; 0 gm fat; 0% calories from fat; 0 mg cholesterol; 2 mg sodium; 34.8 gm carbohydrate; 0 gm protein; 3.4 mg calcium; 0.1 mg iron; 0.5 RE vitamin A; 13 mg vitamin C

POMEGRANATE FREEZE

12 parts pomegranate juice (6 oz.)
10 parts grapefruit juice (5 oz.)
2 parts white grape juice (1 oz.)

Combine ingredients with cracked ice in a blender and blend until slushy. Pour into chilled old-fashioned glasses. Serves two.

114 calories; 0.4 gm fat; 3% calories from fat; 0 mg cholesterol; 4.5 mg sodium; 28 gm carbohydrate; 1.5 gm protein; 11 mg calcium; 0.5 mg iron; 0.8 RE vitamin A; 33.9 mg vitamin C

POMEGRANATE SPARKLER

8 parts pomegranate
   juice (4 oz.)
1 tsp. fresh-squeezed lemon juice
Sparkling white grape juice
Lemon twist, for garnish

Combine juices with cracked ice in a cocktail shaker and shake well. Strain into a chilled wineglass and fill the glass with the sparkling grape juice. Stir gently and garnish with the lemon twist. Serves one.

115 calories; 0.4 gm fat; 3% calories from fat; 0 mg cholesterol; 5.2 mg sodium; 29 gm carbohydrate; 1.5 gm protein; 7.2 mg calcium; 0.5 mg iron; 0.3 RE vitamin A; 11 mg vitamin C

POMO PUNCH

8 parts pomegranate
   juice (4 oz.)
8 parts cantaloupe juice (4 oz.)
1 tbsp. fresh-squeezed lime juice
Lime slice, for garnish

Combine juices in a blender and blend until smooth. Pour into a chilled collins glass and garnish with the lime slice. Serves one.

141 calories; 0.8 gm fat; 4% calories from fat; 0 mg cholesterol; 14.6 mg sodium; 35.2 gm carbohydrate; 2.4 gm protein; 18.1 mg calcium; 365.9 RE vitamin A; 61 mg vitamin C

163

POND SCUM

1 tbsp. fresh-squeezed lime juice
1 tsp. sugar
Ginger beer
Fresh mint sprig, for garnish

Combine the lime juice and sugar in the bottom of a chilled pilsner glass. Fill the glass with the ginger beer and stir gently. Garnish with the mint sprig. Serves one.

88 calories; 0 gm fat; 0% calories from fat; 0 mg cholesterol; 14.1 mg sodium; 22.8 gm carbohydrate; 0.1 gm protein; 18.1 mg calcium; 0.7 mg iron; 365.9 RE vitamin A; 61 mg vitamin C

PONY EXPRESS

10 parts tomato juice
  (5 oz.)
8 parts carrot juice (4 oz.)
6 parts celery juice (3 oz.)
4 parts broccoli juice (2 oz.)
4 parts turnip juice (2 oz.)
1 part beet juice (½ oz.)
1 tbsp. fresh-squeezed lemon juice
1 tbsp. fresh-squeezed lime juice

Combine all ingredients in a blender and blend until smooth. Pour into chilled highball glasses. Serves two.

62 calories; 0.3 gm fat; 4% calories from fat; 0 mg cholesterol; 14.1 mg sodium; 22.8 gm carbohydrate; 0.1 gm protein; 7.4 mg calcium; 0.3 mg iron; 0.2 RE vitamin A; 4.5 mg vitamin C

POP DRINK '95

Sparkling apple cider
1 tbsp. blackberry syrup
Lime twist, for garnish

Fill a chilled wineglass with the sparkling apple cider and add the syrup. Stir gently and garnish with the lime slice. Serves one.

107 calories; 0.1 gm fat; 1% calories from fat; 0 mg cholesterol; 4.4 mg sodium; 28.8 gm carbohydrate; 0.1 gm protein; 18.4 mg calcium; 1.3 mg iron; 0 RE vitamin A; 1.1 mg vitamin C

POPEYE'S PUNCH

10 parts spinach juice (5 oz.)
8 parts carrot juice (4 oz.)
Carrot sticks, for garnish

Combine juices in a blender and mix well. Pour into chilled old-fashioned glasses and garnish with the carrot sticks. Serves two.

39 calories; 0.4 gm fat; 9% calories from fat; 0 mg cholesterol; 35.3 mg sodium; 7.7 gm carbohydrate; 2.5 gm protein; 103.4 mg calcium; 1.9 mg iron; 2,082 RE vitamin A; 14.9 mg vitamin C

POWER SHOT

4 parts spinach juice (2 oz.)
4 parts wheatgrass juice
  (2 oz.)

Combine juices in a cocktail shaker and shake well. Pour into a chilled shot glass. Serves one.

13 calories; 0.3 gm fat; 15% calories from fat; 0 mg cholesterol; 15.1 mg sodium; 1.9 gm carbohydrate; 1.6 gm protein; 71.8 mg calcium; 1.3 mg iron; 497.6 RE vitamin A; 0.1 mg vitamin C

PRUNE FREEZER

12 parts prune juice (6 oz.)
2 scoops vanilla frozen yogurt
Cream soda

Combine prune juice and yogurt in a blender and blend until smooth. Pour mixture into chilled highball glasses and fill the glasses with cream soda. Stir gently. Serves two.

189 calories; 4 gm fat; 19% calories from fat; 2 mg cholesterol; 69.8 mg sodium; 36 gm carbohydrate; 3.3 gm protein; 114.6 mg calcium; 1.2 mg iron; 41.3 RE vitamin A; 4.1 mg vitamin C

PRUNE MORNING SMOOTHIE

8 parts prune juice (4 oz.)
8 parts nonfat yogurt (4 oz.)
4 parts fresh-squeezed orange
   juice (2 oz.)
1 banana, sliced

Combine all ingredients in a blender
and blend until smooth. If mixture
is too thick, add more prune juice
until desired consistency is achieved.
Pour into chilled highball glasses.
Serves two.

*136 calories; 0.3 gm fat; 2% calo-
ries from fat; 43 mg sodium;
30.8 gm carbohydrate; 4.4 gm protein; 125.8 mg calcium; 0.9 mg
iron; 10.5 RE vitamin A; 21.7 mg
vitamin C*

PRUNE WHIP

12 parts prune juice (6 oz.)
1 scoop vanilla ice cream

Combine juice and ice cream in a
blender and blend until smooth but
not watery. Pour into frosted glass
and serve with a drinking straw.
Serves one.

*213 calories; 5.7 gm fat; 23% calo-
ries from fat; 39 mg cholesterol;
32.8 mg sodium; 39.3 gm carbohydrate; 32.8 mg sodium; 39.3 gm
carbohydrate; 2.8 gm protein; 77
mg calcium; 2.1 mg iron; 67.1 RE
vitamin A; 7.3 mg vitamin C*

PUCKER UPPER

10 parts lemonade (5 oz.)
   (see Traditional
   Lemonade, page 207)
1 tsp. fresh-squeezed lemon juice
1 scoop lemon sorbet
Lemon slice, for garnsih

Combine lemonade and lemon juice
in a mixing glass and stir well. Place
lemon sorbet in a chilled wineglass
and add lemonade mixture. Garnish
with the lemon slice. Serves one.

*167 calories; 0 gm fat; 0% calories
from fat; 0 mg cholesterol; 0.1 mg
sodium; 44.4 gm carbohydrate;
0.2 gm protein; 4 mg calcium;
0 mg iron; 1 RE vitamin A; 23.3
mg vitamin C*

PUMPKIN PIE

16 parts apple juice (8 oz.)
8 parts pumpkin
   puree (4 oz.)
1 tbsp. fresh-squeezed lemon juice
1 tbsp. maple syrup
1½ tsp. pumpkin pie spice
½ tsp. alcohol-free vanilla extract

Combine all ingredients in a blender
and blend until frothy. Pour into
chilled wineglasses. Serves two.

*102 calories; 0.2 gm fat; 2% calo-
ries from fat; 0 mg cholesterol; 7.3
mg sodium; 25 gm carbohydrate;
0.7 gm protein; 33.2 mg calcium;
1.3 mg iron; 1,250 RE vitamin A;
52.4 mg vitamin C*

PUMPKIN SHAKE

16 parts apple juice (8 oz.)
10 parts pumpkin
   puree (5 oz.)
2–3 scoops vanilla ice cream
1 tbsp. fresh-squeezed lemon juice
2 tsp. pumpkin pie spice
1 tsp. maple syrup

Combine all ingredients in a blender
and blend until smooth. Pour into
chilled highball glasses. Serves two.

*180 calories; 5.9 gm fat; 28% calo-
ries from fat; 39 mg cholesterol;
33.4 mg sodium; 31.3 gm carbohydrate; 2.6 gm protein; 86.7 mg
calcium; 1.5 mg iron; 1,629 RE
vitamin A; 53.2 mg vitamin C*

PURPLE HAZE

4 parts blueberry juice
   (2 oz.)
4 parts coconut milk (2 oz.)
4 parts strawberry juice or
   puree (2 oz.)

Combine all ingredients with cracked
ice in a cocktail shaker. Strain into
a chilled old-fashioned glass.
Serves one.

*224 calories; 16.6 gm fat; 65%
calories from fat; 0 mg cholesterol;
13.6 mg sodium; 17.7 gm carbohydrate; 2.5 gm protein; 18.2 mg
calcium; 1.1 mg iron; 10.1 RE
vitamin A; 43.2 mg vitamin C*

PURPLE LEMONADE

4 parts apricot nectar (2 oz.)
2 parts black-currant syrup
  (1 oz.)
1 tbsp. fresh-squeezed lime juice
Lemonade (see Traditional
  Lemonade, page 207)
Fresh mint sprig, for garnish

Combine all the ingredients except the
lemonade and mint with cracked ice
in a cocktail shaker and shake well.
Strain over ice cubes into a chilled
collins glass and fill the glass with the
lemonade. Stir and garnish with the
mint sprig. Serves one.

*196 calories; 0 gm fat; 0% calories
from fat; 0 mg cholesterol; 5.1 mg
sodium; 52 gm carbohydrate;
0.5 gm protein; 42.5 mg calcium;
2.3 mg iron; 75.9 RE vitamin A;
44.4 mg vitamin C*

PURPLE PASSION

8 parts concord grape juice
  (4 oz.)
8 parts passion-fruit juice (4 oz.)
2 parts fresh-squeezed lime
  juice (1 oz.)
Lime slices, for garnish

Combine juices with cracked ice in a
cocktail shaker and shake well. Strain
into chilled cocktail glasses and garnish with the lime slices. Serves two.

*72 calories; 0 gm fat; 0% calories
from fat; 0 mg cholesterol; 5.2 mg
sodium; 18 gm carbohydrate; 0.8
gm protein; 8.7 mg calcium; 0.3
mg iron; 137.2 RE vitamin A; 14.5
mg vitamin C*

PURPLE
PEOPLE-EATER

8 parts concord grape juice
  (4 oz.)
1 part fresh-squeezed lime
  juice (½ oz.)
Sparkling mineral water
Lime slice, for garnish

Combine juices with cracked ice in a
cocktail shaker and shake well. Pour
over ice cubes into a chilled collins
glass. Fill the glass with the sparkling
mineral water and stir gently. Garnish
with the lime slice. Serves one.

*73 calories; 0.1 gm fat; 1% calories
from fat; 0 mg cholesterol; 3.5 mg
sodium; 18.2 gm carbohydrate;
0.7 gm protein; 11.5 mg calcium;
0.3 mg iron; 1 RE vitamin A;
4.3 mg vitamin C*

PURPLE RAIN

10 parts pear juice (5 oz.)
8 parts blueberry juice (4 oz.)
½ tsp. alcohol-free vanilla extract
Fresh blueberries, for garnish

Combine ingredients except fresh
blueberries with cracked ice in a
blender and blend until slushy. Pour
into a chilled highball glass and garnish with fresh blueberries. Serves one.

*171 calories; 0.6 gm fat; 3% calo-
ries from fat; 0 mg cholesterol; 13.6
mg sodium; 43.1 gm carbohydrate;
1.1 gm protein; 14.7 mg calcium;
0.6 mg iron; 14.2 RE vitamin A;
20 mg vitamin C*

PURPLE PEOPLE-EATER

PUT DE LIME IN DE COCONUT

6 parts coconut milk (3 oz.)
4 parts fresh-squeezed lime
   juice (2 oz.)
Sparkling mineral water
Fresh mint sprig, for garnish

Combine coconut milk and lime juice
in a cocktail shaker and shake well.
Pour over ice cubes into a chilled
collins glass. Fill the with the
sparkling mineral water and stir
gently. Garnish with the mint sprig.
Serves one.

*252 calories; 24.2 gm fat; 84%
calories from fat; 0 mg cholesterol;
12.5 mg sodium; 7.6 gm carbohydrate; 3.6 gm protein; 12.8 mg calcium; 1.1 mg iron; 0.6 RE vitamin
A; 16.6 mg vitamin C*

QUESTION MARK

12 parts apple cider (6 oz.)
8 parts nonfat yogurt (4 oz.)
4 parts fresh-squeezed lemon
   juice (2 oz.)
1 tbsp. bee pollen

Combine all ingredients in a blender
and blend well. Pour into a chilled
collins glass. Serves one.

*159 calories; 0.2 gm fat; 1% calo-
ries from fat; 2.5 mg cholesterol;
85.6 mg sodium; 37.4 gm carbohydrate; 6.8 gm protein; 239 mg calcium; 0.9 mg iron; 1.1 RE vitamin
A; 27.7 mg vitamin C*

*(Bee pollen not included in nutri-
tional analysis.)*

QUIET PASSION

QUICK-AND-FANCY
LEMONADE FOR
UNEXPECTED COMPANY

1 can frozen lemonade concentrate
16 parts unsweetened cherry
   cider (8 oz.)
8 parts unsweetened cranberry
   juice (4 oz.)
Lemon slices, for garnish
Lime slices, for garnish

Prepare lemonade according to the
instructions on can. Pour into a large
punch bowl. Add cherry cider and
cranberry juice and stir well. Add ice.
Float lemon and lime slices on top.
Serve in highball glasses over ice
cubes. Serves twelve.

*73 calories; 0.3 gm fat; 4% calories
from fat; 0 mg cholesterol; 5.1 mg
sodium; 18.2 gm carbohydrate;
0.4 gm protein; 15 mg calcium; 0.2
mg iron; 6.7 RE vitamin A; 3.9 mg
vitamin C*

QUIET PASSION

8 parts white grape juice (4 oz.)
8 parts grapefruit juice (4 oz.)
2 parts passion-fruit juice (1 oz.)

Combine ingredients with cracked ice
in a cocktail shaker and shake well.
Strain over ice cubes into a chilled
collins glass. Serves one.

*130 calories; 0.3 gm fat; 2% calo-
ries from fat; 0 mg cholesterol; 6.2
mg sodium; 31.5 gm carbohydrate;
1.4 gm protein; 21.3 mg calcium;
0.6 mg iron; 70.3 RE vitamin A;
48.4 mg vitamin C*

R

RABBIT SEASON

8 parts apple juice (4 oz.)
6 parts celery juice (3 oz.)
4 parts spinach juice (2 oz.)
2 parts parsley juice (1 oz.)

Combine all ingredients with cracked ice in a cocktail shaker and shake well. Strain over ice cubes into a chilled collins glass. Serves one.

91 calories; 0.8 gm fat; 7% calories from fat; 0 mg cholesterol; 108 mg sodium; 20 gm carbohydrate; 3.1 gm protein; 152.6 mg calcium; 3.8 mg iron; 656.1 RE vitamin A; 98.3 mg vitamin C

RADICAL TOMATO

10 parts tomato juice (5 oz.)
4 parts cucumber juice (2 oz.)
3 parts red radish juice (1½ oz.)
1 tsp. fresh-squeezed lime juice
Cucumber slices, for garnish

Combine juices in a blender and blend until smooth. Pour over ice cubes into chilled old-fashioned glasses. Garnish with the cucumber slices. Serves two.

21 calories; 0.2 gm fat; 8% calories from fat; 0 mg cholesterol; 262.8 mg sodium; 5.1 gm carbohydrate; 0.9 gm protein; 16.5 mg calcium; 0.6 mg iron; 41.2 RE vitamin A; 14.2 mg vitamin C

RAISIN-ABLE DOUBT

12 parts fresh-squeezed orange juice (6 oz.)
8 parts rehydrated raisins (4 oz.)
1 banana, sliced
1 scoop vanilla frozen yogurt
½ tsp. alcohol-free almond extract
Raisins, for garnish

Combine all ingredients except four raisins in a blender and blend until smooth. Pour into a chilled collins glass and sprinkle with remaining raisins. Serves one.

635 calories; 5.3 gm fat; 7% calories from fat; 2 mg cholesterol; 79 mg sodium; 149.7 gm carbohydrate; 8.9 gm protein; 196.6 mg calcium; 3.3 mg iron; 86 RE vitamin A; 99.8 mg vitamin C

RASPBERRY BRACER

8 parts raspberry juice or puree (4 oz.)
6 parts peach juice (3 oz.)
4 parts fresh-squeezed orange juice (2 oz.)
Orange slice, for garnish

Combine juices with cracked ice in a cocktail shaker and shake well. Strain into chilled highball glass and garnish with the orange slice. Serves one.

127 calories; 0.8 gm fat; 5% calories from fat; 0 mg cholesterol; 6.3 mg sodium; 30.9 gm carbohydrate; 1.7 gm protein; 35.6 mg calcium; 0.9 mg iron; 48.1 RE vitamin A; 61.2 mg vitamin C

RASPBERRY FREEZE

8 parts raspberry juice (4 oz.)
2 parts raspberry syrup (1 oz.)
1 tsp. fresh-squeezed lemon juice
Fresh raspberries, for garnish

Combine all ingredients except fresh raspberries with cracked ice in a blender and blend until slushy. Pour into a chilled wineglass and garnish with fresh raspberries. Serves one.

131 calories; 0.6 gm fat; 4% calories from fat; 0 mg cholesterol; 1.5 mg sodium; 32.8 gm carbohydrate; 1 gm protein; 42.3 mg calcium; 1.6 mg iron; 14.9 RE vitamin A; 30.7 mg vitamin C

RASPBERRY GINGER ALE

6 parts raspberry juice (3 oz.)
1 part ginger juice (½ oz.)
Ginger ale
Lemon wedge, for garnish

Combine juices in a mixing glass.
Pour over ice cubes into a chilled
collins glass. Fill the glass with the
ginger ale and stir gently. Garnish
with the lemon wedge. Serves one.

*101 calories; 0.5 gm fat; 4% calo-
ries from fat; 0 mg cholesterol; 6.5
mg sodium; 25.4 gm carbohydrate;
0.8 gm protein; 20.4 mg calcium;
0.9 mg iron; 11.9 RE vitamin A;
22.1 mg vitamin C*

RASPBERRY PARADE

8 parts raspberry puree
   (4 oz.)
4 parts fresh-squeezed orange
   juice (2 oz.)
2 parts fresh-squeezed lime
   juice (1 oz.)
1 scoop raspberry sorbet
Fresh raspberries, for garnish

Combine juices, puree, and sorbet in a
blender and blend until smooth. Pour
into a chilled collins glass and garnish with fresh raspberries.

*215 calories; 1.1 gm fat; 4% calo-
ries from fat; 0 mg cholesterol; 1.1
mg sodium; 53.7 gm carbohydrate;
2.1 gm protein; 47.5 mg calcium;
1.1 mg iron; 34.4 RE vitamin A;
80.5 mg vitamin C*

RASPBERRY REVOLUTION

8 parts raspberry
   juice (4 oz.)
4 parts fresh-squeezed orange
   juice (2 oz.)
1 tsp. fresh-squeezed lemon juice
1 tsp. coconut syrup
Sparkling mineral water
Lemon slice, for garnish

Combine all ingredients except
sparkling mineral water and lemon
slice in a blender and blend until

smooth. Pour over ice cubes into a
chilled collins glass and fill the glass
with the sparkling mineral water. Stir
gently and garnish with the lemon
slice. Serves one.

*99 calories; 0.7 gm fat; 6% calories
from fat; 0 mg cholesterol; 0.8 mg
sodium; 23.8 gm carbohydrate;
1.5 gm protein; 35.4 mg calcium;
0.9 mg iron; 26.2 RE vitamin A;
59.1 mg vitamin C*

RASPBERRY SHAKE

8 parts raspberries frozen (4 oz.)
12 parts nonfat yogurt (6 oz.)
1 tbsp. unsweetened raspberry
   preserves
Nonfat milk

Combine all ingredients except milk
in a blender and blend until smooth.
Pour into a chilled collins glass. For
a thinner shake, add nonfat milk until
desired consistency is achieved.
Serves one.

*196 calories; 1.1 gm fat; 5% calo-
ries from fat; 4.7 mg cholesterol;
149.1 mg sodium; 36.4 gm carbohydrate; 13.3 gm protein; 445.6 mg
calcium; 1 mg iron; 57.5 RE vitamin A; 44.4 mg vitamin C*

RASPBERRY TINGLER

8 parts raspberry juice
   (4 oz.)
2 parts fresh-squeezed lemon
   juice (1 oz.)
Sparkling mineral water
Lime slice, for garnish

Combine juices with cracked ice in a
mixing glass and stir well. Strain over
ice cubes into a chilled highball glass
and fill the glass with the sparkling
mineral water. Garnish with the lime
slice. Serves one.

*63 calories; 0.6 gm fat; 8% calories
from fat; 0 mg cholesterol; 0.3 mg
sodium; 15.5 gm carbohydrate; 1.1
gm protein; 27 mg calcium; 0.7 mg
iron; 15.3 RE vitamin A; 41.4 mg
vitamin C*

RASPBERRY-MANGO ECSTASY

8 parts mango nectar
  (4 oz.)
8 parts raspberry juice (4 oz.)
1 tbsp. honey
1 banana, sliced
White grape juice (optional)

Combine ingredients in a blender and blend until smooth. If mixture is too thick, add white grape juice until desired consistency is achieved. Pour into chilled highball glasses. Serves two.

165 calories; 0.9 gm fat; 4% calories from fat; 0 mg cholesterol; 2.4 mg sodium; 42.2 gm carbohydrate; 1.6 gm protein; 26.8 mg calcium; 0.7 mg iron; 289.8 RE vitamin A; 42.6 mg vitamin C

(White grape juice not included in nutritional analysis.)

RAZZLE DAZZLE

8 parts raspberry puree,
  chilled (4 oz.)
8 parts blueberry puree, chilled (4 oz.)
8 parts blackberry puree, chilled
  (4 oz.)
8 oz. vanilla frozen yogurt
Raspberry soda
Fresh berries, for garnish

Combine purees and frozen yogurt in a blender and blend until slushy. Pour mixture into a chilled collins glasses. Slowly add raspberry soda to glasses, stirring gently. Garnish with fresh berries and serve with drinking straws. Serves two.

269 calories; 7 gm fat; 22% calories from fat; 3.2 mg cholesterol; 5.7 gm protein; 49.2 gm carbohydrate; 5.7 gm protein; 196.3 mg calcium; 1.1 mg iron; 87 RE vitamin A; 34.4 mg vitamin C

RED APPLE SUNSET

RED APPLE SUNSET

4 parts apple juice (2 oz.)
4 parts grapefruit juice
  (2 oz.)
3–5 dashes grenadine

Combine all ingredients with cracked ice in a cocktail shaker and shake well. Strain into a chilled cocktail glass. Serves one.

66 calories; 0.1 gm fat; 2% calories from fat; 0 mg cholesterol; 11.7 mg sodium; 16.2 gm carbohydrate; 0.3 gm protein; 12.9 mg calcium; 0.6 mg iron; 0.6 RE vitamin A; 44.8 mg vitamin C

RED FIZZ

4 parts red grape juice (2 oz.)
Ginger ale
Orange peel, for garnish

Pour grape juice into a chilled wine-glass and fill the with ginger ale. Stir gently and garnish with the orange peel. Serves one.

83 calories; 0 gm fat; 0% calories from fat; 0 mg cholesterol; 11.7 mg sodium; 20.8 gm carbohydrate; 0.3 gm protein; 9.4 mg calcium; 0.4 mg iron; 0.4 RE vitamin A; 0.1 mg vitamin C

RED LINE COOLER

4 parts unsweetened cherry
  cider (2 oz.)
8 parts fresh-squeezed orange
  juice (4 oz.)
Ginger ale
Bing cherry, for garnish

Combine all ingredients except ginger
ale and the bing cherry with cracked
ice in a cocktail shaker and shake
well. Strain over ice cubes into a
chilled highball glass. Fill the glass
with ginger ale and stir gently.
Garnish with the bing cherry.
Serves one.

*121 calories; 0.8 gm fat; 5% calories from fat; 0 mg cholesterol; 6.9
mg sodium; 28.6 gm carbohydrate;
1.5 gm protein; 23.2 mg calcium;
0.6 mg iron; 34.9 RE vitamin A;
60.7 mg vitamin C*

RED LINE COOLER

*2 gm protein; 20.2 mg calcium; 1.1
mg iron; 0.7 RE vitamin A; 56 mg
vitamin C*

RED MENACE

8 parts red grape juice (4 oz.)
Natural cherry soda

Pour grape juice over ice cubes into a
chilled collins glass. Fill glass with the
cherry soda and stir gently. Serves one.

*93 calories; 0.3 gm fat; 2% calories
from fat; 0 mg cholesterol; 7.9 mg
sodium; 22.4 gm carbohydrate;
0.8 gm protein; 10.2 mg calcium;
0.3 mg iron; 0.9 RE vitamin A;
0.1 mg vitamin C*

RED PLANET SQUISHY

8 parts apple juice (4 oz.)
6 parts red grape juice (3 oz.)
4 parts pomegranate juice (2 oz.)
Lemon slice, for garnish

Combine ingredients with cracked
ice in a blender and blend until
slushy. Pour into a chilled collins
glass and garnish with the lemon
slice. Serves one.

*210 calories; 0.7 gm fat; 3% calories from fat; 0 mg cholesterol; 10.6
mg sodium; 52.4 gm carbohydrate;*

REDWOOD HIGHWAY

8 parts apple juice (4 oz.)
8 parts peach juice (4 oz.)
4 parts white grape juice (2 oz.)
Lemon twist, for garnish

Combine juices with cracked ice in a
cocktail shaker and shake well. Pour
into a chilled collins glass and garnish with the lemon twist. Serves one.

*149 calories; 0.2 gm fat; 1% calories from fat; 0 mg cholesterol; 12.8
mg sodium; 37.5 gm carbohydrate;
0.7 gm protein; 19 mg calcium;
0.8 mg iron; 29.7 RE vitamin A;
52.6 mg vitamin C*

REFRIGERATOR CLEANER

8 parts tomato juice
  (4 oz.)
6 parts carrot juice (3 oz.)
4 parts red or green bell-pepper
  juice (2 oz.)
4 parts celery juice (2 oz.)
4 parts cucumber juice (2 oz.)
4 parts scallion juice (2 oz.)
4 parts fennel juice (2 oz.)
2 parts fresh-squeezed lemon
  juice (1 oz.)

REFRIGERATOR TEA

Combine all ingredients in a blender and blend until smooth. Pour into chilled old-fashioned glasses. Serves two.

57 calories; 0.3 gm fat; 4% calories from fat; 0 mg cholesterol; 257.6 mg sodium; 13.9 gm carbohydrate; 1.9 gm protein; 51.8 mg calcium; 0.8 mg iron; 1,138 RE vitamin A; 73.9 mg vitamin C

REFRIGERATOR TEA

60 parts water (30 oz.)
6 tsp. loose tea of your choice
10–15 fresh mint leaves, crushed
  (optional)
Sugar or honey, to taste

Combine loose tea and water (and mint leaves if desired) in a large glass jar and cover. Refrigerate overnight. Strain over ice cubes into a chilled collins glasses and sweeten to taste with sugar or honey. Serves five.

65 calories; 0 gm fat; 0% calories from fat; 0 mg cholesterol; 6.1 mg sodium; 17.7 gm carbohydrate; 0.1 gm protein; 1 mg calcium; 0.1 mg iron; 0 RE vitamin A; 0.2 mg vitamin C.

RHUBARB REFRESHER

10 parts apple juice (5 oz.)
10 parts pear juice (5 oz.)
8 parts cooked rhubarb (4 oz.)
8 parts strawberry puree (4 oz.)
2 tbsp. honey

Combine all ingredients in a blender and blend until smooth. If mixture is too thick, add more apple juice until desired consistency is achieved. Pour into chilled highball glasses. Serves two.

174 calories; 0.5 gm fat; 2% calories from fat; 0 mg cholesterol; 9.8 mg sodium; 44.5 gm carbohydrate; 1.3 gm protein; 90.3 mg calcium; 1.3 gm protein; 90.3 mg calcium; 1 mg iron; 9.9 RE vitamin A; 69.1 mg vitamin C

RICHTER SCALE

10 parts pineapple juice (5 oz.)
10 parts fresh-squeezed orange juice (5 oz.)
6 parts coconut milk (3 oz.)
2 parts fresh-squeezed lime juice (1 oz.)
3 scoops vanilla ice cream
1 tbsp. shredded coconut

Combine ingredients in a blender and blend until smooth. For a thinner shake, add more pineapple juice. Pour into chilled highball glasses. Serves two.

329 calories; 20.6 gm fat; 55% calories from fat; 50.7 mg cholesterol; 48.8 mg sodium; 33.5 gm carbohydrate; 4.3 gm protein; 98.8 mg calcium; 1.1 mg iron; 101.1 RE vitamin A; 47.6 mg vitamin C

ROAD RUNNER

6 parts carrot juice (3 oz.)
6 parts fresh-squeezed orange juice (3 oz.)
6 parts papaya juice (3 oz.)
6 parts pineapple juice (3 oz.)
1 tbsp. fresh-squeezed lime juice
Orange slices, for garnish

Combine juices in a blender and blend until smooth. Pour into chilled wineglasses and garnish with the orange slices. Serves two.

86 calories; 0.3 gm fat; 3% calories from fat; 0 mg cholesterol; 15.3 mg sodium; 21.1 gm carbohydrate; 0.9 gm protein; 27 mg calcium; 0.5 mg iron; 1,108 RE vitamin A; 33 mg vitamin C

ROADSIDE RASPBERRY FIZZ

8 parts fresh raspberries (4 oz.)
1 scoop raspberry sorbet
1 scoop lemon sorbet
Sparkling mineral water
Fresh raspberries, for garnish

Combine raspberries and sorbet in a blender and blend until smooth. Pour into highball glasses and fill the glasses with the sparkling mineral water. Stir gently and garnish with fresh raspberries. Serves two.

259 calories; 0.7 gm fat; 2% calories from fat; 0 mg cholesterol; 1.1 mg sodium; 66.3 gm carbohydrate; 1.2 gm protein; 28.7 mg calcium; 0.7 mg iron; 15.9 RE vitamin A; 43.6 mg vitamin C

ROARING CAMP COCKTAIL

6 parts sauerkraut juice (3 oz.)
4 parts tomato juice (2 oz.)
1 tsp. fresh-squeezed lemon juice
½ tsp. white horseradish
Pinch of hot paprika
Cocktail olive, for garnish

Combine all ingredients except the cocktail olive with cracked ice in a cocktail shaker and shake well. Strain into a chilled cocktail glass and garnish with the cocktail olive. Serves one.

30 calories; 0.2 gm fat; 4% calories from fat; 0 mg cholesterol; 849.1 mg sodium; 7.2 gm carbohydrate; 1.3 gm protein; 35.5 mg calcium; 1.6 mg iron; 33.4 RE vitamin A; 20.9 mg vitamin C

ROCKET SCIENTIST

8 parts apple juice (4 oz.)
6 parts blackberry juice
  (3 oz.)
2 parts unsweetened cherry
  juice (1 oz.)
Fresh blackberries, for garnish

Combine juices with cracked ice in a
cocktail shaker and shake well. Strain
over ice cubes into a chilled collins
glass and garnish with the fresh
blackberries. Serves one.

*118 calories; 0.7 gm fat; 5% calo-
ries from fat; 0 mg cholesterol;
3.4 mg sodium; 28.8 gm carbohydrate; 1 gm protein; 39.4 mg
calcium; 1 mg iron; 20.1 RE vitamin A; 66.4 mg vitamin C*

ROMAN REFRESHER

6 parts apple cider vinegar (or vinegar
  of your choice) (3 oz.)
Ginger ale or sparkling mineral water

Pour vinegar over ice cubes into a
chilled collins glass. Fill the glass
with the ginger ale and stir gently.
Serves one.

*41 calories; 0 gm fat; 0% calories
from fat; 0 mg cholesterol; 6.8 mg
sodium; 12.4 gm carbohydrate; 0
gm protein; 7.7 mg calcium; 0.7
mg iron; 0 RE vitamin A; 0 mg vitamin C*

*(Nutritional analysis calculated
with sparkling mineral water.)*

ROOT BEER FLOAT

3 scoops vanilla ice cream or
  frozen yogurt
Root beer

Put ice cream in a chilled collins
glass. Fill with root beer. Serve with a
drinking straw. Serves one.

*316 calories; 17.1 gm fat; 47%
calories from fat; 117 mg cholesterol; 84.7 mg sodium; 37.4 gm
carbohydrate; 5.5 gm protein;
169.5 mg calcium; 0.3 mg iron;
199.5 RE vitamin A; 0.9 mg vitamin C*

ROSY CHEEKS

8 parts cranberry juice
  cocktail (4 oz.)
8 parts pear juice (4 oz.)
4 parts apple juice (2 oz.)
1 tbsp. honey
½ tsp. cinnamon
Cinnamon sticks, for garnish

Combine all ingredients except cinnamon sticks with cracked ice in a
blender and blend until slushy. Pour
into chilled wineglasses and garnish
with the cinnamon sticks. Serves two.

*111 calories; 0.1 gm fat; 1% calo-
ries from fat; 0 mg cholesterol; 5.7
mg sodium; 29.1 gm carbohydrate;
0.1 gm protein; 8.1 mg calcium;
0.4 mg iron; 0 RE vitamin A; 32.5
mg vitamin C*

ROSY DAWN

4 parts fresh-squeezed
  orange juice (2 oz.)
2 parts fresh-squeezed lemon
  juice (1 oz.)
2 parts fresh-squeezed lime
  juice (1 oz.)
1 part cream of coconut (½ oz.)
1 tsp. grenadine
1 tsp. orgeat (almond) syrup

Combine all ingredients with cracked
ice in a blender and blend until
smooth. Pour into a chilled margarita
glass. Serves one.

ROSY DAWN

178 calories; 10 gm fat; 48% calories from fat; 0 mg cholesterol; 6.4 mg sodium; 23.6 gm carbohydrate; 0.7 gm protein; 19.4 mg calcium; 0.8 mg iron; 13.8 RE vitamin A; 49.7 mg vitamin C

ROUSTABOUT

10 parts apple juice
  (5 oz.)
6 parts celery juice (3 oz.)
1 tbsp. fresh-squeezed lemon juice
Celery stick, for garnish

Combine juices in a cocktail shaker with cracked ice and shake well. Strain into a chilled highball glass and garnish with the celery stick. Serves one.

89 calories; 0.3 gm fat; 3% calories from fat; 0 mg cholesterol; 102.9 mg sodium; 22 gm carbohydrate; 1 gm protein; 56.4 mg calcium; 1 mg iron; 15.1 RE vitamin A; 73.1 mg vitamin C

RUBY TUESDAY

8 parts unsweetened cherry
  juice (4 oz.)
1 tbsp. peppermint syrup
½ tsp. fresh-squeezed lemon juice
Fresh mint sprig, for garnish

Combine liquid ingredients with cracked ice in a cocktail shaker and shake well. Strain into a chilled cocktail glass and garnish with the mint sprig. Serves one.

154 calories; 1.4 gm fat; 7% calories from fat; 0 mg cholesterol; 1 mg sodium; 36.9 gm carbohydrate; 1.7 gm protein; 32.6 mg calcium; 1.2 mg iron; 30.5 RE vitamin A; 11.2 mg vitamin C

RUSSIAN RIVER SPARKLER

4 parts unsweetened cranberry
  juice (2 oz.)
4 parts grapefruit juice (2 oz.)
4 parts pineapple juice (2 oz.)
Ginger ale
Orange slice, for garnish

Combine juices in a mixing glass and stir until well-blended. Pour over ice cubes into a chilled collins glass and fill the glass with the ginger ale. Stir gently and garnish with the orange slice. Serves one.

115 calories; 0.3 gm fat; 2% calories from fat; 0 mg cholesterol; 5.9 mg sodium; 28.8 gm carbohydrate; 0.8 gm protein; 22.6 mg calcium; 0.5 mg iron; 4.7 RE vitamin A; 39.1 mg vitamin C

S

SACRAMENTO EXPRESS

12 parts tomato juice (6 oz.)
6 parts carrot juice (3 oz.)
2 parts fresh-squeezed lemon
juice (1 oz.)
1 part onion juice (½ oz.)
1 part parsley juice (½ oz.)
½ tsp. pureed garlic
½ tsp. pureed jalapeño pepper
3–5 dashes Worcestershire sauce
Salt, to taste
Freshly ground black pepper, to taste
Carrot sticks, for garnish

Combine all ingredients except salt, pepper, and carrot sticks in a blender and blend until well mixed. Pour over ice cubes into highball glasses. Add salt and pepper to taste and garnish with the carrot sticks. Serves two.

46 calories; 0.2 gm fat; 4% calories from fat; 0 mg cholesterol; 356.9 mg sodium; 10.9 gm carbohydrate; 1.7 gm protein; 43.1 mg calcium; 1.7 mg iron; 1,217 RE vitamin A; 38.2 mg vitamin C

SAFFRON-CITRUS ENCHANTMENT

12 parts fresh-squeezed orange
juice (6 oz.)
4 parts fresh-squeezed lemon
juice (2 oz.)
1 tbsp. honey
4 saffron threads
Lemon twist, for garnish

Combine all ingredients except lemon twist in a saucepan and simmer for about twenty minutes. Serve in a warmed mug and garnish with the lemon twist. Serves one.

108 calories; 0.1 gm fat; 1% calories from fat; 0 mg cholesterol; 19.1 mg sodium; 29.5 gm carbohydrate; 1.6 gm protein; 20.7 mg calcium; 1.2 mg iron; 96.7 RE vitamin A; 57.4 mg vitamin C

SALSA IN A GLASS

10 parts tomato juice
(5 oz.)
6 parts tomatillo juice (3 oz.)
2 parts fresh-squeezed lime
juice (1 oz.)
1 part onion juice (½ oz.)
1 tbsp. fresh cilantro, chopped
½ tsp. jalapeño pepper juice
½ tsp. pureed garlic
Freshly ground black pepper
Salt, to taste
Fresh cilantro sprigs, for garnish

Combine all ingredients except salt and cilantro sprigs in a blender and blend until well mixed. Pour over ice cubes into chilled highball glasses and add salt to taste. Garnish with the cilantro sprigs. Serves two.

20 calories; 0.1 gm fat; 3% calories from fat; 0 mg cholesterol; 301.8 mg sodium; 5.1 gm carbohydrate; 0.8 gm protein; 15.8 mg calcium; 0.6 mg iron; 71.8 RE vitamin A; 11.6 mg vitamin C

SALTY PUPPY

Coarse salt
Granulated sugar
Lime wedge
Grapefruit juice

Mix salt and sugar together in a saucer. Moisten rim of chilled old-fashioned glass with lime wedge. Dip the rim into the salt-sugar mixture and discard lime. Fill the glass with ice cubes and the grapefruit juice. Stir well. Serves one.

70 calories; 0.2 gm fat; 2% calories from fat; 0 mg cholesterol; 214.9 mg sodium; 16.5 gm carbohydrate; 0.9 gm protein; 16.8 gm calcium; 0.3 mg iron; 1.7 RE vitamin A; 64.7 mg vitamin C

SALTY PUPPY

SAN ANDREAS FAULT

8 parts nonfat plain
    yogurt (4 oz.)
8 parts fresh-squeezed orange
    juice (4 oz.)
½ tsp. jalapeño pepper juice
Salt, to taste
Freshly ground black pepper, to taste
Orange peel, for garnish

Combine yogurt and juices in a
blender and blend until smooth.
Season with salt and pepper to taste
and pour into a chilled collins glass.
Garnish with the orange peel. Serves
one.

*81 calories; 0.1 gm fat; 1% calories
from fat; 2.5 mg cholesterol; 174.3
mg sodium; 14 gm carbohydrate;
7.4 gm protein; 236.4 mg calcium;
0.9 mg iron; 68.5 RE vitamin A;
21.6 mg vitamin C*

SAN DIEGO FREEWAY

4 parts apple juice
    (2 oz.)
4 parts grapefruit juice (2 oz.)
4 parts fresh-squeezed orange
    juice (2 oz.)
4 parts pineapple juice (2 oz.)
4 parts tangerine juice (2 oz.)
1 part fresh-squeezed lime
    juice (½ oz.)
1 tsp. cilantro juice
Fresh cilantro sprig, for garnish

Combine juices with cracked ice in a
cocktail shaker and shake well. Strain
into a chilled cocktail glass and
garnish with the fresh cilantro.
Serves one.

*135 calories; 0.4 gm fat; 3% calo-
ries from fat; 0 mg cholesterol; 4.9
mg sodium; 32.6 gm carbohydrate;
4.9 mg sodium; 40.3 mg calcium;
0.8 mg iron; 47.2 RE vitamin A;
101.4 mg vitamin C*

SAN FRANCISCO DAYS

6 parts sparkling apple cider
    (3 oz.)
6 parts sparkling white grape
    juice (3 oz.)
½ tsp. fresh-squeezed lemon juice
Lemon slice, for garnish

Stir juices together in a chilled wineglass and garnish with lemon slice.
Serves one.

*64 calories; 0.1 gm fat; 1% calories
from fat; 0 mg cholesterol; 3.4 mg
sodium; 16.5 gm carbohydrate;
0.4 gm protein; 8.7 mg calcium;
0.4 mg iron; 0.5 RE vitamin A;
1.8 mg vitamin C*

SAN JUAN CAPISTRANO

SAN JUAN
CAPISTRANO

4 parts grapefruit juice
   (2 oz.)
2 parts coconut milk (1 oz.)
2 parts fresh-squeezed lime juice (1 oz.)
Lime twist, for garnish

Combine all ingredients with cracked
ice in a blender and blend until
smooth. Pour into a chilled wineglass
and garnish with the lime twist.
Serves one.

109 calories; 0.1 gm fat; 65% calories from fat; 0 mg cholesterol; 4.8 mg sodium; 8.6 carbohydrate;1.2 gm protein; 10.2 mg calcium; 0.5 mg iron; 0.9 RE vitamin A; 29.9 mg vitamin C

SAN SIMEON

SANGRITA SECA

SAN SIMEON

4 parts guava nectar (2 oz.)
4 parts fresh-squeezed lime
   juice (2 oz.)
2 parts half-and-half (1 oz.)
1 part sugar syrup (½ oz.)

Combine all ingredients with cracked
ice in a blender and blend at low
speed until smooth. Pour into a
chilled champagne flute. Serves one.

*118 calories; 3.7 gm fat; 25% calo-
ries from fat; 10.4 mg cholesterol;
14.5 mg sodium; 22.7 gm carbohydrate; 1.6 gm protein; 54.7 mg
calcium; 0.7 mg iron; 82.4 RE
vitamin A; 120.8 mg vitamin C*

SANGRITA SECA

32 parts tomato juice (16 oz.)
16 parts cup fresh-squeezed orange
   juice (8 oz.)
6 parts fresh-squeezed lime
   juice (3 oz.)
Jalapeño pepper, seeded and chopped
   fine
1 part Tabasco sauce
2 tsp. Worcestershire sauce (2 tsp.)
½ tsp. white pepper
Celery salt, to taste

Pour all ingredients into a large pitcher and stir. Chill for at least one hour.
When ready to serve strain into a fresh
pitcher and pour over ice into chilled
highball glasses. Serves six to eight.

*36 calories; 0.1 gm fat; 3% calories
from fat; 0 mg cholesterol; 368.8
mg sodium; 8.9 gm carbohydrate;
1 gm protein; 15.1 mg calcium;
0.8 mg iron; 55.8 RE vitamin A;
34.4 mg vitamin C*

SANTA ANA COOLER

8 parts pineapple juice
   (4 oz.)
4 parts fresh-squeezed orange
   juice (2 oz.)
4 parts fresh lemonade (2 oz.) (see
   Traditional Lemonade, page 207)
1 tbsp. passion-fruit syrup
Pineapple spear, for garnish
Orange slice, for garnish

Combine juices and lemonade with
cracked ice in a cocktail shaker and
shake well. Strain over ice cubes into
a chilled collins glass. Slowly pour
passion-fruit syrup into drink,
creating a swirling effect. Do not stir.
Garnish with the pineapple spear and
orange slice. Serves one.

*281 calories; 0.2 gm fat; 1% calo-
ries from fat; 0 mg cholesterol; 5.9
mg sodium; 78 gm carbohydrate;*

SANTA CRUZ BOARDWALK

*0.9 gm protein; 74.9 mg calcium;
3.2 mg iron; 12.8 RE vitamin A;
61.5 mg vitamin C*

SANTA CRUZ
BOARDWALK

4 parts fresh-squeezed
  lemon juice (2 oz.)
½ tsp. bar sugar
½ fresh peach, peeled, pitted,
  and diced
Sparkling mineral water
Fresh raspberries, for garnish

Combine all ingredients except the
raspberries and sparkling mineral
water with cracked ice in a blender
and blend until slushy. Pour into a
chilled highball glass. Fill the glass
with the sparkling mineral water and
stir gently. Garnish with the fresh
raspberries. Serves one.

*21 calories; 0.2 gm fat; 2% calories
from fat; 0 mg cholesterol; 0.6 mg
sodium; 19.3 gm carbohydrate;
1 gm protein; 13.7 mg calcium;
0.3 mg iron; 49.8 RE vitamin A;
37.8 mg vitamin C*

SAUERKRAUT COCKTAIL

8 parts sauerkraut juice (4 oz.)
1 part fresh-squeezed lemon
    juice (½ oz.)
1 garlic clove, peeled
Freshly ground black pepper, to taste
Cocktail onion, for garnish

Combine juices with cracked ice in a cocktail shaker. Extract garlic essence with a garlic press and add to juices. Shake well and strain into a chilled cocktail glass. Sprinkle with pepper and garnish with the cocktail onion. Serves one.

30 calories; 0.2 gm fat; 4% calories from fat; 0 mg cholesterol; 750.2 mg sodium; 7.1 gm carbohydrate; 1.3 gm protein; 40.4 mg calcium; 1.7 mg iron; 2.6 RE vitamin A; 24.1 mg vitamin C

SAVORY CUCUMBER SMOOTHIE

12 parts cucumber juice (6 oz.)
10 parts nonfat plain yogurt (5 oz.)
4 parts onion juice (2 oz.)
2 parts watercress juice (1 oz.)
1 tbsp. fresh dill, chopped
1 tsp. garlic puree
½ tsp. white horseradish
Fresh dill sprigs, for garnish

Combine ingredients in a blender and blend until smooth. Pour into chilled highball glasses and garnish with the dill sprigs. Serves two.

57 calories; 0.2 gm fat; 3% calories from fat; 1.6 mg cholesterol; 102.1 mg sodium; 9.5 gm carbohydrate; 5.3 gm protein; 186.7 mg calcium; 0.5 mg iron; 173.7 RE vitamin A; 15.4 mg vitamin C

SAVORY LEMON TONIC

4 parts fresh-squeezed
    lemon juice (2 oz.)
1 tsp. parsley juice
1 tsp. sugar
3–5 dashes Worcestershire sauce
Freshly ground black pepper, to taste
Sparkling mineral water
Lemon twist, for garnish

Combine all ingredients except sparkling mineral water with cracked ice in a cocktail shaker and shake well. Strain over ice cubes into a chilled highball glass and fill the glass with sparkling mineral water. Stir gently and garnish with the lemon twist. Serves one.

32 calories; 0 gm fat; 0% calories from fat; 0 mg cholesterol; 20.9 mg sodium; 9.5 gm carbohydrate; 0.3 gm protein; 7.7 mg calcium; 0.2 iron; 8.3 RE vitamin; 31.3 mg vitamin C

SAVORY WATERMELON COOLER

8 parts watermelon juice (4 oz.)
4 parts cucumber juice (2 oz.)
4 parts tomato juice (2 oz.)
2 parts onion juice (1 oz.)
Cocktail onions, for garnish

Combine juices with cracked ice in a cocktail shaker and shake well. Strain into chilled cocktail glasses and garnish with the cocktail onion. Serves two.

30 calories; 0.3 gm fat; 9% calories from fat; 0 mg cholesterol; 119.3 mg sodium; 6.8 gm carbohydrate; 1 gm protein; 19.8 mg calcium; 0.5 mg iron; 90 RE vitamin A; 12 mg vitamin C

SCARECROW

12 parts carrot juice (6 oz.)
8 parts pumpkin puree (4 oz.)
4 parts still spring water (2 oz.)
½ tsp. alcohol-free almond extract
½ tsp. alcohol-free vanilla extract
Dash of cinnamon
Dash of ginger
Dash of nutmeg

Combine all ingredients in a blender and blend until smooth. Pour into chilled old-fashioned glasses. Serves two.

63 calories; 0.4 gm fat; 5% calories from fat; 0 mg cholesterol; 27.7 mg sodium; 13.7 gm carbohydrate; 1.5 gm protein; 38.5 mg calcium; 1.3 mg iron; 34.4 RE vitamin A; 9.7 mg vitmain C.

SCARLET FEVER

10 parts celery juice (5 oz.)
4 parts red radish
 juice (2 oz.)
4 parts red-cabbage juice (2 oz.)
Celery sticks, for garnish

Combine all juices with cracked ice in a cocktail shaker and shake well. Strain over ice cubes into chilled old-fashioned glasses and garnish with the celery sticks. Serves two.

17 calories; 0.2 gm fat; 7% calories from fat; 0 mg cholesterol; 67 mg sodium; 3.9 gm carbohydrate; 0.8 gm protein; 37.8 mg calcium; 0.4 mg iron; 11.7 RE vitamin A; 11.8 mg vitamin C

SCOTTY'S PALACE BLEND

12 parts pineapple juice
 (6 oz.)
8 parts coconut milk (4 oz.)
6 parts rehydrated dates,
 chopped (3 oz.)
1 banana, sliced
1 tsp. bee pollen
½ tsp. alcohol-free almond extract

Combine all ingredients in a blender and blend until smooth. Pour into chilled highball glasses. Serves two.

388 calories; 16.4 gm fat; 38% calories from fat; 0 mg cholesterol; 10.6 mg sodium; 57.6 gm carbohydrate; 3.5 gm protein; 46.5 mg calcium; 1.5 mg iron; 14.8 RE vitamin A; 14.3 mg vitamin C

(Bee pollen not included in nutritional analysis.)

SEBASTOPOL SPECIAL

10 parts Gravenstein
 apple juice (5 oz.)
6 parts raspberry juice (3 oz.)
4 parts grapefruit juice (2 oz.)
4 parts orange juice (2 oz.)
2 parts lemon juice (1 oz.)
Lemon slices, for garnish
Orange slices, for garnish

Combine juices in a blender and mix well. Pour over ice cubes into chilled highball glasses and garnish with the lemon and orange slices. Serves two.

88 calories; 0.5 gm fat; 5% calories from fat; 0 mg cholesterol; 2.8 mg sodium; 21.6 gm carbohydrate; 1 gm protein; 24.1 mg calcium; 0.7 mg iron; 13.6 RE vitamin A; 74.7 mg vitamin C

SEPTEMBER HARVEST

8 parts cranberry juice
 cocktail (4 oz.)
8 parts white grape juice (4 oz.)
Seedless grapes, for garnish

Combine juices with ice cubes in a mixing glass and stir well. Strain over ice cubes into chilled old-fashioned glass and garnish with the seedless grapes. Serves one.

134 calories; 0.2 gm fat; 15 calories from fat; 0 mg cholesterol; 7.9 mg sodium; 33.3 gm carbohydrate; 0.6 gm protein; 13.6 mg calcium; 0.4 mg iron; 0.9 RE vitamin A; 40.3 mg vitamin C

SEQUOIA SUNDOWN

10 parts pear juice (5 oz.)
8 parts pomegranate juice (4 oz.)
Lime slice, for garnish

Combine juices with cracked ice in a cocktail shaker and shake well. Strain over ice cubes into a chilled collins glass and garnish with the lime slice. Serves one.

181 calories; 0.4 gm fat; 2% calories from fat; 0 mg cholesterol; 9.4 mg sodium; 46.6 gm carbohdrate; 1.5 gm protein; 10.5 mg calcium; 0.8 mg iron; 0 RE vitamin A; 10.2 mg vitamin C

183

SHANGRI-LA

4 parts fresh-squeezed lemon
    juice (2 oz.)
2 parts black-currant syrup (1 oz.)
1 tsp. alcohol-free mint extract
Sparkling mineral water
Lemon slice, for garnish

Combine lemon juice, black-currant
syrup, and mint extract in a chilled
highball glass. Add ice cubes and fill
the glass with the sparkling mineral
water. Stir gently and garnish with the
lemon slice. Serves one.

*103 calories; 0 gm fat; 0% calories
from fat; 0 mg cholesterol; 2 mg
sodium; 25.6 gm carbohydrate; 0.2
gm protein; 21 mg calcium; 1 mg
iron; 1.1 RE vitamin A; 26 mg vitamin C*

SHARON'S SPECIAL
FRUIT PUNCH

64 parts apple cider (32 oz.)
24 parts fresh-squeezed orange
    juice (12 oz.)
16 parts raspberry juice or
    puree (8 oz.)
16 parts fresh grapefruit juice (8 oz.)
4 parts fresh-squeezed lemon
    juice (2 oz.)
1 orange, sliced thinly
1 apple, sliced thinly
1 lemon, sliced thinly
12–15 fresh raspberries, for garnish
1 liter ginger ale
1 liter sparkling mineral water or
    lemon-lime soda

Combine fruit juices in a large punch
bowl. Stir well and add ice. Garnish
with the fresh fruit. Add the ginger ale
and sparkling mineral water just
before serving and stir again. Serves
twenty.

*68 calories; 0.2 gm fat; 3% calories
from fat; 0 mg cholesterol; 5.5 mg
sodium; 17.8 gm carbohydrate;
0.5 gm protein; 16.3 mg calcium;
0.5 mg iron; 7.1 RE vitamin A;
25.8 mg vitamin C*

SHARP CARROT
COCKTAIL

8 parts carrot juice (4 oz.)
3 parts red-radish juice (1½ oz.)
Carrot curl, for garnish

Combine juices with cracked ice in a
cocktail shaker and shake well. Strain
into a chilled cocktail glass and garnish with the carrot curl. Serves one.

*53 calories; 0.4 g fat; 6% calories
from fat; 0 mg cholesterol; 43.1 mg
sodium; 12.1 gm carbohydrate; 1.3
gm protein; 36.1 mg calcium; 0.6
mg iron; 2,920 RE vitamin A; 19.4
mg vitamin C*

SHIRLEY TEMPLE

2 parts fresh-squeezed
    lemon juice (2 oz.)
1 part sugar syrup (½ oz.)
1 part grenadine (½ oz.)
Ginger ale
Maraschino cherry, for garnish
Orange slice, for garnish

Combine all ingredients except cherry,
orange slice, and ginger ale with
cracked ice in a cocktail shaker and
shake well. Strain over ice cubes into a
chilled old-fashioned glass. Fill the
glass with the ginger ale and stir gently. Garnish with the cherry and
orange slice. Serves one.

SHIRLEY TEMPLE

83 calories; 0 gm fat; 0% calories from fat; 0 mg cholesterol; 7.3 mg sodium; 22.7 gm carbohydrate; 0.2 gm protein; 15.3 mg calcium; 0.7 mg iron; 1.6 RE vitamin A; 26.1 mg vitamin C

SHOWER PUNCH

16 parts apple juice (8 oz.)
16 parts cranberry juice
   cocktail (8 oz.)
16 parts pineapple juice (8 oz.)
8 parts fresh-squeezed lime
   juice (4 oz.)
1½ liters ginger ale
Pineapple slices, for garnish

Combine juices in a large punch bowl. Just before serving, add ginger ale and stir gently. Add ice and float pineapple slices on top. Serves eight.

115 calories; 0.1 gm fat; 1% calories from fat; 0 mg cholesterol; 16 mg sodium; 29.4 gm carbohydrate; 0.2 gm protein; 14.7 mg calcium; 0.5 mg iron; 0.3 RE vitamin A; 28.9 mg vitamin C

SILKEN SMOOTHIE

12 parts pear juice
   (6 oz.)
8 parts unsweetened cherry
   juice (4 oz.)
1 frozen banana, broken in chunks
1 tbsp. honey
1 tsp. bee pollen
1 tsp. fresh-squeezed lemon juice

Combine all ingredients in a blender and blend until smooth. Add more pear juice if mixture is too thick until desired consistency is achieved. Pour into chilled wineglasses. Serves two.

187 calories; 1 gm fat; 4% calories from fat; 0 mg cholesterol; 4.1 mg sodium; 47.4 gm carbohydrate; 1.6 gm protein; 18.4 mg calcium; 0.7 mg iron; 19.9 RE vitamin A; 12.3 mg vitamin C

(Bee pollen not included in nutritional analysis.)

SLEEPING BULL

SIMPLE CARROT COCKTAIL

10 parts carrot juice
   (5 oz.)
1 tbsp. fresh-squeezed lemon juice
Dash of Tabasco sauce
Lemon twist, for garnish

Combine all ingredients except the lemon twist with cracked ice in a cocktail shaker and shake well. Strain into a chilled cocktail glass and garnish with the lemon twist. Serves one.

61 calories; 0.2 gm fat; 3% calories from fat; 0 mg cholesterol; 47.8 mg sodium; 14.5 gm carbohydrate; 1.4 gm protein; 35.1 mg calcium; 0.7 mg iron; 3,651 RE vitamin A; 20.1 mg vitamin C

SLEEPING BULL

8 parts beef bouillon (4 oz.)
8 parts tomato juice (4 oz.)
1 part fresh-squeezed lime
   juice (½ oz.)
¼ tsp. Worcestershire sauce
Tabasco sauce, to taste
Celery salt, to taste
Freshly ground pepper, to taste

Combine all ingredients in a saucepan. Heat well, stirring occasionally, but do not boil. Adjust seasonings and pour into a warmed mug. Serves one.

185

55 calcium; 0.1 gm fat; 1% calories from fat; 0 mg cholesterol; 534.5 mg sodium; 13.5 gm carbohydrate; 1.5 gm protein; 20.9 mg calcium; 1.2 mg iron; 75.4 RE vitamin A; 16.5 mg vitamin C

S.L.O. SMOOTHIE

8 parts apple juice (4 oz.)
8 parts strawberry puree (4 oz.)
6 parts coconut milk (3 oz.)
6 parts peach juice (3 oz.)
4 parts papaya juice (2 oz.)
4 parts pineapple juice (2 oz.)
1 tbsp. fresh-squeezed lime juice
1 Haas avocado, peeled, pitted, and chopped

Combine ingredients in a blender and blend until smooth. Pour into chilled highball glasses. Serves two.

372 calories; 27.4 gm fat; 63% calories from fat; 0 mg cholesterol; 23.4 mg sodium; 32.5 gm carbohydrtae; 3.7 gm protein; 35.8 mg calcium; 2.3 mg iron; 68.9 RE vitamin A; 70.7 mg vitamin C

SOMETHING WILD

10 parts lemon-verbena tea, chilled (5 oz.)
8 parts apple juice (4 oz.)
4 parts licorice-root tea, chilled (2 oz.)
Lemon twist, for garnish

Combine all ingredients except the lemon twist with cracked ice in a cocktail shaker and shake well. Strain over ice cubes into a chilled collins glass and garnish with the lemon twist. Serves one.

55 calories; 0.1 gm fat; 2% calories from fat; 0 mg cholesterol; 9.4 mg sodium; 13.8 gm carbohydrate; 0.1 gm protein; 8 mg calcium; 0.5 mg iron; 0 RE vitamin A; 46.5 mg vitamin C

SONOMA SMOOTHIE

16 parts nonfat plain yogurt (8 oz.)
14 parts tomato juice (7 oz.)
4 parts celery juice (2 oz.)
2 parts garlic puree (1 oz.)
1 tsp. white horseradish
Celery sticks, for garnish

Combine all ingredients except celery sticks in a blender and blend until smooth. Pour into chilled collins glasses and garnish with the celery sticks. Serves two.

85 calories; 0.1 gm fat; 1% calories from fat; 2.5 mg cholesterol; 490 mg sodium; 19.9 gm carbohydrate; 7.6 gm protein; 249.3 mg calcium; 0.7 mg iron; 59 RE vitamin A; 10.9 mg vitamin C

SONORA SUNRISE

8 parts cranberry juice cocktail (4 oz.)
6 parts fresh-squeezed orange juice (3 oz.)
1 scoop lemon sorbet
1 tbsp. fresh-squeezed lime juice
Lime twist, for garnish

Combine all ingredients except lime twist in a blender and blend until smooth. Pour into a chilled highball glass and garnish with the lime twist. Serves one.

216 calories; 0.3 gm fat; 1% calories from fat; 0 mg cholesterol; 6.2 mg sodium; 55.8 gm carbohydrate; 0.9 gm protein; 17.7 mg calcium; 0.4 mg iron; 18.1 RE vitamin A; 109.6 mg vitamin C

SOUTH BAY SHAKE-UP

10 parts pineapple juice (5 oz.)
8 parts fresh-squeezed orange juice (4 oz.)
8 parts strawberry puree (4 oz.)
8 parts plain nonfat yogurt (4 oz.)
1 banana, sliced

Combine all ingredients in a blender and blend until smooth. If mixture is too thick, add more orange juice until desired consistency is achieved. Pour into chilled highball glasses. Serves two.

165 calories; 0.7 gm fat; 3% calories from fat; 1.2 mg cholesterol; 42.2 mg sodium; 37.5 gm carbohydrate; 4.8 gm protein; 142.1 mg calcium; 0.7 mg iron; 17.8 RE vitamin A; 73.3 mg vitamin C

SOUTH OF SUNSET

6 parts passion-fruit juice (3 oz.)
2 parts fresh-squeezed lemon juice (1 oz.)
Sparkling mineral water
Lemon slice, for garnish

Combine fruit juices in a mixing glass and pour over ice cubes into a chilled highball glass. Fill the glass with the sparkling mineral water and stir gently. Garnish with the lemon slice. Serves one.

58 calories; 0.2 gm fat; 2% calories from fat; 0 mg cholesterol; 5.4 mg sodium; 14.7 gm carbohydrate; 0.7 gm protein; 5.4 mg calcium; 0.3 mg iron; 205.4 RE vitamin A; 28.5 mg vitamin C

SPARKLING ICED COFFEE

16 parts espresso or strong-brewed black coffee, chilled (8 oz.)
1 tsp. fresh-squeezed lemon juice
1 tsp. alcohol-free vanilla extract
Sparkling mineral water
Peel of one lemon, halved
Sugar (optional)

Combine coffee, lemon juice, and vanilla extract in a mixing glass with cracked ice and stir well. Strain over ice cubes into chilled collins glasses. Fill the glass with the sparkling mineral water and stir gently. Add sugar to taste and garnish with the lemon peel. Serves one.

14 calories; 0 gm fat; 0% calories from fat; 0 mg cholesterol; 2.3 mg sodium; 2.4 gm carbohydrate; 0.2 gm protein; 10.5 mg calcium; 0.1 mg iron; 0 RE vitamin A; 8.9 mg vitamin C

(Sugar not included in nutritional analysis.)

SPARKLING PEACH MELBA

SPARKLING PEACH MELBA

8 parts peach nectar (4 oz.)
4 parts raspberry puree (2 oz.)
Sparkling mineral water
Fresh raspberries, for garnish

Combine peach nectar with raspberry puree in a cocktail shaker and shake well. Pour into a chilled collins glass and fill the glass with the sparkling water. Stir gently. Garnish with the fresh raspberries. Serves one.

103 calories; 0.5 gm fat; 4% calories from fat; 0 mg cholesterol; 7.7 mg sodium; 25.6 gm carbohydrate; 1.1 gm protein; 24.7 mg calcium; 0.7 mg iron; 40.4 RE vitamin A; 27.3 mg vitamin C

SPARKLING PEAR

6 parts pear juice (3 oz.)
1 tbsp. fresh-squeezed lime juice
Sparkling cranberry juice
Lime twist, for garnish

Combine pear and lime juices in a cocktail shaker with cracked ice and shake well. Strain into a chilled wineglass and fill the glass with the sparkling cranberry juice. Stir gently and garnish with the lime twist. Serves one.

71 calories; 0.1 gm fat; 1% calories from fat; 0 mg cholesterol; 4.3 mg sodium; 18.9 gm carbohydrate; 0.2 gm protein; 6 mg calcium; 0.3 mg iron; 0.2 RE vitamin A; 15.5 mg vitamin C

SPELLBINDER

8 parts pineapple juice
  (4 oz.)
6 parts pear juice (3 oz.)
½ tsp. alcohol-free almond extract

Combine all ingredients with cracked ice in a blender and blend until slushy. Pour into a chilled highball glass. Serves one.

122 calories; 0.1 gm calories from fat; 0 mg cholesterol; 4.2 mg sodium; 29.8 gm carbohydrate; 0.5 gm protein; 23 mg calcium; 0.5 mg iron; 0.5 RE vitamin A; 13.1 mg vitamin C

SPICED COCOA

4 parts unsweetened chocolate
  (2 solid oz.)
16 parts boiling water (8 oz.)
8 parts cup sugar (4 oz.)
½ tsp. ground cloves
½ tsp. grated cinnamon
½ tsp. ground ginger
16 parts half-and-half, warm (8 oz.)
1 tsp. alcohol-free vanilla extract
Chocolate shavings, for garnish

Melt unsweetened chocolate in a microwave or a double-boiler. In the double boiler combine the melted chocolate, boiling water, sugar, and spices and continue to warm over low to medium heat until mixture is hot and well blended. Add warm half-and-half and vanilla. Serve in warmed coffee cups. Sprinkle with the chocolate shavings. Serves two.

493 calories; 28.1 gm fat; 47% calories from fat; 41.7 mg cholesterol; 48.9 mg sodium; 65.5 gm carbohydrate; 6.4 gm protein; 151.4 mg calcium; 2.4 mg iron; 153.1 RE vitamin A; 1.4 mg vitamin C

SPICED ICED COFFEE

4 cinnamon sticks
12 whole cloves
3 tbsp. honey
1 tsp. ground nutmeg
1 tsp. ground ginger
Peels of 2 lemons and 2 oranges cut
  into thin strips
64 parts strong-brewed black coffee,
  hot (32 oz.)

Combine the spices, honey, and fruit peel in a heat-proof pitcher. Add the hot coffee and stir. Chill in the refrigerator. Serve over ice in chilled highball glasses. Serves six to eight.

45 calories; 0.3 gm fat; 5% calories from fat; 0 mg cholesterol; 4.5 mg sodium; 11.4 gm carbohydrate; 0.4 gm protein; 18.9 mg calcium; 0.3 mg iron; 2.5 RE vitamin A; 11 mg vitamin C

SPICED ICED TEA

16 parts fresh-squeezed orange
  juice (8 oz.)
6 Cinnamon sticks
12 whole cloves
1 tsp. ground nutmeg
1 tsp. ground ginger
Peels of 2 lemons and 2 oranges cut
  into thin strips
Lemon slices, for garnish
48 parts strong-brewed black tea, hot
  (24 oz.)

Combine the juice, spices, and fruit peel in a heat-proof pitcher. Add the hot tea and stir. Chill in the refrigerator. Serve over ice in chilled highball glasses. Garnish with the lemon slices. Serves six to eight.

30 calories; 0.3 gm fat; 9% calories from fat; 0 mg cholesterol; 4.8 mg sodium; 6.8 gm carbohydrate; 0.5 gm protein; 24.1 mg calcium; 0.4 mg iron; 10.1 RE vitamin A; 29.9mg vitamin C

SPICED ICED COFFEE

SPICY GRAPE

16 parts white grape
  juice (8 oz.)
1 tsp. honey
½ tsp. ground cinnamon
½ tsp. ground ginger
½ tsp. ground cardamom
Ground nutmeg, for garnish

Combine all ingredients except the
nutmeg in a mixing glass and let
steep for about thirty minutes. Strain
into a chilled wineglass and sprinkle
with the nutmeg. Serves one.

*169 calories; 0.6 gm fat; 3% calo-
ries from fat; 0 mg cholesterol;
9.1 mg sodium; 41.3 gm carbohydrate; 1.4 gm protein; 35.2 mg calcium; 1 mg iron; 2.4 RE vitamin A;
1 mg vitamin C*

SPIKED TOMATO

8 parts tomato juice (4 oz.)
6 parts carrot juice (3 oz.)
3–5 dashes Worcestershire sauce
3–5 dashes Tabasco sauce
Carrot stick, for garnish
Freshly ground black pepper, for
  garnish

Combine all ingredients except carrot stick and black pepper with cracked ice in a cocktail shaker and shake well. Strain over ice cubes into a chilled highball glass. Garnish with the carrot stick and sprinkle with black pepper. Serves one.

54 calories; 1 gm fat; 3% calories from fat; 0 mg cholesterol; 447.5 mg sodium; 12.9 gm carbohydrate; 1.7 gm protein; 31.6 mg calcium; 1.1 mg iron; 2,254 RE vitamin A; 18.8 mg vitamin C

SPINOUT

4 parts fresh-squeezed
  orange juice (2 oz.)
2 parts guava juice (1 oz.)
2 parts grapefruit juice (1 oz.)
2 parts pineapple juice (1 oz.)
2 parts fresh-squeezed lemon
  juice (1 oz.)
1 tbsp. raspberry syrup
½ banana, sliced
Sparkling mineral water
Pineapple spear, for garnish

Combine all ingredients except the sparkling mineral water and pineapple spear with cracked ice in a blender and blend until slushy. Pour into a chilled collins glass and fill the glass with the sparkling mineral water. Stir gently and garnish with the pineapple spear. Serves one.

177 calories; 0.6 gm fat; 3% calories from fat; 0 mg cholesterol; 3.6 mg sodium; 44.7 gm carbohydrate; 1.6 gm protein; 36.3 mg calcium; 1.2 mg iron; 39.4 RE vitamin A; 112.3 mg vitamin C

SPRING BREAK

12 parts grapefruit juice (6 oz.)
4 parts strawberry puree (2 oz.)
1 tbsp. honey
Fresh mint sprig, for garnish

Combine juices and honey in a blender and blend until smooth. Pour into a chilled highball glass and garnish with the mint sprig. Serves one.

147 calories; 0.4 gm fat; 2% calories from fat; 0 mg cholesterol; 3.3 mg sodium; 36.8 gm carbohydrate; 1.3 gm protein; 24.3 mg calcium; 0.7 mg iron; 3.3 RE vitamin A; 97 mg vitamin C

SPRING MOON

8 parts cantaloupe juice
  (4 oz.)
4 parts peach juice (2 oz.)
4 parts plum juice (2 oz.)
Fresh mint sprigs, for garnish

Combine all ingredients except mint sprig with cracked ice in a cocktail shaker and shake well. Strain over ice cubes into chilled old-fashioned glasses and garnish with the mint sprigs. Serves two.

58 calories; 0.4 gm fat; 6% calories from fat; 0 mg cholesterol; 7 mg sodium; 14.2 gm carbohydrate; 0.9 gm protein; 9.4 mg calcium; 0.2 mg iron; 203.8 RE vitamin A; 29.5 mg vitamin C

SPRUCE GOOSE

10 parts apple juice (5 oz.)
6 parts celery juice (3 oz.)
2 parts red cabbage juice (1 oz.)
Celery stick, for garnish

Combine all ingredients except celery stick with cracked ice in a cocktail shaker and shake well. Strain over ice cubes into a chilled highball glass and garnish with the celery stick. Serves one.

86 calories; 0.3 gm fat; 3% calories from fat; 0 mg cholesterol; 83.5 mg sodium; 21 gm carbohydrate; 1 gm protein; 53.4 mg calcium; 1 mg iron; 13.5 RE vitamin A; 71 mg vitamin C

STAIRWAY TO HEAVEN

10 parts cucumber juice
(5 oz.)
1 tbsp. peppermint juice
½ tsp. bar sugar
Fresh mint sprig, for garnish

Combine all ingredients except mint sprig with cracked ice in a cocktail shaker. Strain over ice cubes into a chilled old-fashioned glass and garnish with the mint sprig. Serves one.

26 calories; 0.2 gm fat; 6% calories from fat; 0 mg cholesterol; 2.9 mg sodium; 6 gm carbohydrate; 1 gm protein; 20.2 mg calcium; 0.4 mg iron; 30.6 RE vitamin A; 7.6 mg vitamin C

STANLEY SPRITZER

4 parts fresh-squeezed lime
juice (2 oz.)
4 parts fresh-squeezed orange
juice (2 oz.)
Ginger ale
Lime slice, for garnish

Combine all ingredients except ginger ale and lime slice with cracked ice in a cocktail shaker and shake well. Strain over ice cubes into a chilled collins glass. Fill the glass with the ginger ale and stir gently. Garnish with the lime slice. Serves one.

60 calories; 0.2 gm fat; 2% calories from fat; 0 mg cholesterol; 5 mg sodium; 15.9 gm carbohydrate; 0.6 gm protein; 13 mg calcium; 0.2 mg iron; 11.9 RE vitamin A; 45 mg vitamin C

STARDUST

4 parts raspberry juice
(2 oz.)
4 parts strawberry juice (2 oz.)
1 tsp. fresh-squeezed lime juice
Sparkling mineral water
Whole strawberry, for garnish

Combine juices in a cocktail shaker with cracked ice and shake well. Strain into a chilled highball glass

STANLEY SPRITZER

over ice cubes. Slowly the fill glass with the sparkling mineral water and stir gently. Garnish with the whole strawberry. Serves one.

69 calories; 0.8 gm fat; 9% calories from fat; 0 mg cholesterol; 0.9 mg sodium; 16.3 gm carbohydrate; 1.3 gm protein; 31.1 mg calcium; 68.6 mg iron; 13.5 RE vitamin A; 71 mg vitamin C

STARGAZER

12 parts apple juice
(6 oz.)
8 parts cooked rhubarb (4 oz.)
8 parts rehydrated raisins, chopped
fine (4 oz.)
1 tbsp. honey
1 tsp. fresh-squeezed lemon juice
½ tsp. ginger juice
Lemon twists, for garnish

Combine all ingredients except lemon twists in a blender and blend until smooth. Pour over ice cubes into chilled highball glasses and garnish with the lemon twists. Serves two.

254 calories; 0.4 gm fat; 1% calories from fat; 0 mg cholesterol; 14.5 mg sodium; 65.9 gm carbohydrate; 2.5 gm protein; 98.3 mg calcium; 1.4 mg iron; 8.4 RE vitamin A; 43.7 mg vitamin C

STATE FAIR

10 parts fresh-squeezed
  orange juice (5 oz.)
6 parts peach juice (3 oz.)
4 parts unsweetened cherry
  cider (2 oz.)
Orange slice, for garnish

Combine juices in a blender with
cracked ice and mix until slushy. Pour
into a chilled collins glass and garnish with the orange slice. Serves one.

171 calories; 1.1 gm fat; 6% calo-
ries from fat; 0 mg cholesterol; 7 mg
sodium; 40.7 gm carbohydrate;
2.2 gm protein; 32.4 mg calcium;
0.8 mg iron; 68.6 RE vitamin A;
81.4 mg vitamin C

STEVE'S SPECIAL SANGRIA

64 parts red grape juice (32 oz.)
32 parts fresh-squeezed orange
  juice (16 oz.)
8 parts fresh-squeezed lemon
  juice (4 oz.)
8 parts fresh-squeezed lime
  juice (4 oz.)
8 parts peach juice (4 oz.)
4 parts sugar syrup (2 oz.)
1 tbsp. alcohol-free brandy extract
Orange slices, for garnish
Lemon slices, for garnish
Lime slices, for garnish

Combine all ingredients except fruit
slices in a punch bowl and stir until
well-mixed. Carefully add ice and
float fruit slices on top. Serves eight.

134 calories; 0.2 gm fat; 1% calo-
ries from fat; 0 mg cholesterol; 5.5
mg sodium; 32.7 gm carbohydrate;
1.2 gm protein; 23.6 mg calcium;
0.7 mg iron; 16.3 RE vitamin A;
39.9 mg vitamin C

STONE-FREE SMOOTHIE

4 parts apricot nectar (2 oz.)
4 parts peach nectar (2 oz.)
4 parts plum juice (2 oz.)
1 banana, sliced
1 tsp. bee pollen

Combine ingredients in a blender
and blend until smooth. If mixture
is too thick, add more plum juice
until desired consistency is achieved.
Pour into chilled highball glasses.
Serves two.

101 calories; 0.5 gm fat; 4% calo-
ries from fat; 0 mg cholesterol; 2.4
mg sodium; 25.6 gm carbohydrate;
1 gm protein; 7.9 mg calcium;
0.4 mg iron; 51.1 RE vitamin A;
17.6 mg vitamin C

(Bee pollen not included in nutri-
tional analysis.)

STRANGE BEDFELLOWS

8 parts apple juice (4 oz.)
8 parts pineapple juice (4 oz.)
8 parts beet juice (4 oz.)
6 parts coconut milk (3 oz.)

Combine ingredients in a blender and
blend until smooth. Pour into chilled
highball glasses. Serves two.

199 calories; 12.3 gm fat; 55%
calories from fat; 0 mg cholesterol;
202.8 mg sodium; 20.8 gm carbo-
hydrate; 2.1 gm protein; 28.1 mg
calcium; 2.2 mg iron; 1 RE vita-
min A; 34.3 mg vitamin C

74 calories; 0.5 gm fat; 6% calories from fat; 0 mg cholesterol; 9 mg sodium; 17.6 gm carbohydrate; 1.1 gm protein; 20.1 mg calcium; 0.6 mg iron; 2.5 RE vitamin A; 49.7 mg vitamin C

STRAWBERRY LEMONADE

32 parts fresh-squeezed lemon juice (16 oz.)
40 parts cold water (20 oz.)
32 parts sugar syrup (16 oz.)
16 parts fresh strawberry puree (8 oz.)
Lemon slices, for garnish
Fresh whole strawberries, for garnish

Combine lemon juice and cold water in a pitcher. Add one cup of the sugar syrup and strawberry puree and stir. Add more sugar to taste. Stir well and add ice. Float lemon slices and whole strawberries on top. Chill well before serving. Serves ten.

137 calories; .08 gm fat; 1% calories from fat; 0 mg cholesterol; 2.9 mg sodium; 36.4 gm carbohydrate; 0.3 gm protein; 33.5 mg calcium; 1.7 mg iron; 1.5 RE vitamin A; 33.7 mg vitamin C

STRAWBERRY STATEMENT

8 parts fresh-squeezed orange juice (4 oz.)
4 parts apple juice (2 oz.)
1 parts fresh-squeezed lemon juice (½ oz.)
1 scoop strawberry sorbet
6 fresh strawberries

Combine all ingredients except one strawberry in a blender and blend until smooth. Pour into a chilled highball glass and garnish with the whole strawberry. Serves one.

222 calories; 0.8 gm fat; 3% calories from fat; 0 mg cholesterol; 4.6 mg sodium; 55.1 gm carbohydrate; 1.8 gm protein; 38.5 mg calcium; 1 mg iron; 27.1 RE vitamin A; 171 mg vitamin C

STRAWBERRY COLADA

STRAWBERRY COLADA

10 parts pineapple juice (5 oz.)
6 fresh strawberries
2 parts cream of coconut (1 oz.)
Pineapple spear, for garnish

Combine all ingredients except pineapple spear and one strawberry with cracked ice in a blender. Blend until smooth and pour into a chilled highball glass. Garnish with the pineapple spear and remaining strawberry. Serves one.

195 calories; 10.2 gm fat; 45% calories from fat; 0 mg cholesterol; 3.3 mg sodium; 26.7 gm carbohydrate; 1.9 gm protein; 37.6 mg calcium; 1.3 mg iron; 2.7 RE vitamin A; 58.2 mg vitamin C

STRAWBERRY GINGER ALE

6 parts strawberry juice (3 oz.)
2 parts ginger juice (1 oz.)
1 tbsp. white grape juice
Ginger ale
Lemon wedge, for garnish

Combine strawberry and ginger juices in a mixing glass. Pour over ice cubes into a chilled collins glass. Fill the glass with the ginger ale and stir gently. Garnish with the lemon wedge. Serves one.

STRAWBERRY VACATION

10 parts pineapple juice (5 oz.)
8 parts strawberry puree (4 oz.)
1 scoop frozen vanilla yogurt
1 scoop strawberry sorbet
Sparkling mineral water or ginger ale
Pineapple spears, for garnish

Combine all ingredients except sparkling mineral water and pineapple spears in a blender and blend until smooth but not watery. Pour the mixture into chilled collins glasses. Slowly fill the glasses with the sparkling mineral water and garnish with the pineapple spears. Serves two.

154 calories; 2.5 gm fat; 14% calories from fat; 1 mg cholesterol; 35 mg sodium; 32.9 gm carbohydrate; 2.2 gm protein; 70.9 mg calcium; 0.7 mg iron; 24.1 RE vitamin A; 74.7 mg vitamin C

STRAWBERRY-BANANA KEFIR

16 parts fresh strawberries (8 oz.)
16 parts vanilla yogurt (8 oz.)
1 banana, sliced
2 parts honey (1 oz.)
16 parts apple juice (8 oz.)
Fresh whole strawberries, for garnish

Combine all ingredients except apple juice in a blender and blend until smooth. Slowly pour apple juice through top of blender while continuing to blend at low speed until desired consistency is achieved. Chill in a pitcher and serve in chilled highball glasses garnished with the fresh strawberries. Serves four.

146 calories; 1.3 gm fat; 8% calories from fat; 3.3 mg cholesterol; 42.7 mg sodium; 31.4 gm carbohydrate; 3.6 gm protein; 94.7 mg calcium; 0.5 mg iron; 3.3 RE vitamin A; 47 mg vitamin C

STRAWBERRY-BANANA SHAKE

16 parts strawberry juice (8 oz.)
2 scoops vanilla frozen yogurt
2 tbsp. strawberry preserves
1 banana, sliced

Combine all ingredients in a blender and blend until smooth. Pour into chilled highball glasses. Serves two.

255 calories; 4.7 gm fat; 16% calories from fat; 2 mg cholesterol; 67 mg sodium; 52.7 gm carbohydrate; 4.2 gm protein; 126.4 mg calcium; 1 mg iron; 49.3 RE vitamin A; 70.5 mg vitamin C

STRAWBERRY-HIBISCUS FREEZE

8 parts hibiscus tea, chilled (4 oz.)
8 parts strawberry puree (4 oz.)
2 parts white grape juice (1 oz.)

Combine all ingredients with cracked ice in a blender until slushy. Pour into a chilled highball glass. Serves one.

81 calories; 2.2 gm fat; 22% calories from fat; 0.5 mg cholesterol; 45.5 mg sodium; 15.4 gm carbohydrate; 1.9 gm protein; 55.7 mg calcium; 0.5 mg iron; 12.6 RE vitamin A; 64.3 mg vitamin C

STRAWBERRY-LEMONADE SPARKLER

4 parts strawberry puree (2 oz.)
4 parts fresh-squeezed lemon
   juice (2 oz.)
1 tbsp. sugar syrup, or to taste
Sparkling mineral water
Lemon slice, for garnish
Fresh strawberry, for garnish

Combine strawberry puree and lemon juice in a mixing glass with the sugar syrup and stir until well blended. Pour into a chilled collins glass and add ice cubes. Fill the glass with the sparkling mineral water and stir gently. Garnish with the lemon slice and fresh strawberry. Serves one.

STRAWBERRY-BANANA KEFIR

82 calories; 0.2 gm fat; 2% calories from fat; 0 mg cholesterol; 2.1 mg sodium; 22 gm carbohydrate; 0.6 gm protein; 23.5 mg calcium; 0.9 mg iron; 2.7 RE vitamin A; 58.2 mg vitamin C

SUMMER FRUIT FREEZE

8 parts fresh-squeezed
    orange juice (4 oz.)
8 parts plum juice (4 oz.)
4 parts blueberry juice (2 oz.)
4 parts mango juice (2 oz.)
Orange slice, for garnish

Combine all juices with cracked ice in a blender and blend until slushy. Pour into a chilled collins glass and garnish with the orange slice. Serves one.

200 calories; 1.4 gm fat; 6% calories from fat; 0 mg cholesterol; 6 mg sodium; 49 gm carbohydrate; 2.5 gm protein; 28.9 mg calcium; 0.5 mg iron; 395.8 RE vitamin A; 98.4 mg vitamin C

SUMMER PLUM TREAT

8 parts plum juice (4 oz.)
6 parts pear juice (3 oz.)
4 parts fresh-squeezed
    orange juice (2 oz.)
Orange slice, for garnish

Combine juices with cracked ice in a cocktail shaker and shake well. Strain over ice cubes into a chilled highball glass and garnish with the orange slice. Serves one.

138 calories; 0.8 gm fat; 5% calories from fat; 0 mg cholesterol; 3.5 mg sodium; 34 gm carbohydrate; 1.4 gm protein; 14.5 mg calcium; 0.4 mg iron; 47.6 RE vitamin A; 40 mg vitamin C

SUMMER PUNCH

2 quarts Strawberry Lemonade
    (see recipe, page 194) (64 oz.)
16 parts fresh-squeezed orange
    juice (8 oz.)
8 parts fresh-squeezed lime
    juice (4 oz.)
2 liters ginger ale
Fresh strawberries, for garnish
Lemon slices, for garnish
Orange slices, for garnish

Prepare 2 quarts of the Strawberry Lemonade recipe. Combine Strawberry Lemonade and juices and ice in a large punch bowl and stir well. Just before serving, add ginger ale and stir gently. Float the fresh fruit on top. Serves twenty.

84 calories; 0.1 gm fat; 1% calories from fat; 0 mg cholesterol; 8.3 mg sodium; 21.7 gm carbohydrate; 0.3 gm protein; 15.4 mg calcium; 0.8 mg iron; 3 RE vitamin A; 16.9 mg vitamin C

SUMMER SOLSTICE

8 parts blueberry juice (4 oz.)
6 parts apricot juice (3 oz.)
6 parts kiwi juice (3 oz.)
6 parts peach juice (3 oz.)
6 parts raspberry juice (3 oz.)
6 parts strawberry puree (3 oz.)
4 parts unsweetened cherry juice (2 oz.)
4 parts fresh figs, chopped fine (2 oz.)
Whole strawberries, for garnish

Combine juices, puree, and figs in a blender and blend until smooth. Pour over ice cubes into chilled highball glasses and garnish with the whole strawberries. Serves four.

97 calories; 0.7 gm fat; 6% calories from fat; 0 mg cholesterol; 5.4 mg sodium; 23.9 gm carbohydrate; 1.3 gm protein; 26.8 mg calcium; 0.6 mg iron; 50.2 RE vitamin A; 56.2 mg vitamin C

SUN TEA

3 tbsp. Loose tea of your choice
60 parts water (30 oz.)
Peel of one lemon
Sugar or honey, to taste
Lemon wedges, for garnish

Combine tea, water, and lemon peel in a 32-ounce glass jar and cover. Set in direct sunlight for at least four hours. Strain into pitcher and chill. Pour over ice cubes in collins glasses. Add sugar or honey to taste. Garnish with the lemon wedges. Serves four.

22 calories; 0 gm fat; 0 % calories from fat; 0 mg cholesterol; 0.6 mg sodium; 5.9 gm carbohydrate; 0 gm protein; 1.7 mg calcium; 0 mg iron; 0 RE vitamin A; 1.3 mg vitamin C

SUN TEA

SUNDAY PUNCH

10 parts watermelon
   juice (5 oz.)
8 parts fresh-squeezed orange
   juice (4 oz.)
1 tbsp. fresh-squeezed lime juice
Lime twists, for garnish

Combine juices with cracked ice in a
blender and blend until slushy. Pour
into chilled wineglasses and garnish
with the lime twists. Serves two.

*50 calories; 0.4 gm fat; 7% calories
from fat; 0 mg cholesterol; 2 mg
sodium; 11.7 gm carbohydrate;
0.9 gm protein; 12.5 mg calcium;
0.2 mg iron; 37.4 RE vitamin A;
37.4 mg vitamin C*

SUNDIAL PUNCH

into a chilled collins glass and garnish with the pineapple spear. Serves one.

142 calories; 0.2 gm fat; 1% calories from fat; 0 mg cholesterol; 7.2 mg sodium; 35.7 gm carbohydrate; 0.4 gm protein; 343.4 mg calcium; 1.2 mg iron; 0.5 RE vitamin A; 35.4 mg vitamin C

SUNDIAL PUNCH

6 parts pineapple juice
  (3 oz.)
2 parts orgeat (almond) syrup (1 oz.)
4 parts fresh-squeezed lime
  juice (2 oz.)
2 parts fresh-squeezed lemon
  juice (1 oz.)
1 part blackberry syrup (½oz.)
Pineapple spear, for garnish

Combine all ingredients except blackberry syrup and pineapple spear with cracked ice in a cocktail shaker and shake well. Pour into a chilled highball glass. Float syrup on top and garnish the with pineapple spear. Serves one.

182 calories; 0.1 gm fat; 1% calories from fat; 0 mg cholesterol; 3.8 mg sodium; 48.2 gm carbohydrate; 0.6 gm protein; 47 mg calcium; 1.8 mg iron; 1.6 RE vitamin A; 38.8 mg vitamin C

SUNNY DAY

8 parts pineapple juice (4 oz.)
8 parts hibiscus tea, chilled (4 oz.)
4 parts apple juice (2 oz.)
1 tbsp. tamarind syrup
Pineapple spear, fr garnish

Combine all ingredients except pineapple spear with cracked ice in a blender and blend until slushy. Pour

SUNSET STRIP

4 parts hazelnut syrup
  (2 oz.)
4 parts fresh-squeezed lemon
  juice (2 oz.)
1 tsp. grenadine
Sparkling mineral water
Orange slice, for garnish

Combine all ingredients except sparkling mineral water and orange slice with cracked ice in a cocktail shaker and shake well. Pour over ice into a chilled highball glass. Fill the glass with the sparkling mineral water and stir gently. Garnish with the orange slice. Serves one.

180 calories; 0 gm fat; 0% calories from fat; 0 mg cholesterol; 3.7 mg sodium; 47.8 gm carbohydrate; 0.2 gm protein; 41.7 mg calcium; 2.3 mg iron; 1.1 RE vitamin A; 26 mg vitamin C

SUNSET STRIP

SUPER BOWL SPECIAL

8 parts pineapple juice (4 oz.)
8 parts apple cider (4 oz.)
8 parts fresh-squeezed orange
   juice (4 oz.)
8 parts coconut milk (4 oz.)
2 bananas, sliced

Combine ingredients in a blender and
blend until smooth. Pour into a
chilled collins glasses. Serves two.

*348 calories; 16.8 gm fat; 48 %
calories from fat; 0 mg cholesterol;
11.7 mg sodium; 49.9 gm carbohydrate; 3.4 gm protein; 31.3 mg
calcium; 1.6 mg iron; 20.8 RE vitamin A; 45.3 mg vitamin C*

SURFER BOY

SUPER C

8 parts tomato juice (4 oz.)
8 parts tangerine juice (4 oz.)
1 tbsp. fresh-squeezed lemon juice

Combine juices with cracked ice in a
cocktail shaker and shake well. Strain
into a chilled highball glass. Add ice if
desired. Serves one.

*72 calories; 0.3 gm fat; 3% calories
from fat; 0 mg cholesterol; 409.7
mg sodium; 17.6 gm carbohydrate;
1.5 gm protein; 31.5 mg calcium;
0.9 mg iron; 111.2 RE vitamin A;
51.2 mg vitamin C*

SURF-CITY SALSA

10 parts tomato juice (5 oz.)
2 parts onion juice (1 oz.)
1 part cilantro juice (½ oz.)
1 part garlic juice (½ oz.)
1 tsp. jalapeño pepper juice
Fresh cilantro, for garnish

Combine all ingredients in a blender
and blend until smooth. Strain over
ice cubes into a chilled highball glass.
Garnish with the fresh cilantro sprig.
Serves one.

*37 calories; 18.1 gm fat; 5% calo-
ries from fat; 0 mg cholesterol;
628.2 mg sodium; 7.8 gm carbohydrate; 2 gm protein; 4.3 mg calcium; 1.5 mg iron; 225.4 RE vitamin
A; 19 mg vitamin C*

SURFER BOY

6 parts pineapple juice
   (3 oz.)
2 parts cream of coconut (1 oz.)
2 parts fresh-squeezed lime juice (1 oz.)
½ tsp. orgeat (almond) syrup
Pineapple spear, for garnish

Combine all ingredients except
pineapple spear with cracked ice in a
blender and blend until slushy. Pour
into a chilled highball glass. Garnish
with the pineapple spear. Serves one.

*257 calories; 18.1 gm fat; 61 %
calories from fat; 21 mg cholesterol;
398.5 mg sodium; 19 gm carbohydrate; 7.5 gm protein; 172 mg
calcium; 1.1 mg iron; 62 RE vitamin A; 18.2 mg vitamin C*

SWEET CARROT COOLER

8 parts carrot juice (4 oz.)
4 parts unsweetened cherry juice (2 oz.)
Sparkling mineral water
Carrot stick, for garnish

Combine juices with cracked ice in a
cocktail shaker and shake well. Strain
over ice cubes into a chilled collins
glass. Top off with the sparkling mineral water and stir gently. Garnish
with the carrot stick. Serves one.

86 calories; 0.7 gm fat; 7% calories from fat; 0 mg cholesterol; 32.9 mg sodium; 20 gm carbohydrate; 1.7 gm protein; 35.5 mg calcium; 0.7 mg iron; 297 RE vitamin A; 13.7 mg vitamin C

SWEET DESTINY

8 parts apple juice
(4 oz.)
8 parts fresh-squeezed orange
juice (4 oz.)
6 parts pear juice (3 oz.)
4 parts grapefruit juice (2 oz.)
2 parts carrot juice (1 oz.)
Orange slices, for garnish

Combine juices in a blender and blend until smooth. Pour into chilled wineglasses and garnish with the orange slice. Serves two.

94 calories; 0.2 gm fat; 2% calories from fat; 0 mg cholesterol; 8.1 mg sodium; 23.2 gm carbohydrate; 0.8 gm protein; 18 mg calcium; 0.6 mg iron; 376.7 RE vitamin A; 64.1 mg vitamin C

SWEET DREAMS

16 parts milk (8 oz.)
1 tbsp. honey
½ tsp. ground cinnamon
½ tsp. ground ginger
½ tsp. ground nutmeg

Heat milk and honey in a saucepan until very hot but not boiling, stirring well to blend. Turn off heat, add spices, and stir again. Serve in a warmed mug. Serves one.

215 calories; 8.1 gm fat; 33% calories from fat; 30.7 mg cholesterol; 113.3 mg sodium; 29.9 gm carbohydrate; 7.7 gm protein; 288.5 mg calcium; 0.8 mg iron; 86.3 RE vitamin A; 2.7 mg vitamin C

SWEET JANE

SWEET JANE

4 parts fresh-squeezed
orange juice (2 oz.)
4 parts fresh-squeezed lime juice (2 oz.)
2 parts cream of coconut (1 oz.)
1 part orgeat (almond) syrup (½ oz.)

Combine all ingredients with cracked ice in a blender. Blend at low speed until smooth. Pour into a chilled wineglass. Serves one.

171 calories; 19 gm fat; 48% calories from fat; 0 mg cholesterol; 2.9 mg sodium; 22.5 gm carbohydrate; 1.7 gm protein; 22.8 mg calcium; 1.3 mg iron; 11.9 RE vitamin A; 45.8 mg vitamin C

SWEET-AND-SOUR COCKTAIL

6 parts apple juice (3 oz.)
6 parts sauerkraut juice (3 oz.)
1 tbsp. beet juice
Lemon slice, for garnish

Combine juices with cracked ice in a cocktail shaker and shake well. Strain into chilled cocktail glass and garnish with the lemon slice. Serves one.

61 calories; 0.2 gm fat; 3% calories from fat; 0 mg cholesterol; 607.1 mg sodium; 14.7 gm carbohydrate; 1 gm protein; 33.8 mg calcium; 1.8 mg iron; 1.9 RE vitamin A; 51.2 mg vitamin C

T

TAHOE SUMMER

8 parts chilled mulled cider (4 oz.)
   (see Mulled Cider, page 141)
Tonic water
Orange twist, for garnish

Prepare recipe for mulled cider and chill overnight. Pour over ice cubes into a chilled collins glass and fill the glass with tonic. Stir gently and garnish with the orange twists. Serves ten.

102 calories; .3 gm fat; 0% calories from fat; 0 mg cholesterol; 11 mg sodium; 34 gm carbohydrate; .5 gm protein; 20 mg calcium; 1 mg iron; .2 RE vitamin A; 1 mg vitamin C

TAMARINDO

TAMARINDO

4 parts tamarind syrup
   (2 oz.)
2 parts grenadine (1 oz.)
2 parts fresh-squeezed lemon
   juice (1 oz.)
Grapefruit juice

Combine all ingredients except grapefruit juice with cracked ice in a cocktail shaker and shake well. Pour over ice cubes into a chilled collins glass. Fill the glass with the grapefruit juice and stir. Serves one.

189 calories; 0.1 gm fat; 0% calories from fat; 0 mg cholesterol; 4 mg sodium; 48.8 gm carbohydrate; 0.5 gm protein; 43.6 mg calcium; 2.2 mg iron; 1.4 RE vitamin A; 45.4 mg vitamin C

TANGERINE BLOSSOM

10 parts hibiscus tea,
   chilled (5 oz.)
4 parts rose-hips tea, chilled (2 oz.)
6 parts tangerine juice (3 oz.)

Combine teas and juices with cracked ice in a cocktail shaker and shake well. Strain over ice cubes into chilled highball glasses. Serves two.

19 calories; 0.1 gm fat; 4% calories from fat; 0 mg cholesterol; 3.3 mg sodium; 4.6 gm carbohydrate; 0.2 gm protein; 7.6 mg calcium; 0.1 mg iron; 17.9 RE vitamin A; 13.2 mg vitamin C

TANGERINE BLUSH

10 parts tangerine juice (5 oz.)
8 parts hibiscus tea, chilled (4 oz.)
4 parts unsweetened cherry
   juice (2 oz.)
Lemon slices, for garnish

Combine all ingredients with cracked ice except lemon slices in a cocktail shaker and shake well. Pour over crushed ice into chilled wineglasses. Garnish with the lemon slices. Serves two.

62 calories; 0.6 gm fat; 8% calories from fat; 0 mg cholesterol; 2.3 mg sodium; 14.4 gm carbohydrate; 0.9 gm protein; 10.9 mg calcium; 0.3 mg iron; 39 RE vitamin A; 25 mg vitamin C

TANGERINE DREAM

8 parts tangerine juice (4 oz.)
8 parts passion-fruit juice (4 oz.)
Fresh mint sprig, for garnish

Combine juices together in a mixing glass and mix well. Pour into a chilled highball glass and garnish with the mint sprig. Serves one.

117 calories; 0.4 gm fat; 3% calories from fat; 0 mg cholesterol; 7.7 mg sodium; 27.9 gm carbohydrate; 1.3 gm protein; 24.7 mg calcium; 0.6 mg iron; 320.9 RE vitamin A; 55.8 mg vitamin C

TEA DANCE PUNCH

32 parts lemon-verbena tea, chilled (16 oz.)
24 parts peppermint tea, chilled (12 oz.)
16 parts hibiscus tea, chilled (8 oz.)
16 parts pureed raspberries (8 oz.)
16 parts fresh-squeezed orange juice (8 oz.)
8 parts fresh-squeezed lemon juice (4 oz.)
Orange slices, for garnish
Fresh raspberries, for garnish

Combine all ingredients except orange slices and fresh raspberries in a large punch bowl. Chill well. Just before serving, add ice and float orange slices and fresh raspberries. Serves six to eight.

42 calories; 0.3 gm fat; 6% calories from fat; 0 mg cholesterol; 5.6 mg sodium; 10.4 gm carbohydrate; 0.7gm protein; 13.8 mg calcium; 0.3 mg iron; 12.9 RE vitamin A; 37 mg vitamin C

TEA SANDWICH

8 parts unsweetened pineapple juice (4 oz.)
8 parts cucumber, peeled, seeded, and chopped (4 oz.)
4 watercress sprigs, chopped
1 fresh mint sprig, chopped
1 parsley sprig, chopped
1 tbsp. fresh-squeezed lime juice

Combine all ingredients except one watercress sprig with cracked ice in a blender and blend until smooth. Pour into a chilled collins glass and garnish with the remaining watercress. Serves one.

88 calories; 0.3 gm fat; 3% calories from fat; 0 mg cholesterol; 17.3 mg sodium; 20.8 gm carbohydrate; 2 gm protein; 74.4 mg calcium; 0.9 mg iron; 177.6 RE vitamin A; 39.9 mg vitamin C

TEMPEST

8 parts mango juice (4 oz.)
4 parts fresh-squeezed lime juice (2 oz.)
Lime twist, for garnish

Combine juices with cracked ice in a blender and blend until slushy. Pour into a chilled highball glass and garnish with the lime twist. Serves one.

108 calories; 0.4 gm fat; 3% calories from fat; 0 mg cholesterol; 3.3 mg sodium; 29.2 gm carbohydrate; 1 gm protein; 19.5 mg calcium; 0.2 mg iron; 552.5 RE vitamin A; 55.9 mg vitamin C

THANKSGIVING TEA

12 parts fresh-squeezed orange juice (6 oz.)
8 parts unsweetened cranberry juice (4 oz.)
4 parts fresh-squeezed lemon juice (2 oz.)
2 tbsp. honey
½ tsp. allspice
½ tsp. ground cinnamon
½ tsp. ground ginger
½ tsp. ground nutmeg
32 parts black tea, hot (16 oz.)
Lemon slices, for garnish

Combine juices, honey, and spices in a saucepan over medium heat. Bring to a boil and then simmer for five minutes. Add brewed tea to mixture and stir well. Serve in warmed mugs garnished with the lemon slices. Serves four.

TEA SANDWICH

74 calories; 0.2 gm fat; 2% calories from fat; 0 mg cholesterol; 4.8 mg sodium; 19.3 gm carbohydrate; 0.5 gm protein; 10.4 mg calcium; 0.3 mg iron; 10.5 RE vitamin A; 32.7 mg vitamin C

THREE C

8 parts carrot juice (4 oz.)
4 parts unsweetened cherry
   juice (2 oz.)
2 parts unsweetened cranberry
   juice (1 oz.)
Carrot stick, for garnish

Combine juices with cracked ice in cocktail shaker and shake well. Strain over ice cubes into a chilled collins glass. Garnish with the carrot stick. Serves one.

135 calories; 1.1 gm fat; 7% calories from fat; 0 mg cholesterol; 33.4 mg sodium; 31.9 gm carbohydrate; 2.3 gm protein; 43.8 mg calcium; 1 mg iron; 2,941 RE vitamin A; 23.3 mg vitamin C

THRUST FAULT

10 parts cantaloupe juice
  (5 oz.)
8 parts apricot juice (4 oz.)
8 parts mango juice (4 oz.)
1 tbsp. honey
½ tsp. alcohol-free mint extract
Orange twists, for garnish

Combine all ingredients except orange twists with cracked ice in a blender and blend until slushy. Pour into chilled wineglasses and garnish with the orange twists. Serves two.

135 calories; 0.4 gm fat; 3% calories from fat; 0 mg cholesterol; 60 mg sodium; 34.7 gm carbohydrate; 1.2 gm protein; 19.5 mg calcium; 0.5 mg iron; 579.3 RE vitamin A; 69 mg vitamin C

THUDPUCKER COCKTAIL

8 parts carrot juice (4 oz.)
6 parts apple juice (3 oz.)
6 parts broccoli juice (3 oz.)
4 parts cucumber juice (2 oz.)
Lemon wedge, for garnish

Combine juices with cracked ice in a cocktail shaker and shake well. Strain over ice cubes into a chilled collins glass and garnish with the lemon wedge. Serves one.

117 calories; 0.6 gm fat; 4% calories from fat; 0 mg cholesterol; 59.6 mg sodium; 26.6 gm carbohydrate; 4 gm protein; 81.9 mg calcium; 1.7 mg iron; 3,054 RE vitamin A; 126.5 mg vitamin C

TIJUANA TOMATO

12 parts tomato juice (6 oz.)
4 parts green bell-pepper juice
  (2 oz.)
3–5 dashes Tabasco sauce
Salt, to taste
Freshly ground black pepper, to taste
Pickled jalapeño peppers, for garnish

Combine juices and Tabasco with cracked ice in a cocktail shaker and shake well. Strain into chilled cocktail glasses and add salt and pepper to taste. Garnish with the pickled jalapeño peppers. Serves two.

22 calories; 0.1 gm fat; 4% calories from fat; 0 mg cholesterol; 311.4 mg sodium; 5.4 gm carbohydrate; 0.9 gm protein; 10.3 mg calcium; 0.6 mg iron; 65.9 RE vitamin A; 32.8 mg vitamin C

TOMATO COCKTAIL

32 parts tomato juice (16 oz.)
2 parts red-wine vinegar (1 oz.)
1 cucumber, peeled and pureed
½ tsp. salt
½ tsp. dried or 1 tbsp. fresh basil
½ tsp. freshly ground black pepper
⅛ tsp. paprika
Lime wedges, for garnish

Combine all ingredients except lime wedges in a large glass pitcher and stir well. Chill and serve over ice cubes in highball glasses. Garnished with the lime wedges. Serves four.

24 calories; 0.1 gm fat; 4% calories from fat; 0 mg cholesterol; 523.8 mg sodium; 6 gm carbohydrate; 1.1 gm protein; 16.5 mg calcium; 0.8 mg iron; 75 RE vitamin A; 10.7 mg vitamin C

TOMATO COOLER

12 parts tomato juice (6 oz.)
8 parts celery juice (4 oz.)
Freshly ground black pepper, to taste
Celery stick, to taste

Combine juices and pepper with cracked ice in a cocktail shaker and shake well. Strain over ice cubes into a chilled collins glass and garnish with the celery. Serves one.

48 calories; 0.3 gm fat; 4% calories from fat; 0 mg cholesterol; 711.5 mg sodium; 11.5 gm carbohydrate; 2.2 gm protein; 61.6 mg calcium; 1.5 mg iron; 109.5 RE vitamin A; 21.8 mg vitamin C

TOMATO MUFFLER

16 parts tomato juice (8 oz.)
1 part fresh-squeezed
    lemon juice (½ oz.)
2 whole cloves
½ tsp. sugar
Salt, to taste
Freshly ground black pepper, to taste

Combine all the ingredients in a
saucepan except the salt and pepper
and heat just to the boiling point.
Lower heat and simmer for five to ten
minutes, stirring occasionally. Strain
into a warmed mug. Add salt and pepper to taste. Serves one.

*50 calories; 0.1 gm fat; 2% calories
from fat; 0 mg cholesterol; 817.4
mg sodium; 12.9 gm carbohydrate;
1.8 gm protein; 21.4 mg calcium;
1.3 mg iron; 126.6 RE vitamin A;
24.6 mg vitamin C*

TOMATO SAUER

8 parts tomato juice (4 oz.)
8 parts sauerkraut
  juice (4 oz.)
½ tsp. fresh-squeezed lime juice
Lemon slice, for garnish

Combine juices in a mixing glass and
stir well. Pour over ice cubes into
chilled collins glass and garnish with
the lemon slice. Serves one.

*41 calories; 0.2 gm fat; 4% calories
from fat; 0 mg cholesterol; 1,158
mg sodium; 9.9 gm carbohydrate;
1.9 gm protein; 44.4 mg calcium;
2.3 mg iron; 65.5 RE vitamin A;
26.5 mg vitamin C*

TOMATO SMOOTHIE

16 parts tomato juice (8 oz.)
8 parts plain nonfat yogurt (4 oz.)
4 parts chopped cucumber (2 oz.)
1 tbsp. fresh basil, chopped fine
3–5 dashes Tabasco sauce
Salt, to taste
Freshly ground black pepper, to taste
Celery stalk, for garnish

Combine all ingredients except salt,
pepper, and celery stalk in a blender.
Blend until well-mixed and pour into
a chilled collins glass. Garnish with
the celery stalk. Serves one.

*106 calories; 0.2 gm fat; 2% calo-
ries from fat; 2.5 mg cholesterol;
907.1 mg sodium; 20.4 gm carbohydrate; 8.6 gm protein; 257.2 mg
calcium; 1.5 mg iron; 130.4 RE vitamin A; 22.1 mg vitamin C*

TOMATO SURPRISE

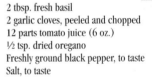

10 parts tomato juice
  (5 oz.)
4 parts fennel juice (2 oz.)
1 tsp. fresh-squeezed lemon juice
½ tsp. garlic puree
Lemon twist, for garnish

Combine juices and puree in a
blender and blend until smooth. Pour
over ice cubes into a chilled highball

glass and garnish with lemon twist.
Serves one.

*48 calories; 0.2 gm fat; 3% calories
from fat; 0 mg cholesterol; 540.7
mg sodium; 11.6 gm carbohydrate;
2 gm protein; 46.6 mg calcium;
0.9 mg iron; 79.1 RE vitamin A;
21.4 mg vitamin C*

TOMATO-AVOCADO COMBO

10 parts tomato juice (5 oz.)
4 parts alfalfa-sprout juice (2 oz.)
1 part scallion juice (½ oz.)
1 Haas avocado, peeled and chopped
1 tsp. pureed garlic
Freshly ground black pepper, to taste

Combine all ingredients in a blender
and blend until smooth. Pour into a
chilled collins glass. Add pepper to
taste. Serves one.

*355 calories; 30.5 gm fat; 20%
calories from fat; 0 mg cholesterol;
536.3 mg sodium; 21.9 gm carbohydrate; 7.4 gm protein; 63.9 mg
calcium; 3.7 mg iron; 264.9 RE
vitamin A; 37 mg vitamin C*

TOMATO-PESTO COCKTAIL

2 tbsp. fresh basil
2 garlic cloves, peeled and chopped
12 parts tomato juice (6 oz.)
½ tsp. dried oregano
Freshly ground black pepper, to taste
Salt, to taste

Puree the basil and garlic in a food
processor or with a mortar and pestle.
Combine with the tomato juice in a
blender and blend. Strain over ice
cubes into chilled a highball glass and
add salt and pepper to taste. Stir gently. Serves one.

*41 calories; 0.2 gm fat; 4% calories
from fat; 0 mg cholesterol; 614 mg
sodium; 9.8 gm carbohydrate;
1.9 gm protein; 43.8 mg calcium;
1.3 mg iron; 98.9 RE vitamin A;
15.4 mg vitamin C*

TOP OF THE WORLD

8 parts carrot juice (4 oz.)
8 parts celery juice (4 oz.)
4 parts onion juice (2 oz.)
Cocktail onions, for garnish

Combine juices with cracked ice in a cocktail shaker and shake well. Strain into chilled cocktail glasses and garnish with the cocktail onions. Serves two.

35 calories; 0.2 gm fat; 5% calories from fat; 0 mg cholesterol; 96.1 mg sodium; 8 gm carbohydrate; 1.3 gm protein; 50 mg calcium; 0.7 mg iron; 1,570 RE vitamin A; 13.3 mg vitamin C

TRADIONAL LEMONADE

TOPPER'S TONIC

6 parts red grape juice (3 oz.)
1 tsp. fresh-squeezed lime juice
Ginger ale
Lime slice, for garnish

Pour grape juice over ice cubes into a chilled highball glass. Add the lime juice and fill the glass with ginger ale. Stir gently and garnish with the lime slice. Serves one.

82 calories; 0.1 gm fat; 1% calories from fat; 0 mg cholesterol; 8.6 mg sodium; 20.6 gm carbohydrate; 0.5 gm protein; 10.7 mg calcium; 0.3 mg iron; 0.7 RE vitamin A; 1.6 mg vitamin C

TOTALLY VEGGED-OUT

8 parts carrot juice (4 oz.)
6 parts tomato juice (3 oz.)
6 parts spinach juice (3 oz.)
4 parts celery juice (2 oz.)
4 parts cucumber juice (2 oz.)
2 parts red-cabbage juice (1 oz.)
2 parts red bell-pepper juice (1 oz.)
1 tbsp. scallion juice
Celery sticks, for garnish

Combine juices in a blender and blend until smooth. Pour into chilled highball glasses and garnish with the celery sticks. Serves two.

58 calories; 0.5 gm fat; 6% calories from fat; 0 mg cholesterol; 209.7 mg sodium; 12.8 gm carbohydrate; 2.9 gm protein; 101.1 mg calcium; 2.1 mg iron; 1,943 RE vitamin A; 40.1 mg vitamin C

TRADITIONAL LEMONADE

40 parts cold water (80 oz. / 10 cups)
32 parts fresh-squeezed lemon juice (16 oz./ 2 cups)
32 parts sugar syrup (16 oz. / 2 cups)
10 fresh mint sprigs
Lemon slices, for garnish

Combine cold water and lemon juice in a large pitcher. Add one cup of the sugar syrup and the mint sprigs and stir. Add more sugar syrup, to taste. Stir well and add ice. Float several lemon slices on top. Serves ten.

Note: To make pink lemonade, add ½ cup of raspberry or strawberry syrup and decrease the amount of sugar syrup accordingly.

174 calories; 0 gm fat; 0% calories from fat; 0 mg cholesterol; 3.6 mg sodium; 46.2 gm carbohydrate; 0.2 gm protein; 40.4 mg calcium; 2.2 mg iron; 1 RE vitamin A; 22.4 mg vitamin C

TRAFFIC JAM

8 parts pineapple juice (4 oz.)
6 parts strawberry puree (3 oz.)
6 parts broccoli juice (3 oz.)
Whole strawberry, for garnish

Combine juices and puree in a blender and blend until smooth. Pour over ice cubes into a chilled collins glass and garnish with the whole strawberry. Serves one.

113 calories; 0.7 gm fat; 5% calories from fat; 0 mg cholesterol; 25 mg sodium; 26.1 gm carbohydrate; 3.4 gm protein; 72 mg calcium; 1.4 mg iron; 134.3 RE vitamin A; 139.6 mg vitamin C

TRIPLE TREMOR

8 parts pineapple juice (4 oz.)
8 parts red grape juice (4 oz.)
8 parts strawberry puree (4 oz.)
Pineapple spears, for garnish

Combine juices and puree in a blender and blend until smooth. Pour into chilled wineglasses and garnish with the pineapple spears. Serves two.

167 calories; 0.6 gm fat; 3% calories from fat; 0 mg cholesterol; 5.7 mg sodium; 40.6 gm carbohydrate; 1.7 gm protein; 45.4 mg calcium; 1 mg iron; 4.6 RE vitamin A; 76.6 mg vitamin C

TROPICAL PLEASURE

8 parts fresh-squeezed
    orange juice (4 oz.)
6 parts papaya juice (3 oz.)
6 parts pineapple juice (3 oz.)
1 banana, sliced

Combine all ingredients in a blender and blend until frothy. Pour into a chilled collins glass. Serves one.

252 calories; 1 gm fat; 3% calories from fat; 0 mg cholesterol; 7 mg sodium; 62.6 gm carbohydrate; 2.4 gm protein; 42.3 mg calcium; 1.1 mg iron; 41.7 RE vitamin A; 78.7 mg vitamin C

TRUE COMPANION

12 parts plum juice
    (6 oz.)
8 parts unsweetened cherry
    juice (4 oz.)
6 parts apple juice (3 oz.)
1 tbsp. fresh-squeezed lemon juice
½ tsp. alcohol-free almond extract
Pinch of ground cloves

Combine all ingredients in a blender and blend until smooth. Pour over ice cubes into chilled highball glasses. Serves two.

113 calories; 1.1 gm fat; 8% calories from fat; 0 mg cholesterol; 1.4 mg sodium; 26.5 gm carbohydrate; 1.4 gm protein; 15.3 mg calcium; 0.5 mg iron; 39.5 RE vitamin A; 33 mg vitamin C

TULARE DUSTBUSTER

Ginger Beer
Natural Cola
Lime wedge, for garnish

Combine the ginger beer and cola in a chilled pilsner glass. Squeeze the lime wedge over drink and drop it in. Stir gently. Serves one.

70 calories; 0 gm fat; 0% calories from fat; 0 mg cholesterol; 11.2 mg sodium; 14.7 gm carbohydrate; 0.1 gm protein; 6.1 mg calcium; 0.1 mg iron; 0 RE vitamin A; 0 mg vitamin C

TUMMY TREAT

10 parts papaya juice
    (5 oz.)
2 parts ginger juice (1 oz.)
1 tsp. alcohol-free mint extract
Sparkling mineral water

Combine juices and extract with cracked ice in a cocktail shaker and shake well. Strain into a chilled collins glass and fill the glass with the sparkling mineral water. Serves one.

116 calories; 0.4 gm fat; 3% calories from fat; 0 mg cholesterol; 7.7 mg sodium; 26.3 gm carbohydrate; 0.7 gm protein; 18.9 mg calcium;

0.6 mg iron; 15.7 RE vitamin A;
5.7 mg vitamin C

TURBULENT PASSION

8 parts fresh-squeezed
   orange juice (4 oz.)
8 parts passion-fruit juice (4 oz.)
2 parts unsweetened cherry
   juice (1 oz.)
Orange slice, for garnish

Combine orange juice and passion-
fruit juice in a cocktail shaker and
shake well. Pour into a chilled highball glass. Slowly pour the cherry juice
into the drink without stirring, creating a red, swirling effect. Garnish with
the orange slice. Serves one.

*139 calories; 0.7 gm fat; 4% calo-
ries from fat; 0 mg cholesterol; 7.7
mg sodium; 32.9 gm carbohydrate;
1.9 gm protein; 21.1 mg calcium;
0.7 mg iron; 301.9 RE vitamin A;
79.4 mg vitamin C*

TWAIN-HARTE TINGLER

4 parts peppermint syrup (2 oz.)
Bitter-lemon soda
Fresh mint sprig, for garnish

Pour syrup over ice cubes into a
chilled highball glass. Fill the glass
with the bitter-lemon soda and stir
gently. Garnish with the fresh mint
sprig. Serves one.

*194 calories; 0 gm fat; 0% calories
from fat; 0 mg cholesterol; 15.3 mg
sodium; 50.3 gm carbohydrate;
0 gm protein; 36.2 mg calcium;
2.1 mg iron; 0 RE vitamin A; 0 mg
vitamin C*

TWENTY-NINE PALMS

8 parts pineapple juice (4 oz.)
6 parts mango juice (3 oz.)
6 parts guava nectar (3 oz.)
4 parts coconut milk (2 oz.)

Combine all ingredients with cracked
ice in a blender and blend until
slushy. Pour into chilled highball
glasses. Serves two.

---

*169 calories; 8.5 gm fat; 43% calo-
ries from fat; 0 mg cholesterol; 6.9
mg sodium; 23.4 gm carbohydrate;
1.6 gm protein; 26.5 mg calcium;
0.7 mg iron; 254.7 RE vitamin A;
99.7 mg vitamin C*

TWENTY-THREE-POINT SPREAD

6 parts apple juice (3 oz.)
6 parts carrot juice (3 oz.)
4 parts cucumber juice (2 oz.)
2 parts red bell-pepper juice (1 oz.)
2 parts spinach juice (1 oz.)
2 parts watercress juice (1 oz.)
Fresh watercress sprigs, for garnish

Combine juices in a blender and
blend until smooth. Pour into chilled
old-fashioned glasses and garnish
with the watercress. Serves two.

*50 calories; 0.3 gm fat; 4% calories
from fat; 0 mg cholesterol; 24.1 mg
sodium; 11.3 gm carbohydrate;
1.4 gm protein; 53.1 mg calcium;
0.8 mg iron; 1,296 RE vitamin A;
43.2 mg vitamin C*

TWO HEARTS

8 parts sparkling apple juice
   (4 oz.)
6 parts sparkling cranberry juice
   cocktail (3 oz.)
Lime slice, for garnish

Slowly pour juices into a chilled wineglass and stir gently. Garnish with the
lime slice. Serves one.

*88 calories; 0.2 gm fat; 2% calories
from fat; 0 mg cholesterol; 1,51.3
mg sodium; 22 gm carbohydrate;
4.6 gm protein; 169.4 mg calcium;
2.8 mg iron; 2,745 RE vitamin A;
65 mg vitamin C*

U-V

UNITED WE VEG

8 parts celery juice (4 oz.)
6 parts carrot juice (3 oz.)
4 parts cucumber juice (2 oz.)
4 parts spinach juice (2 oz.)
4 parts green bell-pepper juice (2 oz.)
4 parts cabbage juice (2 oz.)

Combine juices in a blender and
blend until completely mixed. Pour
over ice cubes into chilled highball
glasses. Serves two.

*100 calories; 0.9 gm fat; 7% calo-
ries from fat; 0 mg cholesterol; 151
mg sodium; 22 gm carbohydrate;
4.6 gm protein; 169.4 mg calcium;
2.8 mg iron; 2,745 RE vitamin A;
90.4 mg vitamin C*

VANILLA COFFEE

12 parts strong-brewed black coffee,
hot (6 oz.)
2 parts vanilla syrup (1 oz.)
2 parts half-and-half (1 oz.)
Whipped cream, for garnish
Grated nutmeg, for garnish
Cinnamon stick, for garnish

Combine coffee with syrup and half-
and half in a warmed mug and stir.
Top with a dollop of whipped cream,
sprinkle with nutmeg, and garnish
with the cinnamon stick. Serves one.

*134 calories; 5.3 gm fat; 34% calo-
ries from fat; 17.2 mg cholesterol;
18.2 mg sodium; 21.5 gm carbohydrate; 1.1 gm protein; 54 mg
calcium; 1.1 mg iron; 58.8 RE
vitamin A; 0.3 mg vitamin C*

VANILLA SUN SHAKE

16 parts fresh-squeezed
orange juice (8 oz.)
2 scoops vanilla frozen yogurt
2 parts orgeat (almond) syrup (1 oz.)

Combine all ingredients in a blender
and blend until smooth. Pour into a
chilled collins glass. Serves one.

*404 calories; 8.5 gm fat; 18% calo-
ries from fat; 4 mg cholesterol;
129.2 mg sodium; 77.7 gm carbohydrate; 7.2 gm protein; 403.9 mg
calcium; 1.9 mg iron; 127.4 RE vitamin A; 114.6 mg vitamin C*

VAQUERO

2 parts fresh-squeezed
lime juice (1 oz.)
2 parts barbecue sauce (1 oz.)
3–5 dashes Worcestershire sauce
Tabasco sauce, to taste
Freshly ground black pepper, to taste
Tomato juice
Pickled jalapeño pepper, for garnish
Lime slice, for garnish

Combine all ingredients except tomato juice, jalapeño pepper, and lime
slice with cracked ice in a cocktail
shaker and shake well. Pour into a
chilled highball glass. Fill the glass
with tomato juice and stir. Garnish
with the jalapeño pepper and the lime
slice. Serves one.

*49 calories; 0.1 gm fat; 1% calories
from fat; 0 mg cholesterol; 219 mg
sodium; 12.4 gm carbohydrate;
0.6 gm protein; 10.5 mg calcium;
0.5 mg iron; 32.9 RE vitamin A;
15.9 mg vitamin C*

VENICE BEACH

4 parts fresh-squeezed lime
juice (2 oz.)
1 tsp. alcohol-free almond extract
Cream soda
Lime slice, for garnish

Combine the lime juice and almond
extract in the bottom of a chilled
highball glass. Fill the glass about
two-thirds full with the cream soda
and stir gently. Add the ice cubes
and garnish with the lime slice.
Serves one.

*88 calories; 0.1 gm fat; 1% calories
from fat; 0 mg cholesterol; 14.2 mg
sodium; 21.6 gm carbohydrate;*

VAQUERO

0.2 gm protein; 10.8 mg calcium;
0.1 mg iron; 0.6 RE vitamin A;
16.6 mg vitamin C

VENTURA
COUNTY LINE

8 parts white grape juice (4
    oz.)
4 parts pineapple juice (2 oz.)
2 parts fresh-squeezed lime
    juice (1 oz.)
Ginger ale
Lime slice, for garnish

Combine juices with cracked ice in a
cocktail shaker and shake well. Strain
over ice cubes into a chilled collins
glass and fill the glass with the ginger
ale. Stir gently and garnish with the
lime slice. Serves one.

*144 calories; 0.2 gm fat; 1% calo-
ries from fat; 0 mg cholesterol; 8.5
mg sodium; 36.2 gm carbohydrate;
1 gm protein; 29 mg calcium;
0.6 mg iron; 1.6 RE vitamin A;
17.5 mg vitamin C*

VERBENA TANGERINA

16 parts lemon-verbena tea, chilled (8 oz.)
4 parts tangerine juice (2 oz.)
Lemon slice, for garnish

Combine tea and juice with cracked ice in a cocktail shaker and shake well. Strain over ice cubes into a chilled collins glass and garnish with the lemon slice. Serves one.

27 calories; 0.1 gm fat; 4% calories from fat; 0 mg cholesterol; 7.3 mg sodium; 6.4 gm carbohydrate; 0.3 gm protein; 10.1 mg calcium; 0.2 mg iron; 23.9 RE vitamin A; 17.6 mg vitamin C

VIGOROUS APRICOT

4 parts apricot juice (2 oz.)
4 parts passion-fruit juice (2 oz.)
Tonic water
Orange slice, for garnish

Combine juices with cracked ice in a cocktail shaker and shake well. Strain over ice cubes into a chilled collins glass and fill the glass with tonic water. Stir gently and garnish with the orange slice. Serves one.

105 calories; 0.2 gm fat; 1% calories from fat; 0 mg cholesterol; 9.6 mg sodium; 26.3 gm carbohydrate; 0.6 gm protein; 7.4 mg calcium; 0.4 mg iron; 211.4 RE vitamin A; 29.3 mg vitamin C

VIRGIN MARY

8 parts tomato juice (4 oz.)
2 parts fresh-squeezed lime juice (1 oz.)
¼ tsp. white horseradish
3–5 dashes Tabasco sauce
3–5 dashes Worcestershire sauce
Freshly ground black pepper, to taste
Salt, to taste
Lime wedge, for garnish

Combine all ingredients except salt, pepper, and the lime wedge with cracked ice in a cocktail shaker and shake well. Pour into a chilled high-ball glass and add salt and pepper to taste. Garnish with the lime wedge. Serves one.

31 calories; 0.1 gm fat; 3% calories from fat; 0 mg cholesterol; 456.1 mg sodium; 8.3 gm carbohydrate; 1.1 gm protein; 18.2 mg calcium; 1 mg iron; 65.5 RE vitamin A; 24.5 mg vitamin C

VIRGIN STRAWBERRY MARGARITA

10 parts strawberry puree (5 oz.)
8 parts fresh-squeezed orange juice (4 oz.)
2 parts fresh-squeezed lemon juice (1 oz.)
2 parts fresh-squeezed lime juice (1 oz.)
Lime slices, for garnish

Combine puree and juices in a blender with cracked ice and blend until slushy. Pour into chilled margarita glasses. Garnish with lime slices. Serves two.

54 calories; 0.4 gm fat; 2% calories from fat; 0 mg cholesterol; 1.5 mg sodium; 13.4 gm carbohydrate; 0.9 gm protein; 18.4 mg calcium; 0.4 mg iron; 13.7 RE vitamin A; 79.2 mg vitamin C

VIRGIN MARY

W-X-Y-Z

WAKE OF THE FLOOD

10 parts fresh-squeezed
orange juice (5 oz.)
2 parts tamarind syrup (1 oz.)
1 tsp. fresh-squeezed lime juice
Lime slice, for garnish

Combine all ingredients except lime
slice with cracked ice in a cocktail
shaker and shake well. Strain over ice
cubes into a chilled highball glass
and garnish with the lime slice.
Serves one.

139 calories; 0.3 gm fat; 2% calories from fat; 0 mg cholesterol; 2.6 mg sodium; 34.5 gm carbohydrate; 1 gm protein; 32.9 mg calcium; 1.3 mg iron; 28.4 RE vitamin A; 72.4 mg vitamin C

WASP'S NEST

12 parts tomato juice
(6 oz.)
2 parts onion juice (1 oz.)
½ tsp. white horseradish
5–7 dashes Tabasco sauce
Ground black pepper, to taste

Combine all ingredients with cracked
ice in a cocktail shaker and
shake well. Strain over ice cubes into
a chilled old-fashioned glass.
Serves one.

43 calories; 0.2 gm fat; 3% calories from fat; 0 mg cholesterol; 648.1 mg sodium; 10.6 gm carbohydrate; 1.8 gm protein; 24.9 mg calcium; 1.2 mg iron; 95.7 RE vitamin A; 17.1 mg vitamin C

WATERMELON FREEZE

12 parts watermelon juice
(6 oz.)
8 parts raspberry puree (4 oz.)
2 scoops lemon sorbet
Fresh raspberries, for garnish

Combine all ingredients except whole
berries in a blender and blend until
smooth. If mixture is too thick, add
more watermelon juice until desired
consistency is achieved. Pour into
chilled highball glasses and garnish
with the fresh raspberries. Serves two.

138 calories; 0.7 gm fat; 4% calories from fat; 0 mg cholesterol; 3.4 mg sodium; 36.7 gm carbohydrate; 1.6 gm protein; 29.1 mg calcium; 0.5 mg iron; 46.1 RE vitamin A; 79.8 mg vitamin C

WATERMELON WAVE

10 parts watermelon juice (5 oz.)
2 parts fresh-squeezed lime
juice (1 oz.)
Lemon-lime soda

Combine juices in a mixing glass and
stir well. Pour over ice cubes into a
chilled collins glass and fill the
glass with the lemon-lime soda. Stir
gently and garnish with the lime slice.
Serves one.

96 calories; 0.8 gm fat; 6% calories from fat; 0 mg cholesterol; 13 mg sodium; 23.6 gm carbohydrate; 1.2 gm protein; 17.9 mg calcium; 0.4 mg iron; 62.5 RE vitamin A; 24.7 mg vitamin C

WATSONVILLE COOLER

8 parts kiwi juice
(4 oz.)
8 parts strawberry puree (4 oz.)
8 parts white grape juice (4 oz.)
1 tbsp. fresh-squeezed lemon juice

Combine all ingredients with cracked
ice in a cocktail shaker and shake vigorously. Strain into a chilled collins
glass over ice cubes. Serves one.

176 calories; 1 gm fat; 5% calories from fat; 0 mg cholesterol; 10.4 mg sodium; 43.1 gm carbohydrate;

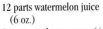

2.5 gm protein; 56.7 mg calcium;
1.2 mg iron; 24.2 RE vitamin A;
182.6 mg vitamin C

WEST L.A. COOLER

4 parts apricot nectar (2 oz.)
Raspberry soda
Orange peel, for garnish
Fresh raspberries, garnish

Pour apricot nectar into a chilled
collins glass almost filled with ice
cubes. Fill the glass with raspberry
soda. Stir gently and garnish with the
orange peel and the fresh raspberries.
Serves one.

93 calories; 0.5 gm fat; 4% calories
from fat; 0 mg cholesterol; 12.9 mg
sodium; 22.4 gm carbohydrate;
0.7 gm protein; 7.3 mg calcium;
0.2 mg iron; 75.8 RE vitamin A;
21.7 mg vitamin C

WESTERN SKY

8 parts apple juice
   (4 oz.)
8 parts pear juice (4 oz.)
6 parts fresh-squeezed orange
   juice (3 oz.)
4 parts rehydrated raisins, chopped
   fine (2 oz.)
1 banana, sliced

Combine all ingredients in a blender
and blend until smooth. Pour into
chilled highball glasses. Serves two.

217 calories; 0.5 gm fat; 2% calo-
ries from fat; 0 mg cholesterol; 8 mg
sodium; 55.3 gm carbohydrate;
1.9 gm protein; 31.6 mg calcium;
1.2 mg iron; 13.6 RE vitamin A;
51.3 mg vitamin C

WHAT A TOMATO

12 parts tomato juice
   (6 oz.)
6 parts carrot juice (3 oz.)
1 tbsp. scallion juice
1 tbsp. parsley juice
½ tsp. jalapeño pepper juice
Fresh parsley sprig, for garnish

Combine ingredients except the
parsley sprig in a blender until well-

mixed. Pour over ice cubes into a
chilled collins glass and garnish with
the parsley sprig. Serves one.

75 calories; 0.3 gm fat; 3% calories
from fat; 0 mg cholesterol; 640.8
mg sodium; 17.8 gm carbohydrate;
2.7 gm protein; 58.2 mg calcium;
2.2 mg iron; 2,446 RE vitamin A;
38.9 mg vitamin C

WHITE GOLD

8 parts papaya juice (4 oz.)
8 parts pineapple juice
   (4 oz.)
½ tsp. alcohol-free almond extract
2 scoops vanilla frozen yogurt
Pineapple spear, for garnish

Combine all ingredients except the
pineapple spear in a blender and
blend until smooth. Add more pineapple juice if mixture is too thick until
desired consistency is achieved.
Pour into a chilled collins glass and
garnish with the pineapple spear.
Serves one.

364 calories; 8.3 gm fat; 20% calo-
ries from fat; 4 mg cholesterol;
132.8 mg sodium; 67.7 gm carbo-
hydrate; 6.1 gm protein; 236.6 mg
calcium; 1.1 mg iron; 95.1 RE vita-
min A; 16.8 mg vitamin C

WHITE RABBIT

10 parts nonfat yogurt (5 oz.)
8 parts carrot juice (4 oz.)
4 parts spinach juice (2 oz.)
2 parts onion juice (1 oz.)
1 tsp. garlic juice
Freshly ground black pepper, to taste
Carrot sticks, for garnish
Celery stalks, for garnish

Combine yogurt and juices in a
blender and blend until smooth. Pour
into chilled highball glasses and garnish with carrot and celery sticks.
Serves two.

76 calories; 0.3 gm fat; 3% calories
from fat; 1.6 mg cholesterol; 74.7
mg sodium; 13.9 gm carbohydrate;
5.7 gm protein; 196.7 mg calcium;
1 mg iron; 1,708 RE vitamin A;
10.4 mg vitamin C

WIDOW'S WALK

8 parts fresh-squeezed
  orange juice (4 oz.)
8 parts cold rose-hips tea (4 oz.)
2 parts peppermint syrup (1 oz.)
Fresh mint sprig, for garnish

Combine all ingredients with cracked
ice in a cocktail shaker. Strain over
ice cubes into a chilled collins glass
and garnish with the mint sprig.
Serves one.

*126 calories; 0.2 gm fat; 2% calo-
ries from fat; 0 mg cholesterol; 5.7
mg sodium; 31.4 gm carbohydrate;
0.8 gm protein; 29.3 mg calcium;
1.3 mg iron; 22.7 RE vitamin A;
56.7 mg vitamin C*

WILD THING

10 parts cranberry juice
  cocktail (5 oz.)
8 parts apricot nectar (4 oz.)
1 tbsp. fresh-squeezed lemon juice
Lemon slice, for garnish

Combine all ingredients except for
the lemon slice with cracked ice in a
cocktail shaker and shake well. Strain
over ice cubes into a chilled collins
glass. Garnish with the lemon slice.
Serves one.

*148 calories; 0.2 gm fat; 1% calo-
ries from fat; 0 mg cholesterol; 9.2
mg sodium; 38 gm carbohydrate;
0.5 gm protein; 13.3 mg calcium;
0.6 mg iron; 149.9 RE vitamin A;
95.1 mg vitamin C*

WINTER TONIC

10 parts fresh-squeezed
  orange juice (5 oz.)
4 parts cream of coconut (2 oz.)
4 parts pineapple juice (2 oz.)
Shredded coconut, for garnish

Combine all ingredients except shredded coconut with cracked ice in a
blender and blend until smooth. Pour
into a chilled collins glass. Sprinkle
with shredded coconut. Serves one.

*282 calories; 20 gm fat; 60% calo-
ries from fat; 0 mg cholesterol; 4.1*

*mg sodium; 26.4 gm carbohydrate;
3.2 gm protein; 31.2 mg calcium;
1.7 mg iron; 28.6 RE vitamin A;
78.5 mg vitamin C*

X-RAY SPEX

4 parts unsweetened cherry
  juice (2 oz.)
2 parts fresh-squeezed lemon
  juice (1 oz.)
Cream soda
Lemon slice, for garnish

Combine juices in a chilled highball
glass. Fill the glass about two-thirds
full with the cream soda and stir gently. Add ice cubes and garnish with the
lemon slice. Serves one.

*91 calories; 0.5 gm fat; 5% calories
from fat; 0 mg cholesterol; 10.5 mg
sodium; 23.1 gm carbohydrate;
0.8 gm protein; 14.6 mg calcium;
0.3 mg iron; 12.7 RE vitamin A;
17 mg vitamin C*

YERBA BUENA FIZZ

10 parts pineapple juice (5 oz.)
1 tsp. alcohol-free mint extract
Ginger ale
Fresh mint sprig, for garnish

Combine pineapple juice and mint
extract with cracked ice in a cocktail
shaker and shake well. Strain into a
chilled highball glass and fill the
glass with the ginger ale. Stir gently
and garnish with the mint sprig.
Serves one.

*113 calories; 0.1 gm fat; 1% calo-
ries from fat; 0 mg cholesterol; 5.4
mg sodium; 26 gm carbohydrate;
0.5 gm protein; 25.8 mg calcium;
0.5 mg iron; 0.7 RE vitamin A;
15.2mg vitamin C*

YOLO COUNTY COOLER

4 parts fresh-squeezed lime juice
  (2 oz.)
4 parts orgeat (almond) syrup (2 oz.)
Sparkling mineral water
Lime slice, for garnish

Combine the juice and syrup in a chilled highball glass. Fill the glass almost two-thirds full with the sparkling mineral water and stir gently. Add ice cubes and garnish with the lime slice. Serves one.

164 calories; 0.1 gm fat; 0 % calories from fat; 0 mg cholesterol; 3.4 mg sodium; 43.7 gm carbohydrate; 0.2 gm protein; 39 mg calcium; 2.1 mg iron; 0.7 RE vitamin A; 15.2 mg vitamin C

YOSEMITE TWILIGHT

6 parts pear juice (3 oz.)
4 parts apple juice (2 oz.)
4 parts peach juice (2 oz.)
Ground nutmeg, for garnish

Combine juices with cracked ice in a cocktail shaker and shake well. Strain over ice cubes into chilled highball glass and sprinkle with nutmeg. Serves one.

110 calories; 0.2 gm fat; 2% calories from fat; 0 mg cholesterol; 8.7 mg sodium; 28.1 gm carbohydrate; 0.3 gm protein; 11.5 mg calcium; 0.6 mg iron; 14.7 RE vitamin A; 27.2 mg vitamin C

YUPPIE-CHOW COCKTAIL

8 parts yellow cherry-
  tomato juice
  (4 oz.)
6 parts mixed baby-lettuce juice (3 oz.)
2 parts radicchio juice (1 oz.)
1 tsp. extra-virgin olive oil
1 tsp. fresh-squeezed lemon juice
½ tsp. balsamic vinegar
Freshly ground black pepper, to taste
Salt, to taste

Combine all ingredients except salt and pepper in a blender and mix well. Pour into chilled cocktail glasses. Serves two.

40 calories; 2.5 gm fat; 52% calories from fat; 0 mg cholesterol; 7.6 mg sodium; 4.3 gm carbohydrate; 1.1 gm protein; 17.5 mg calcium; 0.5 mg iron; 76.7 RE vitamin A; 15.9 mg vitamin C

ZABRISKIE POINT

12 parts carrot juice (6 oz.)
6 parts celery juice (3 oz.)
4 parts beet juice (2 oz.)

Combine all ingredients with cracked ice in a cocktail shaker and shake well. Strain into chilled old-fashioned glasses. Serves two.

54 calories; 0.2 gm fat; 4% calories from fat; 0 mg cholesterol; 83.3 mg sodium; 12.3 gm carbohydrate; 1.6 gm protein; 42.1 mg calcium; 0.8 mg iron; 2,196 RE vitamin A; 11.2 mg vitamin C

ZEN COOLER

8 parts white grape juice
  (4 oz.)
2 parts fresh-squeezed lemon
  juice (1 oz.)
Ginger ale
Lemon twist, for garnish

Combine juices with cracked ice in a cocktail shaker and shake well. Strain over ice cubes into a chilled highball glass. Fill the glass with the ginger ale and stir gently. Garnish with the lemon twist. Serves one.

96 calories; 0.1 gm fat; 1% calories from fat; 0 mg cholesterol; 7.7 mg sodium; 24.3 gm carbohydrate; 0.7 gm protein; 13.9 mg calcium; 0.4 mg iron; 1.5 RE vitamin A; 13.1 mg vitamin C

ZERO GRAVITY

8 parts fresh-squeezed orange
   juice (4 oz.)
8 parts ginger beer (4 oz.)
Orange peel, for garnish

Pour orange juice over ice cubes into
a chilled collins glasss. Add the ginger
beer and stir gently. Twist orange peel
over the drink and drop it in.
Serves one.

*91 calories; 0.2 gm fat; 2% calories
from fat; 0 mg cholesterol; 8.9 mg
sodium; 22.2 gm carbohydrate;
0.8 gm protein; 19.1 mg calcium;
0.4 mg iron; 23.7 RE vitamin A;
59.4 mg vitamin C*

ZESTY COOLER

4 parts fresh-squeezed lime
   juice (2 oz.)
Ginger beer
Lime wedge, for garnish

Pour lime juice over ice cubes into a
chilled beer mug. Fill the glass with
the ginger beer and stir gently.
Garnish with the lime wedge.
Serves one.

*54 calories; 0.1 gm fat; 1% calories
from fat; 0 mg cholesterol; 8.5 mg
sodium; 15 gm carbohydrate;
8.5 gm protein; 8.5 mg calcium;
0.2 mg iron; 0.6 RE vitamin A;
16.6 mg vitamin C*

ZIG-ZAG

8 parts carrot juice (4 oz.)
6 parts apple juice (3 oz.)
6 parts broccoli juice (3 oz.)
4 parts celery juice (2 oz.)
4 parts cucumber juice (2 oz.)
Lemon wedge, for garnish
Broccoli floret, for garnish
Carrot stick, for garnish

Combine juices with cracked ice in a
cocktail shaker and shake well. Strain
over ice cubes and garnish with the
lemon wedge, broccoli floret, and carrot stick. Serves one.

*126 calories; 0.7 gm fat; 5% calo-
ries from fat; 0 mg cholesterol;
108.8 mg sodium; 28.7 gm carbohydrate; 4.4 gm protein; 104.6 mg
calcium; 2 mg iron; 3,061 RE vitamin A; 130.5 mg vitamin C*

ZIPPY'S COOLER

10 parts apple juice (5 oz.)
4 parts broccoli juice (2 oz.)
2 parts beet juice (1 oz.)
Broccoli florets, for garnish

Combine juices with cracked ice in a
cocktail shaker and shake well. Strain
into chilled old-fashioned glasses
and garnish with broccoli florets.
Serves two.

*48 calories; 0.2 gm fat; 4% calories
from fat; 0 mg cholesterol; 20.6 mg
sodium; 11.2 gm carbohydrate;
1.1 gm protein; 20.9 mg calcium;
0.6 mg iron; 44.3 RE vitamin A;
56 mg vitamin C*

ZESTY COOLER

INDEX

Half-and-half 24, 99, 150, 156, 180, 188, 209

Hazelnut syrup 146, 210

Honey 24, 25, 26, 27, 29, 33, 36, 40, 41, 48, 49, 50, 54, 55, 58, 63, 66, 73, 80, 85, 94, 98, 99, 106, 108, 110, 113, 117, 120, 123, 124, 129, 132, 134, 140, 141, 142, 148, 152, 154, 160, 171, 173, 174, 175, 177, 185, 188, 189, 190, 191, 192, 196, 198, 200, 202, 204

Honeydew juice 93, 110, 111, 130, 131, 132, 135, 143, 144, •163

Horseradish, white 61, 50, 92, 112, 149, 162, 174, 182, 186, 212, 213, 214

Hot chocolate 213

Ice cream, chocolate 36, 42, 93

Ice cream, vanilla 30, 36, 42, 44, 65, 84, 93, 137, 148, 157, 165, 174

Iced tea 125, 175

Italian syrup 138

Jalapeño pepper 109, 115

Jalapeño pepper, pickled 177, 204

Jalapeño pepper juice 91, 129, 150, 177, 178, 180, 199, 214

Jalapeño pepper puree 215

Kiwi juice 39, 48, 81, 85, 92, 110, 121, 122, 142, 196, 210, 213

Lemon 142, 180, 183, 184, 192, 194, 196, 201, 202, 215

Lemon juice 25, 26, 27, 28, 29, 31, 34, 39, 40, 42, 43, 44, 47, 48, 49, 50, 51, 52, 53, 55, 57, 58, 59, 60, 63, 66, 68, 70, 71, 73, 74, 75, 76, 77, 80, 81, 87, 89, 90, 91, 92, 93, 96, 98, 99, 100, 106, 107, 108, 109, 110, 111, 113, 118, 120, 121, 122, 123, 124, 125, 126, 130, 132, 136, 142, 143, 144, 145, 148, 153, 156, 157, 158, 160, 163, 165, 167, 169, 170, 172, 174, 175, 176, 177, 178, 181, 182, 183, 184, 185, 186, 187, 190, 191, 192, 194, 195, 198, 199, 201, 202, 206, 207, 208, 213, 215, 216, 217

Lemon juice, meyer 49, 60, 129

Lemon peel 80, 128, 151, 187, 188

Lemon sorbet 163, 188

Lemon-lime soda 96, 123, 184

Lemonade 34, 39, 44, 63, 117, 125, 126, 165, 166, 214

Lettuce juice, mixed baby 216

Lime 104, 166, 168, 192, 217

Lime juice 24, 29, 31, 32, 33, 39, 41, 50, 52, 53, 55, 57, 60, 61, 63, 64, 65, 66, 67, 72, 74, 75, 76, 77, 78, 80, 82, 84, 86, 88, 95, 96, 102, 103, 105, 107, 109, 110, 112, 114, 116, 118, 121, 122, 123, 125, 126, 127, 128, 129, 130, 132, 133, 136, 138, 143, 146, 148, 149, 150, 154, 157, 158, 160, 163, 166, 167, 169, 170, 174, 175, 177, 178, 179, 180, 185, 186, 187, 191, 192, 196, 197, 198, 199, 200, 202, 204, 206, 207, 210, 211, 213

Limeade 104, 163

Loganberry juice 183

Malted milk powder 86

Mango 128, 129, 137, 154

Mango chutney 153

Mango juice 27, 40, 46, 122, 128, 129, 160, 195, 202, 204

Mango nectar 25, 42, 65, 79, 99, 143, 170, 209

Maple syrup 43, 60, 98, 111, 129, 136, 140, 158, 165, 170

Milk 23, 28, 30, 31, 36, 40, 42, 44, 45, 47, 48, 50, 58, 59, 62, 65, 66, 78, 83, 84, 111, 114, 124, 125, 129, 130, 136, 137, 140, 146, 152, 156

Milk, steamed 48, 170

Mineral water, sparkling 25, 28, 29, 31, 39, 40, 46, 49, 50, 53, 56, 57, 60, 67, 68, 70, 74, 76, 80, 93, 94, 95, 99, 100, 108,